Oracle Press™

Java® EE Applications on Oracle Java Cloud

Develop, Deploy, Monitor, and Manage Your Java Cloud Applications

Harshad Oak

New York Chicago San Francisco
Athens London Madrid Mexico City
Milan New Delhi Singapore Sydney Toronto

Library of Congress Cataloging-in-Publication Data
Oak, Harshad.

Java EE applications on Oracle Java Cloud : develop, deploy, monitor, and manage your Java cloud applications / Harshad Oak.

pages cm

Includes index.

ISBN 978-0-07-181715-8 (alk. paper) — ISBN 0-07-181715-8 (alk. paper) 1. Cloud computing. 2. Java (Computer program language) 3. Oracle (Computer file) I. Title.

QA76.585.O24 2015

004.67'82—dc23

2014026774

McGraw-Hill Education books are available at special quantity discounts to use as premiums and sales promotions, or for use in corporate training programs. To contact a representative, please visit the Contact Us pages at www.mhprofessional.com.

Java® EE Applications on Oracle Java Cloud: Develop, Deploy, Monitor, and Manage Your Java Cloud Applications

1 2 3 4 5 6 7 8 9 0 DOC DOC 1 0 9 8 7 6 5 4

ISBN 978-0-07-181715-8
MHID 0-07-181715-8

Sponsoring Editor
Brandi Shailer

Editorial Supervisor
Janet Walden

Project Manager
Kritika Kaushik, Cenveo® Publisher Services

Acquisitions Coordinator
Amanda Russell

Technical Editors
Markus Eisele and Arun Gupta

Copy Editor
Bart Reed

Proofreader
Lisa McCoy

Indexer
Jack Lewis

Production Supervisor
George Anderson

Composition
Cenveo Publisher Services

Illustration
Cenveo Publisher Services

Art Director, Cover
Jeff Weeks

To the two men who shaped me:

My father, Achyut (Baba), my pillar of strength, who against great odds ensured that I had a happy upbringing and the gumption to rise.

Gandhi, who helped me realize the power of love, truth, and nonviolence.

About the Author

Harshad Oak is the founder of IndicThreads and Rightrix Solutions. IndicThreads.com is an online developer magazine and hosts some of the most reputable technology conferences in India on topics such as Java, cloud computing, software quality, and mobile software. Before starting his own venture, Harshad was part of i-flex Solutions and Cognizant Technology Solutions.

In addition to this work, he has authored *Oracle JDeveloper 10g: Empowering J2EE Development* and *Pro Jakarta Commons*, and co-authored *J2EE 1.4 Bible*. Harshad has spoken at conferences in India, the United States, Sri Lanka, Thailand, and China. He has been working to build active Java communities in India and has organized as well as spoken at many Java user group meetings. Additionally, Harshad teaches Enterprise Java to Master's candidates in Computer Science at Symbiosis University, India. Harshad has been recognized as an Oracle ACE Director and a Java Champion for his contributions to the technology and the community.

Harshad writes about technology on IndicThreads.com and its social streams. He writes about social and other matters at HarshadOak.com and on twitter @HarshadOak. He can be reached at harshad@rightrix.com.

About the Technical Editors

Markus Eisele is a software architect, developer, and consultant. He works daily with customers and projects dealing with Enterprise-level Java and infrastructures, including the Java platform and various web-related technologies on a variety of platforms using products from different vendors. An expert in Java EE servers, Markus is an Oracle ACE Director, a Java Champion, and a member of the Java EE 7 expert group, and is a frequent speaker at industry conferences. Follow him on Twitter (@myfear) or read his blog (http://blog.eisele.net).

Arun Gupta is Director of Developer Advocacy at Red Hat and focuses on JBoss middleware. He was a founding member of the Java EE team at Sun Microsystems. At Oracle, Arun led a cross-functional team to drive the global launch of the Java EE 7 platform. After authoring approximately 1,400 blogs at blogs.oracle.com/arungupta on different Java technologies, he continues to promote Red Hat technologies and products at blog.arungupta.me. Arun has extensive speaking experience in 35+ countries on myriad topics.

Contents at a Glance

Contents

Foreword

The move to the cloud has become a seemingly overwhelming direction in which companies and technologists are finding themselves driven in the ongoing effort to achieve better economies of scale and a faster pace of business innovation in using enterprise technology.

This has been clearly illustrated by the rapid rise and adoption of Software as a Service and Infrastructure as a Service, but has been unusually light or limited for the application software infrastructure—enterprise-scale databases and enterprise-scale middleware—itself. This has not been for the lack of trying, but it simply represents a really hard problem that is only now being solved.

The emergence of Oracle Java Cloud Service and its capabilities is a major step forward in this journey to enterprise-class cloud infrastructure. It represents part of a major strategic investment from Oracle to bring to market the industry's first Platform as a Service offering that combines enterprise-class middleware, Oracle WebLogic Server, and an enterprise-class database, Oracle Database, into a highly productive, simple, easy-to-use application development and deployment environment that is proven for large-scale, mission-critical application deployments.

Given my role in the development and project management of Oracle WebLogic Server, Oracle Coherence, and Oracle Java Cloud Services, and given the opportunity by Harshad Oak, the author of this book, I wanted to share my perspective of how this investment is proceeding, in hopes that it frames how you read and understand this book.

It starts frankly in the "middle" of all infrastructures—the application server. In that space, Oracle offers Oracle WebLogic Server, our Java server for building custom and bespoke Java EE applications and for hosting third-party Java applications. It is complemented by Oracle Coherence, our in-memory grid for scaling out infrastructures within and across data centers.

Over the last five to six years, my team has made a huge investment to continue the technical journey of evolving Oracle WebLogic Server and Oracle Coherence to operate in large-scale environments of hundreds to, in many cases, thousands of servers. We have focused on hard problems such as scalability, reliability, availability, and performance, complemented by large-scale administrative and management investments.

The cloud has brought a new set of unique challenges to solve: management through restful interfaces (solved by JAX-RS APIs available for managing WebLogic Server), elastic scalability (solved by dynamic clusters in WebLogic Server and Coherence), self-service provisioning (now available in the Oracle Java Cloud Service!), advances in security concerns (addressed by ongoing investment in new security features in WebLogic Server and lockdown guides to deploying it securely), and, more recently, a focus on solving multitenancy issues in conjunction with Oracle Database 12*c* and its recent support for multitenancy.

But it wasn't enough to evolve the infrastructure of WebLogic Server to be more enterprise and cloud ready. Oracle went to the next step and made Oracle WebLogic Server and Oracle Database available in the Oracle Cloud at http://cloud.oracle.com. The family of Java services built around Oracle WebLogic Server is called *Oracle Java Cloud Services* and for the Database, the *Oracle Database Cloud Services*.

At the time of this book's publication, Oracle has one Java Cloud Service, formally named *Oracle Java Cloud Service – SaaS Extension*. This is the first service in middleware that Oracle has made available and is focused on enabling customers to build and deploy applications rather than having to understand how to manage and operate Oracle WebLogic Server.

Java Cloud Service – SaaS Extension is a remarkably easy and complete Java service and is the focus of this book. It is sometimes simply called Java Cloud Service and, more recently, I have heard people colloquially refer to it as JCS-SX. On its release several years ago, it broke new ground by offering a true enterprise-class version of WebLogic Server that was uniquely integrated out-of-the-box with the Oracle Database.

"SaaS Extension" refers to a characteristic of that service, which is the ability to extend the Oracle SaaS applications that are offered in Oracle Cloud, as well as for pure custom development of Java applications. All lifecycle activities—patching, backup, and restore—are taken care of by Oracle in Oracle Datacenters, and your focus as a developer or application manager is primarily to deploy and run your application. Simple! And Harshad will show you how.

Coming in calendar year 2014, Java Cloud Service – SaaS Extension will be added to several other Java Services that are geared even more toward custom application development to put far more control in the hands of the operators of the underlying Oracle WebLogic Server and Oracle Coherence. These new offerings are formally named *Java Cloud Service – Virtual Image* and *Java Cloud Service* (with no additional descriptor suffix).

These services together are referred to as *Oracle Java Cloud Services* and, as noted earlier, form the basis of moving all Oracle Fusion Middleware into the Oracle Cloud. This is a massive investment by Oracle, with many other services coming focused in areas such as messaging, document management, developer productivity, business process management, and much, much more. It is one of the most exciting times in middleware for Oracle in the last 10 years.

In summary, I would like to say it is my distinct pleasure to write this foreword to Harshad Oak's book on Oracle Java Cloud Services with a focus on Oracle Java Cloud Service – SaaS Extension. Harshad has been a long-time leading Oracle expert driving the understanding of key Oracle technologies and how customers can achieve the most success using them.

Oracle has mobilized to drive its entire software portfolio into the cloud, and getting the foundational middleware and database into the cloud was the first step to enable the rapid rollout of new innovative cloud services on that foundation. Harshad was one of the first people who understood this service was more than a trial balloon for Oracle.

I hope you enjoy this book as much as I did. As in the mid-to-late '90s when everything seemed new with the start of the Internet, we technologists are once again in a very exciting time of change as world-class enterprise software for running real transactional workloads has finally arrived in the cloud. Enjoy!

~ *Mike Lehmann*
Vice President Product Management
Oracle WebLogic Server, Oracle Coherence, and Oracle Java Cloud Services

Acknowledgments

This book has been a wonderful journey, where so many have chipped in to make it a reality.

I would like to thank Markus Eisele and Arun Gupta for their insightful reviews. Thank you Brandi Shailer and Amanda Russell for ensuring that the book stayed on track and in line with the best publishing standards. Thanks to Bart Reed, Janet Walden, Kritika Kaushik, and Tanya Punj for their vital role in shaping the book's content.

Thank you Mike Lehmann for your thoughtful foreword and your inputs throughout the book's writing. Thank you Diby Malakar and Anand Kothari for your help with information and access at Oracle.

This book would have been impossible without the support of my family. It's quite amazing that my father (*Baba*), wife (Sangeeta), sister (Charu), and even my in-laws somehow always seem to have faith in me, regardless of the little I do and the lot that I don't do. Thank you!

Sangeeta in particular has to tolerate a lot of my pondering and at times groaning about a million different things. But like some spiritual guru, she always seems to have a succinct one-liner that addresses my concern and drives me forward. Thank you!

Thanks to my five-year-old son, Tej. *Tej* means brilliance/radiance in Marathi, and Tej has lit up our lives in every sense of the word. He competed with the book for attention and invariably won, but was perceptive enough to let go of his catch and allow me to write. Thank you, Tej.

Introduction

Java EE and the cloud are arguably the two most important technologies today when it comes to building software for enterprises. In this book, you will understand what makes both these technologies tick and how you can leverage them to build and deploy applications on one of the key players in the Java Cloud space: the Oracle Java Cloud Service. You will not only learn to build with Java EE, but also to look at the nuances and the characteristics of the Oracle Java Cloud.

With this book you will get a holistic understanding of Java EE and cloud computing and their role in modern software development.

- Understand how you can go about building and deploying applications using Java EE technologies such as Servlets, JSP, JSF, EJB, and JPA, with an awareness of the cloud platform, its merits, and its limitations.
- Use the Oracle Java Cloud along with the Oracle Database Cloud to fulfill the persistence requirement of your application.
- See how you need to adapt your software development process for the constraints of the cloud as well as the mixed environment offered by the Oracle Java Cloud.
- Learn how to utilize the NetBeans IDE to streamline your cloud development.

Chapter 1: Java EE and Cloud Computing In this chapter, you will get a sound understanding of Java EE and cloud computing, their origins, and their current standing. You will see the benefits and drawbacks of choosing Java EE on the cloud, as compared to traditional Java EE implementations. You will also review the solutions provided by various Java PaaS (Platform as a Service) cloud vendors as well as other competing technologies.

Chapter 2: The Oracle Java Cloud In this chapter, you will look at the specifics of Oracle's cloud. You will review the Oracle SaaS, IaaS, and PaaS offerings and then dive into the finer details, such as the pricing, features, and restrictions of Oracle Java Cloud Service. You will also see how you can integrate NetBeans, Eclipse, and JDeveloper IDEs with the Oracle Java Cloud.

Chapter 3: Build and Deploy with NetBeans In this chapter, you will start building your first Java EE cloud application using the NetBeans IDE. You will understand the structure of a Java EE web application and how you can package a Java EE application.

Chapter 4: Servlets, Filters, and Listeners In this chapter, you will look at Servlets, the configuration of Servlet-based Java EE applications, sharing data, session management, filters, and listeners. You will then deploy applications to the Oracle Java Cloud and see how you can monitor your application and access the Java logs on the Oracle Java Cloud.

Chapter 5: JavaServer Pages, JSTL, and Expression Language In this chapter, you will learn about JavaServer Pages (JSP), JSTL, and Expression Language and how together they can help you generate powerful web pages using streamlined, efficient coding and increase developer productivity.

Chapter 6: JavaServer Faces In this chapter, you will explore JavaServer Faces (JSF), which is the preferred web technology for Java EE applications today. You will see how JSF offers a neat and feature-rich way of building server-side web applications with a UI component model, event handling, validation framework, structured page navigation, and internationalization. You will also see how to use templates for a consistent look and styling for your JSF applications. You will build and deploy JSF applications on the Oracle Java Cloud and see your full-featured JSF application work fine on the cloud.

Chapter 7: Enterprise JavaBeans (Session Beans) In this chapter, you will look at Enterprise JavaBeans and how it can get your business logic code running efficiently, accurately, and securely. You will build enterprise applications that include multiple EJBs and web applications, all packed together into one application. You will use the rich functionality of stateless and stateful session beans and also see how to get the container to manage transactions in your application.

Chapter 8: Web Services In this chapter, you will look at the need for and the benefits of using SOAP and RESTful web services. You will learn how to get around some of the constraints while running web services on a cloud environment such as the Oracle Java Cloud. You will then build web services using both SOAP and REST and deploy them on the Oracle Java Cloud Service.

Chapter 9: Persistence Using the Oracle Database Cloud Service In this chapter, you will explore the Oracle Database Cloud and use the Java Persistence API to persist data to your database on the Oracle Database Cloud Service. You will use the Java Persistence API to create tables as well as retrieve, update, and delete data. Oracle is best known for its database, and you will see how the Oracle Database Cloud puts all that power and capability at your disposal from within your Oracle Java Cloud Service applications.

In addition to the chapters, there are three appendixes:

- Appendix A provides a listing of all Java EE 5, 6, and 7 technologies and their corresponding Java Specification Requests (JSRs).
- Appendix B lists application servers compatible with Java EE 5, 6, and 7.
- Appendix C lists the technologies supported on the Oracle Java Cloud Service as well relevant technologies and APIs that are explicitly not supported.

Intended Audience

This book is suitable for the following readers:

- Developers looking to learn Java EE and cloud computing
- Developers looking to build and deploy Java EE applications on the Oracle Java Cloud

- Users of Oracle Middleware technologies looking to build applications with Java EE on the Oracle Java Cloud
- Business users, technical managers, or consultants who need an introduction to Java EE, Java Cloud, and the Oracle Java Cloud Service

No prior knowledge of Java EE or cloud computing is assumed. You only need to be familiar with Java programming. Everything you need to know to pick up Java EE and Java cloud computing is contained in this book.

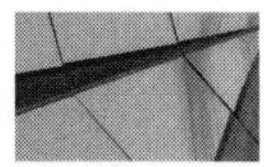

NOTE
The data center name, identity domain, and service names shown in screenshots are based on Oracle data center setups and may vary in screenshots throughout the book. These values should have no direct impact on your usage. Your trial setup will have different values anyway, based on the data you enter in your trial signup form.

Retrieving the Examples

The NetBeans projects for each chapter can be downloaded from the Oracle Press website at www.OraclePressBooks.com. The files are contained in a ZIP file. Once you've downloaded the ZIP file, you need to extract its contents. This will create a directory named Oracle_Java_Cloud_Book that contains the subdirectories for each chapter.

CHAPTER 1

Java EE and Cloud Computing

This book looks at Java Enterprise Edition (Java EE) and cloud computing and how you can best get them working for you on the Oracle Java Cloud Service. In each chapter, we review the various aspects of Java EE and then walk through how to get those pieces up and running on the Oracle Java Cloud Service. This initial chapter provides background on both Java EE and cloud computing. We survey the benefits and drawbacks of choosing Java EE on the cloud, as compared to traditional Java EE implementations on private servers. We then review solutions provided by various Java PaaS (Platform as a Service) cloud vendors and discuss some of the competing technologies.

Java Editions

Java has been around for a long time. Considering the pace at which technologies tend to get outdated, Java's 18-year journey has been most remarkable and highlights the capabilities and the staying power of the technology.

Java 1.0 was released in 1995, and back then, Java had no such thing as an enterprise edition. Only in 1999 was the idea of Java editions (Java SE and Java EE) introduced. Fast-forward to today, and we have three editions of Java:

- **Java Standard Edition (Java SE)** Most Java beginners tend to think of Java SE as Java. However, Java SE as such is a software development platform that provides the Java language, the Java Virtual Machine (JVM), and development and deployment tools for building Java applications.
- **Java Enterprise Edition (Java EE)** Java EE is what we encounter the most in this book. It was first introduced in 1999 as J2EE (or Java 2 Platform, Enterprise Edition). J2EE's mission was to enable enterprises to build highly available, secure, reliable, scalable, multitier, distributed applications. Each subsequent version has sought to enhance these capabilities. The Enterprise Edition continued to be known as J2EE until J2EE 1.4, released in 2003. However, the naming convention was changed in 2006, so what would have been J2EE 1.5 became Java EE 5. Java EE 6 was released in December 2009, and Java EE 7 in June 2013.
- **Java Micro Edition (Java ME)** Java ME was the edition created to address the need for a slimmer version of Java that would work well on the hardware constraints of devices such as mobile phones.

Although most people tend to think of the micro edition as the mobile edition, in reality, the micro edition is used not just for mobile phones, but for all kinds of devices, such as television sets, printers, smartcards, and more. Java ME provides an API and a small-footprint Java Virtual Machine (JVM) for running Java applications.

NOTE

Oracle has announced that their longer-term strategy is to converge Java ME and Java SE and provide a modularized solution. The project that aims to design and implement the standard module system is known as Project Jigsaw and is expected to be part of Java 9. Although modularization with Java 9 is still some way away, Java SE 8 has introduced compact profiles. Compact profiles are three subset profiles of the full Java SE 8 specification that could be used by applications that do not require the full platform.

Java EE Applications

Although the official definitions may differ, for all practical purposes, Java EE is the Java platform for building web and distributed applications. It is essentially a set of libraries that provide most of the core functionality you would require while building your application, which in most cases, is a web-based application. Although you will often hear these applications referred to as "enterprise applications," do not let "enterprise" scare you away from building a Java EE application. The "enterprise" in EE is simply meant to denote an application that offers some mix of security, reliability, speed, scalability, distribution, transaction, and portability. In an age when mainstream applications were standalone, desktop based, and isolated, the denotation of "enterprise" made sense. However, today, almost all software is meant to be online, social, scalable, and, in a sense, "enterprise."

As shown in Figure 1-1, Java EE sits on top of the basic Java platform (Java SE). Because most developers begin learning Java with Java SE, it is important to note that all the things learned with Java SE will continue to be true with Java EE.

You will build Java EE applications using your knowledge of the Java language and your understanding of the libraries provided by Java EE. While building

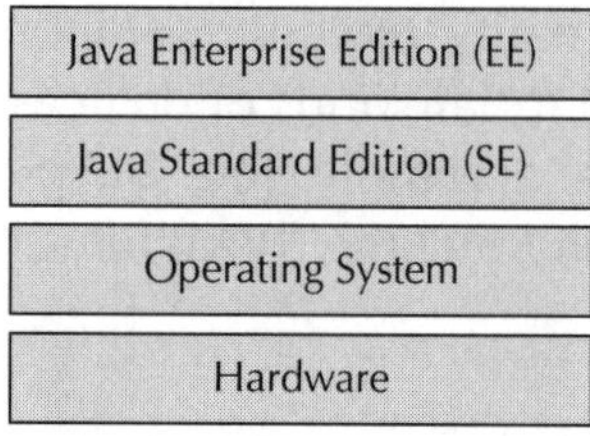

FIGURE 1-1. *Java EE*

these applications, you also need to adhere to certain rules and conventions defined by Java SE and Java EE. With the help of a Java EE application server to work its magic, your application will be up and running in no time.

Application Servers

The application server is the workhorse of Java EE. This is the software that implements Java EE and runs a Java EE application that has been developed, as specified by Java EE, and has been deployed on the application server. Application servers have to stick to the Java EE specification to be Java EE compatible. We will talk more about "specification" and "compatible" later in this chapter, but for the time being, you can proceed with the common English meaning of both terms.

Application servers come in all shapes and sizes and are provided by various vendors, both commercial and open source.

Open Source vs. Commercial

Although many Java EE application servers charge top dollar, there are also many open-source Java EE application servers. If you are wondering why someone would pay for a commercial version, the answer lies in the additional features, tools, and services that come with the paid version. Paid versions provide one or more add-ons, such as Control Dashboard, 24x7 Support, Priority Bug Fixes and Patches, Additional Caching, and Performance Tuning.

You can certainly get all the standard Java EE functionality with an open-source server, but in the case where you need that little bit extra for your enterprise applications, you can opt for the commercial versions. GlassFish, Apache Geronimo, Apache TomEE, Caucho Resin, and JBoss (now WildFly) are some of the popular open-source application servers. With many open-source servers, you find that the same vendor also offers a paid commercial version with add-ons.

Oracle WebLogic, SAP NetWeaver, and IBM WebSphere are popular commercial application servers. The commercial servers often come at a significant cost and are also often customized for specific business needs or even bundled as part of other commercial products.

Oracle WebLogic is Oracle's commercial application server product and the one that runs on Oracle Java Cloud.

NOTE
The open-source servers are freely available for download and use. However, even most commercial servers, such as Oracle WebLogic, offer a trial/developer license that will enable you to download and use the server. Oracle introduced an OTN Free Developer License for WebLogic in 2012, which makes it even easier for developers to try out WebLogic.

Application servers vary primarily on the following factors:

- **Licensing** Software licenses are a vast topic. There are many kinds of commercial licenses and many kinds of open-source licenses, so there are times when a server might fulfill all the requirements of an organization and yet not be considered for adoption because of some license terms and conditions.
- **Support services** Many server vendors, especially those offering commercial variants of open-source servers, rely on support services for their revenues. The quality of the support services is often a crucial factor when deciding which server to adopt.
- **Cost** Application server costs vary drastically. Also, you find that each vendor has its own way of pricing a server. Costs can vary based on many factors, such as number of server instances, number of processors, number of users, and more.

- **Ease of use** Although some servers are easy to install, use, and manage, with some servers, just getting them up and running might be a tough task.
- **Reporting and management features** The richness of the administration UI and its reporting capability vary a lot across servers. Whereas some servers will give you fancy charts, graphs, and timelines, others will have you digging through log files.
- **Standalone/bundled** Application servers are often bundled as part of a larger software suite. For example, if a company buys a certain Oracle application suite, they also get WebLogic bundled with it because it is the foundation for all their products.
- **Disk and memory requirements** Some servers seem to do a much better job at managing disk and memory requirements. These differences are, at times, only visible when a server is tested with large loads.
- **Performance** As with memory management, some servers are simply better at performance. You will find vendors claiming that their server is the fastest based on the results of certain benchmark tests. For example, in 2012, Oracle announced that WebLogic had set a world record for two processor results with an industry-standard benchmark designed to measure the performance of application servers. These results tend to be used to pitch a product as a faster alternative and a better buy for customers.
- **Backward compatibility** Although the Java EE specification itself provides for backward compatibility, some vendors go beyond Java EE backward-compatibility requirements and, at times, even support seemingly outdated technologies. This, however, can be an important feature for companies with legacy software setups but still wanting to migrate to newer versions of the application server.

Let's now look at an application server that is, in a sense, a first among equals: the reference implementation application server.

Reference Implementation

The reference implementation is a definitive implementation of a specification and is developed concurrently with the specification. The reference implementation for Java EE is the GlassFish Server Open Source Edition, which is available for download at www.glassfish.org.

Because the Java EE reference implementation is developed alongside the specification, it not only shows that the specification can be implemented, but also makes the implementation available as soon as the final specification is released. So although GlassFish 3 was the production version for Java EE 6, GlassFish 4 was being developed while the Java EE 7 specification was being finalized. The day Java EE 7 released, GlassFish 4, the reference implementation, was readily available for developers to try out Java EE 7.

Once the final specification is released, most vendors release their own implementations of the latest version of Java EE. Because these implementations have historically taken up to a year or two, developers looking to try out the latest technologies often opt for GlassFish. GlassFish has grown rapidly over the past few years and is today a popular application server that is used in many production applications.

We will now take a closer look at how the Java Community Process (JCP) works, how a specification is finalized, and what it takes for a server to get certified for a Java EE specification. This process is one of the key factors that makes Java EE stand out from competing technologies (both open source and commercial).

API and Technology Specification

Java EE isn't one big block of code or a single technology, but a collection of technologies brought together under the banner of Java EE. Java EE is commonly thought of as an end-to-end technology platform that comes with numerous features and the software providing those features. In reality, however, Java EE is simply a set of specifications about things that need to be done and how they need to be done. Although Java EE is all about building software, the Java EE specification, as such, does not include any code. The specification only provides rules, instructions, and guidelines on which the code is to be written.

You can even think of Java EE specifications as a set of PDF files available for download on the Java Community Process (JCP) website (http://jcp.org).

Having said that, the specification is released along with a reference implementation (RI) and the Technology Compatibility Kit (TCK). The RI is a code implementation that proves the specification can actually be implemented. The TCK consists of tests to check the implementation.

Java Community Process (JCP) and Java EE

Java EE, like all Java technologies, is driven by the JCP. Rather than having one organization make all the decisions, the JCP process involves the developer community and industry in the development of Java specifications. An Expert Group, consisting of members of various companies (such as Oracle, Red Hat, IBM, and SAP) and independent Java EE experts, is elected to manage each new iteration of the Java EE specification. This Expert Group is charged with inviting suggestions from other developers and drafting the specification for a Java Specification Request (JSR). Each version of the specification has a corresponding JSR to which you can refer for complete information about the specification.

For example, JSR 316 is the umbrella JSR for Java EE 6; it lists a high-level view of Java EE 6 and documents the technologies that comprise the specification. JSR 342 covers Java EE 7, whereas JSR 244 covers Java EE 5. All Java EE 5, 6, and 7 technologies and JSRs are listed in Appendix A for reference.

The executive committee is responsible for approving the final specification. The vendor companies usually compete on the actual implementation of that specification.

If you download JSR 316 or 342, all you get is a PDF file. How a company implements the specifications of that PDF makes all the difference in the marketplace. As long as the developer develops as per the specification, his code should work fine on all the Java EE–compatible implementations.

So if Java EE is just a PDF file, where is the code? Where is the implementation? You will remember from the previous section that the application server actually implements the specification. So the application server is where the implementation code is. The server vendors are responsible for writing the code to implement the specification.

NOTE

Although there are specific JSRs for the various Java EE versions, please note that one JSR does not provide the specifications for all Java EE technologies. The Java EE JSR refers to various other JSRs for details on the various technologies in Java EE. Do check out the JCP FAQ at https://jcp.org/en/introduction/faq for more about the journey of the JSR from proposal stage to the final release.

Java EE Compatible

The implementation of the Java EE specification is considered compatible only if it clears the compatibility tests for Java EE that are part of the Java EE Compatibility Test Suite (CTS).

All JSRs need to provide the following:

- The specification
- The reference implementation of the specification
- The Technology Compatibility Kit (TCK)

The fact that all certified Java EE servers will run your Java EE application is one of the key features of Java EE. It brings portability to the platform and drastically reduces vendor lock-in, both vital features for large enterprises. Portability here means the option of migrating to a different application server or a different vendor if required.

However, for a customer to be assured of this portability, all the application servers that claim to be Java EE compatible need to have passed a definite set of compatibility tests. Therefore, Oracle supplies a comprehensive Java EE Compatibility Test Suite (CTS) to Java EE licensees. Only if a server passes the tests in the CTS is it certified as Java EE compatible. This certification for a certain version is a guarantee to the end customer that a server supports Java EE as mandated by the specification for which it has been certified.

NOTE

All Java EE–compatible application servers (that is, all application servers that fulfill the Java EE licensing and compatibility testing procedure) are listed on the "Java EE Compatibility" page on the Oracle Technology Network (OTN) website at http://j.mp/JavaEE-Compatibility.

I would like to reiterate that although the various Java EE server vendors agree on the specifications, they are free to innovate on the actual implementation, as long as it does not interfere with the specified behavior.

NOTE
Oracle Java Cloud Service is not certified for any particular version of Java EE, but supports a mix of Java EE 5 and Java EE 6 technologies that Oracle determined was appropriate for enterprise customers.

Refer to Appendix B for a list of implementations compatible with Java EE 5, 6, and 7.

Profiles

Until Java EE 5, you had no choice but to go with a full-blown Java EE application server, which had support for all the technologies that have made it to Java EE over a decade or so. However, the Java community saw that although most Java EE applications were using only a subset of the technologies, they still had to lug the baggage of all Java EE technologies.

So in Java EE 6, the idea of profiles was introduced. Profiles enabled the creation of smaller Java EE subsets based on requirement. Although it was expected that many profiles would emerge, considering the support and maintenance implications, Java EE 6 and Java EE 7 have only one profile, the Web Profile. So with Java EE 6 and Java EE 7, you can choose the full Java EE server or the slimmer Java EE Web Profile Server.

Web Profile

The Web Profile specification lists only 15 technologies as required components. This naturally leads to a slimmer application server that packs more than enough punch for most web applications. The Web Profile excludes several technologies from the full Java EE specification. However, with Enterprise Java Beans (EJBs), the Web Profile introduces a trimmed-down version called EJB Lite. Download size is not a definite indicator of the difference between versions. However, it is worth noting that the full Java EE (English, Windows) version of GlassFish 3.1.2.2 is 53MB, whereas the Web Profile (English, Windows) version is merely 33MB.

Refer to Appendix A for list of Web Profile technologies in Java EE 6 and 7.

Cloud Computing

There has been immense buzz around cloud computing over the past few years. As seen in Figure 1-2, a Google Trends search for "cloud computing" reveals that cloud computing first gained popularity in 2009 and was at its peak in 2010/2011. By 2012/2013, we see the trend maturing past buzz and into real products, action, and adoption.

It's fair to say that most software developers have at least taken a cursory look at cloud computing. However, the number of actual cloud users is still small, so let's quickly review the fundamental ideas underlying cloud computing.

Going Around in Circles

Someone building software in the 1980s and then checking back today might be amused to see the fuss about cloud computing. To him, the cloud was always the most obvious way to go; he would have heard of it as time-sharing, client/server architecture, or thin clients. Even ideas such as hosted services, utility computing, and grid computing from a few years back were closely aligned with what we now know as cloud computing. In each case, you have minimal data and processing on the device at the user's end and

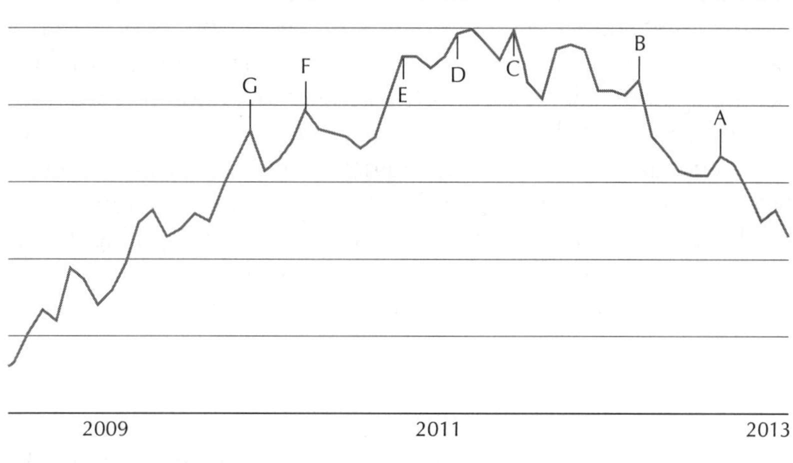

FIGURE 1-2. *Cloud computing on Google Trends*

most of the heavy lifting being done on remote hardware that is far more powerful and capable. The computing power and data were supplied to the user's device on demand.

So what's different with cloud computing? The primary difference is the universal Internet connectivity. Whereas in the past, networks were limited to a campus or an area, today, each of us can access information from any corner of the globe. Hosting my data or my application server on some remote corner of the planet and relying on Internet connectivity for access was previously impossible; not so with cloud computing.

Cloud computing is also possible today because data centers are highly scalable and because of virtualization. Virtualization, as the name suggests, is primarily about creating virtual machines (VMs) that don't run on the actual hardware but instead run on top of the operating system that's actually talking to the hardware. So a single hardware box that has a Linux operating system can have many VMs running on it—some running Windows, some running other flavors of Linux, and more. Each of these VMs could be used by one or many different users.

What Is Cloud Computing?

Cloud computing, in layman terms, stands for renting computing power and data storage capability as per your requirements at a certain point in time. You could be renting hardware, foundation software platforms running on that hardware, or full-fledged software applications.

As core business needs and developer roles evolve, business owners want to avoid buying expensive hardware, software developers want to avoid worrying about setting up and maintaining a software platform, and users want to avoid building software all together; they just want to use it. So business owners, developers, and users would all much rather rent what they need and then customize it, instead of setting up and managing the infrastructure.

These benefits have led to different types of cloud computing, where, in each type, you rent a different set of software or hardware. The most prominent types of cloud computing are IaaS, PaaS, and SaaS.

IaaS

Infrastructure as a Service (IaaS), also at times referred to as "Hardware as a Service," got the ball rolling for cloud computing. Around 2009, when we first started hearing the term "cloud computing," most of the talk was about IaaS and, to a large extent, fueled by Amazon successfully renting out capacity via its Elastic Compute Cloud (EC2) service. EC2 lets you rent virtual computers on which you can install, deploy, and run software.

With IaaS, the vendor just provides the hardware, and the user is responsible for setting up the software platforms as required. Although this provides great flexibility to the user, it also necessitates that the IaaS user has the expertise on board to set up and manage the rented hardware.

PaaS

Although just renting hardware might suffice at times, developers often don't just want the hardware, but also the basic software platform, installed and running. This brings great value to software teams because they now only need to focus on building their software application and don't have to worry about the hardware or even the basic software platform setup. Enter Platform as a Service (PaaS).

NOTE
Usually, software developers and network administrators are distinct teams. Not having to worry about the hardware setup and management means that developers are well placed to run the show on their own.

If a software team was looking to build a Java, .NET, or PHP application, wouldn't it be much easier if they got the hardware along with the operating system, as well as the Java/PHP/.NET software platform preinstalled and set up? How about also having an application server running, optimized, and highly scalable?

Whereas the first wave of cloud computing was around IaaS, the next was around PaaS. PaaS, however, is a much trickier space than IaaS, primarily because the PaaS vendor has to provide for the hundreds of ways in which software gets built. Many PaaS vendors, in an attempt to streamline and secure the software being built on their service, have defined strict dos and don'ts as well as the capabilities they can and cannot support. Having such a policy in place can be both a feature and a limitation. It is a feature because you can be sure that other users with whom you are sharing the platform are not free to do whatever they want and jeopardize your setup. However, it's also a major limitation because you have to build your application as per the rules set by the PaaS provider.

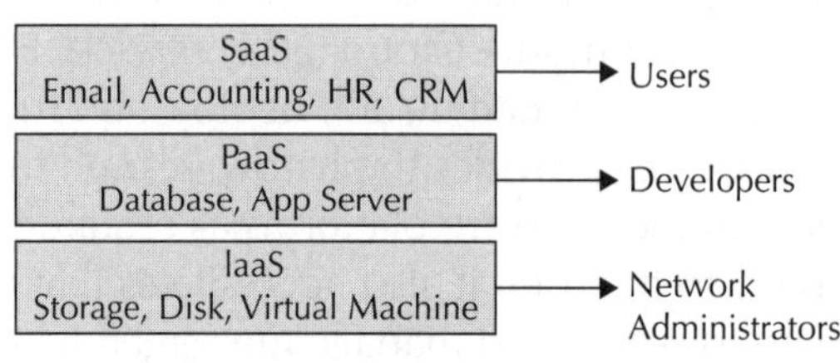

FIGURE 1-3. *The "as a Service" (aaS) types*

PaaS adoption should grow over time, as one would expect organizations to look to delegate the hardware setup and management but continue to want a say on the software that is built and run on the hardware.

SaaS

The term "Software as a Service (SaaS)" has actually been around longer than the term "cloud computing." I recall discussing SaaS in 2006, when cloud computing was unheard of. The meaning still stays pretty much the same, just that it is now thought of as a type of cloud computing.

If your business is using an online third-party service for accounting, email, invoicing, online campaigns, and email marketing, it is utilizing SaaS. SaaS is where you don't bother renting the hardware or even the software platform on which to build your application. You directly rent the actual software application you need. You pay based on your expected usage, or in some cases, you pay as you go. SaaS is especially popular with startups because it significantly reduces their startup and running cost, while still giving the fledgling business all the flexibility it requires.

As shown in Figure 1-3, a SaaS offering builds over the capabilities of a PaaS, which in turn runs over the IaaS. For this book, we will mostly be working with PaaS.

Why Cloud Computing?

The top reasons for the interest and adoption of cloud computing are

- **Technology** Setting up and maintaining your own hardware and software can be an extremely expensive and tedious affair. Most would much rather have someone else do it.

- **People** Most business owners would like to minimize/avoid the expense and effort of inducting, training, and retaining additional personnel.
- **Non-core** Running and maintaining hardware and software is not a core business for most enterprises. Given the choice, most enterprises would rather focus on their core business and rent computing power from a large, reliable provider.
- **Scale as required** You can rent capacity if and when it is required, and get to scale up and, just as importantly, scale down if required.
- **Pay as you go** Businesses need not provision expensive resources to provide for possible future demand.

Concerns About Cloud Computing

The primary concerns with cloud computing are

- **Security** Most surveys show security as businesses' primary concern with cloud computing. Many businesses are uncomfortable putting sensitive data on shared cloud environments.
- **Availability** If the Amazon Cloud goes down, it takes with it a horde of websites and services. An Amazon outage in October 2012 took down many popular websites such as Reddit, Foursquare, and Pinterest.
- **Connectivity issues** Although Internet connectivity has greatly improved over the past few years, it is still unreliable in most developing countries.
- **Lock-in and dependence on vendor** A few large cloud vendors hold a bulk of the cloud market share, and as yet there is little standardization on cloud services, so you can easily get locked into a vendor.
- **Rigid** Using a cloud service significantly limits the flexibility you enjoy if you were to run your own hardware and software. Most cloud vendors define fairly strict rules of operation to which users must adhere. You even need to build your applications with these limitations in mind.
- **Legal** The cloud comes with its own set of legal implications based on locations and jurisdictions. This is a major factor, especially for large enterprises with sensitive data.

Private, Public, and Hybrid Clouds

Although the cloud is usually thought of as a public, shared setup, such a setup might not work in cases where there are serious security implications or where the applications would not work in a shared environment.

In such cases, you can opt for private clouds, which work on pretty much the same lines as public clouds, but with exclusive access for a particular organization, with the consumers being the various business units within the organization. Private clouds are usually run in an internal data center or "on premises." However, that need not always be the case. A hybrid cloud is one that uses a mix of public and private clouds.

An important aspect of the cloud that often gets ignored is the cloud's great ability to provide a level playing field for software development companies and developers.

Cloud as a Leveler

Today, we see that by using various cloud services, small software companies can build and run enterprise-grade Java EE software that is as fast, secure, and reliable as any application built by the mega software companies. Similarly, the cloud expertise of a solo developer or someone working in a three-member company is pretty much the same as a developer in a mega corporation and working in a team of hundreds. This is an important reason for developers to look at adopting the cloud. The cloud has drastically leveled the playing field for software companies and developers.

Now that we have had a look at Java EE and the cloud, let's consider how Java EE is placed as a cloud platform and how it compares with some of the alternatives.

Java EE on the Cloud

Java EE has been the mainstay of server-side software development for over a decade and still today is one of the most widely used software platforms. It is arguably even the most prominent software platform on the cloud. So although there are no cloud-centric specifications or standards in the current Java EE version to date, many vendors are already offering robust Java EE solutions on the cloud. Today's Java Cloud offers a number of service options, opening the doors wide for Java EE application development, deployment, and use.

Until recently, Java EE applications were thought of as applications that enterprises built and ran on their own dedicated server infrastructure. If a company built a Java EE application, it was presumed that the company would also set up the requisite hardware infrastructure and the teams to manage and monitor that setup. It was some time before the idea of shared hosting, which has been popular for a while with technologies such as PHP, was considered suitable for Java's enterprise nature and demands.

We talked earlier of the benefits and drawbacks of cloud computing. You will find that most of the concerns with the cloud are features of a dedicated private Java EE setup, and vice versa.

Apart from the pros and cons for enterprises, one of the major issues with dedicated Java EE servers was that smaller businesses stayed away from Java EE because they did not want to set up and manage their own server infrastructure.

However, in almost all cases, enterprises used to run their Java on dedicated servers and hardly ever on a shared/cloud environment. Prior to the cloud wave, few web hosting providers bothered to offer decent shared Java hosting or cloud-like solutions for Java.

Once it was apparent that even enterprises were looking to go along the cloud path and spend big in the process, Java started being featured in every new hosting/cloud solution. Within no time, Java became one of the most widely used and supported languages on the cloud.

Java's foray into the cloud has changed Java EE for good, as well as Java EE's perception among the developer community. Developers, architects, and customers of all sizes are today increasingly looking to leverage Java on the cloud.

Competing Technologies: Alternatives to Java on the Cloud

Java EE is just one of the many technologies you can use to build software. Considering that technology is just a means to an end, whenever a new project is initiated, developers have a choice of which technologies to use. Multiple technology platforms can enable a developer to build all kinds of software: Java, .NET, Ruby, Python, and PHP would figure to be at the top of the list of software platforms.

Although a number of Java EE hosting and Java PaaS solutions are available today, that number pales in comparison to the number of cloud/hosted solutions for other web technologies. PHP, .NET, Python, and Ruby all continue to enjoy good traction among the developer community.

PaaS-like PHP hosting solutions have been around for quite some time—it's just that they weren't called PaaS back then. PHP works well even within a shared hosting setup, so a PHP app running on a fairly cheap, shared hosting solution has been the mainstay of web applications over the past decade. In comparison, Java has always struggled with shared hosting. Few hosting providers offered Java on a shared environment, and even those few usually offered a tightly sandboxed Tomcat instance that hardly ever worked out for real applications. Most hosting providers asked you to switch to a dedicated server as soon as you uttered the word Java or Java EE.

Oddly, back then, hardly anyone seemed bothered by Java's absence from the shared hosting space. Only because the cloud triggered a surge in enterprises looking at shared cloud environments have we seen the emergence of many Java PaaS solutions.

Not Just Java and .NET for the Enterprise

The Java platform has often scored over the likes of PHP, Python, and Ruby because Java was thought of as "enterprise ready," unlike many other technologies. However, with many large players now offering PaaS solutions for PHP, Python, and other technologies, we now see technologies around PHP, Python, and Ruby, as well as other JVM languages, offering much stiffer competition to conventional Java EE for the enterprise.

Whereas earlier, "enterprise software development" was primarily a two-horse race between Java EE and .NET, today we see many other technologies being considered. This is, to a large extent, due to the availability of enterprise-grade PaaS solutions for these other technologies.

Although each platform has its pros and cons, here are a few things that especially work in favor of Java EE on the cloud:

- Java EE was always meant for robust, scalable, distributed, multitier applications, precisely the things that you expect from a cloud application. This makes Java EE a great fit for the cloud.
- Java EE is already a mature platform on the cloud. You have many vendors, lots of choices, and all kinds of pricing models at your disposal.

- The talent pool of Java EE developers is immense. Getting these developers to use Java EE on the cloud is a lot easier than building an entirely new skill set.
- The Java EE community is vibrant and Java EE technology continues to get better and easier to use with every new version. Therefore, Java EE on the cloud is arguably the safest long-term choice on the cloud.

Standards and Java EE 7

Although Java EE is supported by several cloud vendors, we find that most such vendors are either supporting bits and pieces of Java EE or have built their own APIs that developers need to conform to. There have been some attempts at Java Cloud standardization, but so far, no clear standards have emerged for Java on the cloud.

Java EE 7 was initially meant to bring to life the long-awaited Java Cloud standardization. However in August 2012, 10 months before Java EE 7 was released, one of the specification leads for Java EE 7, wrote in her Java EE 7 Roadmap blog (https://blogs.oracle.com/theaquarium/entry/java_ee_7_roadmap) that it was felt that "providing standardized PaaS-based programming and multitenancy would delay the release of Java EE 7." PaaS enablement and multitenancy support was moved out of Java EE 7 and is now targeted for Java EE 8.

Although there is no official Java EE Cloud standard being released soon, it is important to note that most Java Cloud vendors are presently looking to support standard Java EE applications.

Java EE Vendors and Alternatives

Although Amazon is credited for largely initiating the cloud computing wave, Amazon was primarily an IaaS vendor. Google App Engine (GAE) was the first PaaS solution that received widespread interest and attention. GAE opened with Python support, but introduced Java about a year later, in April 2009. We have been in a constant Java PaaS race since, with many vendors, new and old, offering Java PaaS products.

The Java Cloud vendor space is one that keeps changing rapidly, as most of the major software companies have either launched a cloud solution or are looking to do so. As of today, the prominent players in the Java Cloud space are Amazon Elastic Beanstalk, Google App Engine, Jelastic, CloudBees, OpenShift from Red Hat, and the Oracle Java Cloud Service.

Many of the PaaS providers run a Tomcat server, and some use Jetty and GlassFish. The Oracle Java Cloud runs on Oracle WebLogic Server release 10.3.6, which is the latest version in the WebLogic Server 11*g* line.

Some of these vendors also offer IaaS solutions where you can install your own Java EE server. However, here we are only looking at their PaaS offerings.

Amazon Elastic Beanstalk Beanstalk is Amazon's PaaS offering. It supports applications built in Java, PHP, Python, Ruby, Node.js, and .NET. There is no additional charge for Elastic Beanstalk, and you only need to pay for the Amazon Web Services (AWS) resources needed to store and run your applications. Beanstalk deploys applications to the Apache Tomcat server and therefore only supports those Java EE technologies that are supported on Tomcat.
http://aws.amazon.com/elasticbeanstalk/

Google App Engine Google App Engine has only partial Java EE support and uses its own customized server and data store. If one intends to use Google App Engine, some vendor-specific learning is essential.
https://developers.google.com/appengine/docs/java/

Jelastic Jelastic began as the "Java Elastic Cloud." It no longer claims to be the "Java Elastic Cloud," as it now supports both Java and PHP. Jelastic supports multiple Java EE servers (Tomcat, TomEE, GlassFish, and Jetty), as well as multiple SQL and NoSQL databases. Its postives are its Java focus and that it does not require you to use its proprietary APIs and technologies.
http://jelastic.com/

CloudBees CloudBees claims to be the Java PaaS company that supports the entire application lifecycle, from development through production. It provides for source control repositories and Maven repositories, as well as continuous-build servers managed by Jenkins. It supports Tomcat, JBoss, GlassFish, WildFly, and Jetty application servers and supports many JVM languages and frameworks.
http://cloudbees.com/

OpenShift OpenShift is the PaaS from Red Hat. It supports Java, Ruby, Node.js, Python, PHP, and Perl. It supports multiple Java EE application servers (JBoss AS 7.1, WildFly 8, JBoss EAP6, Tomcat, and GlassFish) and MySQL, MongoDB, and PostgreSQL databases. OpenShift's support for a wide range of languages, servers, frameworks, and databases, is its major positive. https://www.openshift.com/get-started/java

Oracle Java Cloud Although this entire book is about OJC, here's a quick description: OJC is a Java PaaS service that runs the Oracle WebLogic server, which is an integral part of Oracle's Fusion Middleware range and its Oracle Cloud Application Foundation. OJC supports a mix of Java EE 5 and 6 features. The WebLogic server, the standards support, the Oracle Database, support for Oracle frameworks such as ADF, and ease of use are some of its highlights. https://cloud.oracle.com/mycloud/f?p=service:java:0a f

Although these are the prominent players in the Java PaaS space, other notable mentions would be Heroku from Salesforce.com and Cloud Foundry from GoPivotal (formerly VMware). Already, a wide range and depth to the Java PaaS offerings is available. These offerings vary on multiple factors, so a close examination of multiple vendors is usually needed before one can pick the right Java PaaS for their requirement.

NOTE
The WebLogic server is integral to Oracle's Fusion Middleware range and its Oracle Cloud Application Foundation, and is the server used on the Oracle Java Cloud Service.

Tens of factors go into why one would choose one PaaS over another. The following are the top considerations (in no particular order) and how the Oracle Java Cloud (OJC) performs on each one. There's a fair bit of overlap between the features that these cloud services offer, but the key points to consider from a purely software development platform point of view are as follows:

- **Pricing and billing** Costs and pricing strategies vary widely across vendors. Some charge based on fine-grained usage details, whereas others provide duration-based subscriptions. You need to evaluate if you would like to go with subscriptions or with a "pay-as-you-go" model.

OJC: Offers a monthly subscription currently starting at $249 for a single WebLogic server instance. It does not offer a "pay-as-you-go" option. OJC offers three broad editions, each of which come with a definitive set of resources. You pick your edition and pay a flat monthly rental for the same.

- **Supported features and technologies** Are the supported technologies and features in line with your requirements? Is your chosen framework officially supported by the cloud vendor? Which version is supported? Is the vendor supporting standards, or do you have to write custom, vendor-specific code? Many vendors support only subsets of Java EE, and in some cases, require you to use and adopt their custom technology/API. If you intend to develop a pure Java EE application, check whether the vendor supports Full Java EE/Java EE Web Profile.
  OJC: Java EE standards support is one of the primary pitches for OJC. It currently supports most of Java EE 5 and many of Java EE 6's capabilities, but isn't yet fully Java EE 6 or even Java EE 6 Web Profile compatible. Its support for the Oracle ADF framework is a plus for those with existing ADF deployments and development setups.
- **Flexibility** Many vendors insist that you develop in a certain way using certain APIs. This isn't always possible or easy to execute unless you have a team adept at developing as per that cloud vendor's requirements.
  OJC: The OJC relies on Java EE standards and does not insist on you using any non-Java EE or Oracle-specific APIs, unless you wish to leverage any features specific to WebLogic or Oracle's cloud.
- **Vendor standing** Considering that you are putting your application and data on the vendor's hardware, you want to be confident with the vendor's credentials and ability to be up and running, say, 10 years from now.
  OJC: Oracle rates highly on this count. The Java Cloud Service should be around for a long time.
- **Tooling and ease of use** Many cloud vendors have rich web-based UIs, and some even provide integration with popular integrated development environments (IDEs). Ease of use is quite important

because some cloud services can be rather confusing and, at times, even intimidating.
OJC: The OJC has a decent browser-based UI and supports integration with popular IDEs, including JDeveloper, NetBeans, and Eclipse.

- **Database support** Most cloud vendors support at least one RDBMS and NoSQL data store. You need to check if it's the one you prefer.
OJC: The OJC supports the Oracle RDBMS, but there's no NoSQL database as of now. However, considering most other vendors are offering a NoSQL option and Oracle has a NoSQL database, it should only be a matter of time before Oracle NoSQL is available on the Oracle Cloud.
- **Open/closed: vendor lock-in** Is the vendor offering a closed stack that would lock you in? Would it be possible for you to migrate to a new server if the need arises, or are you getting locked in to a particular vendor?
OJC: OJC fares well on this count because of its emphasis on Java EE standards-based development. Migrating from the Oracle Cloud to a dedicated server or another PaaS vendor should be possible.
- **Java friendly** Whereas some vendors are focused Java Cloud players, there are others that support many different technologies. This does seem to affect the features, the documentation, and the overall priority areas for that service.
OJC: Being a purely Java Cloud service, OJC is certainly Java friendly. The UI, features, and capabilities all seem to be built with a Java developer in mind.
- **Skill building** How difficult would it be to build a team capable of developing and deploying for a PaaS?
OJC: Again, due to OJC's focus on Java EE standards, it is much easier to build a team for OJC than for other PaaS solutions, which require skill building on a vendor-specific technology.

Apart from the software platform issue, there are, of course, other non-software issues such as support, service level agreements (SLAs), and server locations that need to be considered.

Summary

In this chapter, we had a look at the basics and origins of Java EE and cloud computing. We discussed the various kinds of cloud services and why Java EE is a great fit for a cloud environment. We took a look at some of the prominent Java Cloud vendors today, as well as the things to consider while picking a Java Cloud.

We also looked at Java EE in more detail, reviewing JSRs, the various application servers, and the Java EE profiles. We followed this up with a discussion on Java EE PaaS and how the Oracle Java Cloud fares on some of the key parameters for a PaaS, concluding with a look at PaaS alternatives on other technologies.

Let's now take off into the Oracle Java Cloud, set up our Java Cloud instance, and start looking at the nuts and bolts of Oracle's Java Cloud offering.

CHAPTER 2

The Oracle Java Cloud

This chapter provides the specifics of Oracle's Cloud offering. We will briefly review the Oracle SaaS, IaaS, and PaaS, then dive into the specifics of pricing and features and restrictions of Oracle Java Cloud (OJC). We will also look at how you can create users and roles so as to best manage your Oracle Cloud. This chapter will also show how to integrate NetBeans, Eclipse, and JDeveloper IDEs with the Oracle Java Cloud so you'll be ready to start development in the next chapter.

Oracle's Cloud Foray

In the early days of the term "cloud computing," when the hype was just starting, Oracle founder Larry Ellison famously said, "[The Cloud] is databases and operating systems and memory and microprocessors and the Internet" and "all the Cloud is, is computers in a network."

Ellison sure had a point. SaaS (Software as a Service) had been around for years, and the cloud as such was nothing new in the technology sense. What was perhaps new was the software development paradigm being spun around the idea of cheap, pay-per-use hardware and software. Another remarkable aspect of the cloud was the stickiness of the term "cloud." For reasons no one is perhaps sure of, the term "cloud" worked. So soon we had marketing gurus from every other company leveraging the term "cloud" to sell their wares. Whereas "grid" and "virtualization" had their brief moments in the limelight, "cloud" made it big time in quick time. Even the mainstream media was talking about the cloud in no time.

Since 2011 we have seen a big cloud push from Oracle. The Oracle Cloud was announced at Oracle OpenWorld 2011, and we have since seen a vast range of cloud solutions being announced and delivered by Oracle. In 2013, Oracle went a step further and even announced dedicated Oracle CloudWorld events across many cities worldwide.

Oracle Cloud Constituents

Oracle defines its cloud as "a broad set of industry-standards based, integrated services that provide customers with subscription-based access to Oracle Platform Services, Application Services, and Social Services, all completely managed, hosted, and supported by Oracle" (https://cloud.oracle.com/mycloud/f?p=service:faq:0#q2). The Oracle Cloud today offers a wide range of cloud solutions in the SaaS, IaaS, and PaaS domains.

SaaS

From day one, the Oracle Cloud has been projected more as a solution provider than a hardware and software rental place. Much of Oracle's focus has been on providing SaaS solutions around verticals such as Enterprise Resource Planning (ERP), Planning and Budgeting, Financial Reporting, Human Capital Management (HCM), Talent Management, Sales and Marketing, and Customer Support. Oracle has a popular product in each segment, and the first cloud push from Oracle was around making these products available as SaaS solutions on the cloud. Apart from the traditional Oracle products, there's also the Oracle Social Network (OSN) on the cloud. The OSN was announced at OpenWorld 2012 and tries to bring social interactions to the enterprise while being tightly integrated with the other Oracle solutions.

IaaS

In January 2013, Oracle also announced Infrastructure as a Service (IaaS) solutions. However, Oracle IaaS is focused on on-premises deployment, rather than being a commodity cloud like Amazon. Oracle IaaS offers customers a monthly rental option to access preconfigured application servers to be deployed in on-premises customer data centers.

PaaS

The Oracle Cloud also offers a wide range of PaaS solutions, some of which are already in General Availability, while others are still in Beta/Preview. One in General Availability, is the Java PaaS, the focus of this book. Other PaaS include Oracle Developer Cloud Service, which offers Project Configuration, Source Control, Defect Tracking, Continuous Build Integration, and Document Collaboration, as well as the Oracle Storage Cloud and the Oracle Messaging Cloud. All of Oracle's PaaS services are meant to be tightly integrated and collaborate with each other. Last but not least is the Oracle Database Cloud, which is an integral part of the Oracle Java Cloud offering. We'll use the Database Cloud in the chapter dealing with persistence.

Java Cloud

A simplistic explanation of the Oracle Java Cloud is that it's Oracle's WebLogic Server integrated with the Oracle Database. So developing and deploying on the Java Cloud is akin to developing and deploying on WebLogic and using an Oracle Database for persistence. However, although the latest versions of WebLogic support all Java EE 6 features, the Java Cloud supports a mix of Java EE 5, Java EE 6, and Oracle WebLogic Server capabilities. For a detailed list of technologies supported by Java Cloud, refer to Appendix B.

NOTE
Oracle has recently introduced "Oracle WebLogic as a Service," which is still in preview mode. Although both the Java Cloud Service and WebLogic as a Service run the WebLogic Server, the primary differentiating factor of "Oracle WebLogic as a Service" is that it offers full administrative and operational control.

Although Java Cloud supports a mixture of features and capabilities, it is important to note that the Java Cloud supports almost all of the most commonly used Java EE technologies. Although it might not support the latest versions of each, there is support for Servlets, JavaServer Pages (JSP), JavaServer Faces (JSF), Enterprise JavaBeans (EJB), Java Persistence API (JPA), Java API for Restful Web Services (JAX-RS), and Java API for XML Web Services (JAX-WS), as well as popular technologies such as ADF.

Another thing to note is that the Java Cloud supports Java SE 6 APIs. Refer to Appendix C for a detailed list of technologies that would trigger a whitelist violation and stop your application from being deployed.

NOTE
A whitelist is a list of those technologies and APIs that fulfill the technical and security requirements of a software/service and have been approved to run on it.

Pricing

Now that you understand the history and position of Oracle Java Cloud, what does it take to get started? Oracle offers three broad editions of cloud subscription; you pick your edition and pay a flat monthly rental.

The Java Cloud prices at the time of writing range from 249 USD per month for a single WebLogic Server instance to 1,499 USD for four WebLogic Server instances. Any of the WebLogic server instances can be a deployment target for your Java EE applications. You can also choose to run multiple Java EE applications on the same WebLogic instance. Considering that multiple Java EE applications can run fine on a single WebLogic server instance, in most cases, the deciding factor for which OJC edition to buy will be based on the memory, storage, and data transfer available in each edition.

A WebLogic Server instance here means a configured instance that's ready to host any applications and resources. You do not have to perform any of the tasks involved in setting up and configuring the WebLogic Server instance.

Also note that one physical hardware box could be running multiple instances of WebLogic, or even one instance could be running over multiple physical boxes. However, the point of the cloud is that it should not matter what the hardware is on which your instance is running. Most cloud vendors do not share or give users any control over what hardware is running underneath their cloud setup.

As seen in Figure 2-1, the user does not gain any further fine-grained control over the setup at the higher price point. Although downsizing is not

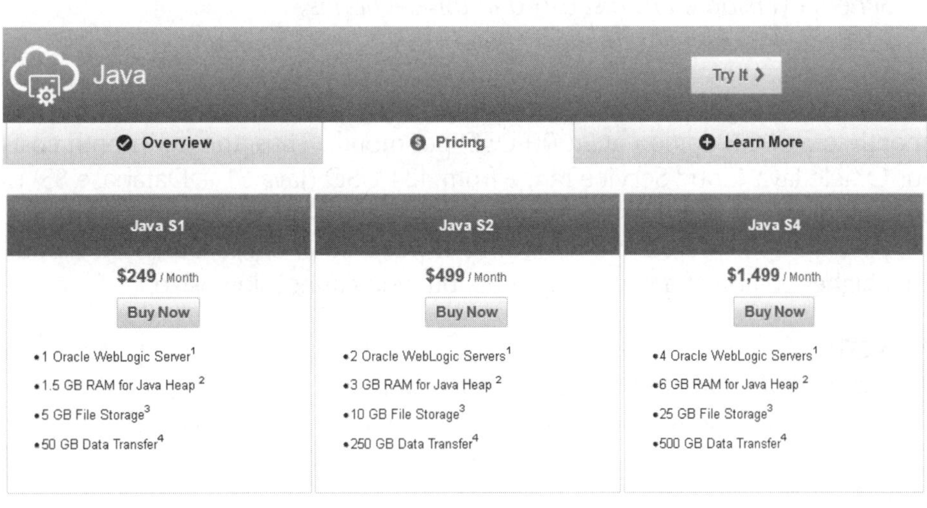

FIGURE 2-1. *Java Cloud pricing*

allowed, users do have the choice to upsize from a lower edition to a higher edition at any point in time.

NOTE
Oracle Java Cloud Service does not expose details on the underlying operating system, middleware, and JVM configurations to its users.

It is important to note that Oracle Java Cloud Service requires the Oracle Database Cloud. The Java Cloud trial we use in this book comes with a trial of the Database Cloud. However, for your real-world enterprise deployments, you will also need to purchase the appropriate Database Cloud edition. You have the choice to mix and match your Java and Database Clouds. You can choose to have a single WebLogic server instance running with the 50GB database edition.

NOTE
Oracle is expected to launch additional versions —Basic, Customer Managed Database Cloud, and Premium Managed Database—of the Database Cloud. However, all of these are still in the preview/concept stage. Only the Managed Schema version that's discussed in this section is available for use with the Java Cloud.

As seen in Figure 2-2, you can choose from a 5GB edition at 175 USD per month to a 50GB edition at 2,000 USD per month. Thus, the per month costs for Oracle Java Cloud Service range from 424 USD (Java S1 + Database S5) to 3,499 USD (Java S4 + Database S50).

As with OJC, you can upsize from a lower edition of the Database Cloud to a higher edition at any point in time, but you cannot downsize.

NOTE
Although the Oracle Database Cloud is a must have for OJC today, one would expect that to change eventually as customers ask for database and NoSQL alternatives.

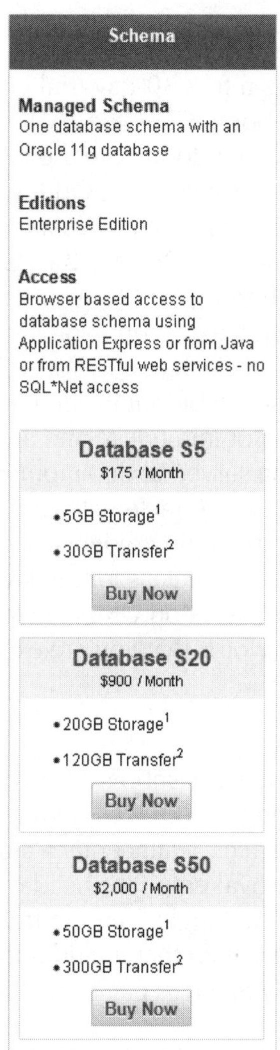

FIGURE 2-2. *Database Cloud pricing*

Trial Signup

You don't have to invest another 400 USD to try out the Oracle Java Cloud with this book. Oracle offers a free 30-day trial of the Java Cloud, which will serve very well for this book. Click the Try It button on the Java Cloud page at https://cloud.oracle.com/ to initiate the trial signup process. With one Oracle WebLogic Server instance, 1.5GB RAM Java Heap, adequate file storage, 5GB of data transfer, unlimited users and applications, along with one schema (Oracle Database 11g Release 2), 1GB of storage, and 6GB data transfer, you get a pretty rich trial setup for your Java Cloud.

If you already have an Oracle account, you'll need to sign in. Otherwise, you need to sign up for an Oracle account. You will need to fill out a few forms, and then your request will be put in "pending" status until it is fulfilled. Note that trial approvals are not immediate and are based on availability and the number of requests being served at that moment.

Once your setup is complete, Oracle will send an email to the account on file with your trial approval and login credentials for the trial setup.

The email will provide service details for the Java Cloud Service, Database Cloud Service, Account Administration URL, and Identity Domain Details. You are provided temporary passwords that you are expected to reset on first login.

My Services

The "My Services" page is like a dashboard for your Oracle Java Cloud. You can either bookmark the "MyServices Administration URL," which will be in the form https://myservices.<datacenter>.cloud.oracle.com/mycloud/f?p=my_services in the approval email, or head over to https://cloud.oracle.com/, log in with your Oracle Single Sign On ID, and access My Services. In both cases, you will see a screen that includes the box shown in Figure 2-3. Note that the URL for the My Services page changes based on the data center associated with it.

Click the link for the Java service and you will get an overview page as shown in Figure 2-4, showing the current service status as well as information about start date, end date, sftp, and more. In the left panel you will find sections titled Overview, Administration, Metrics, and Associations.

NOTE

Curiously, as of the time of this writing, the link only works if opened in the same tab and does not work if you attempt opening it in a new tab/window.

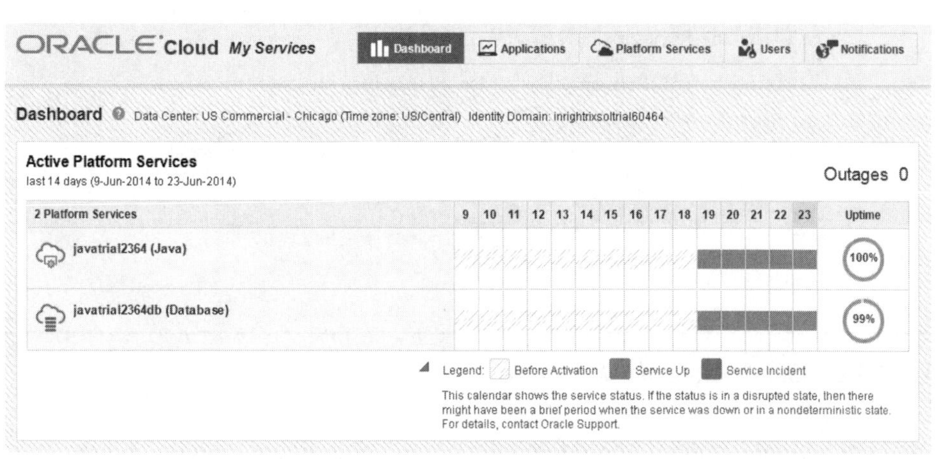

FIGURE 2-3. *My Services*

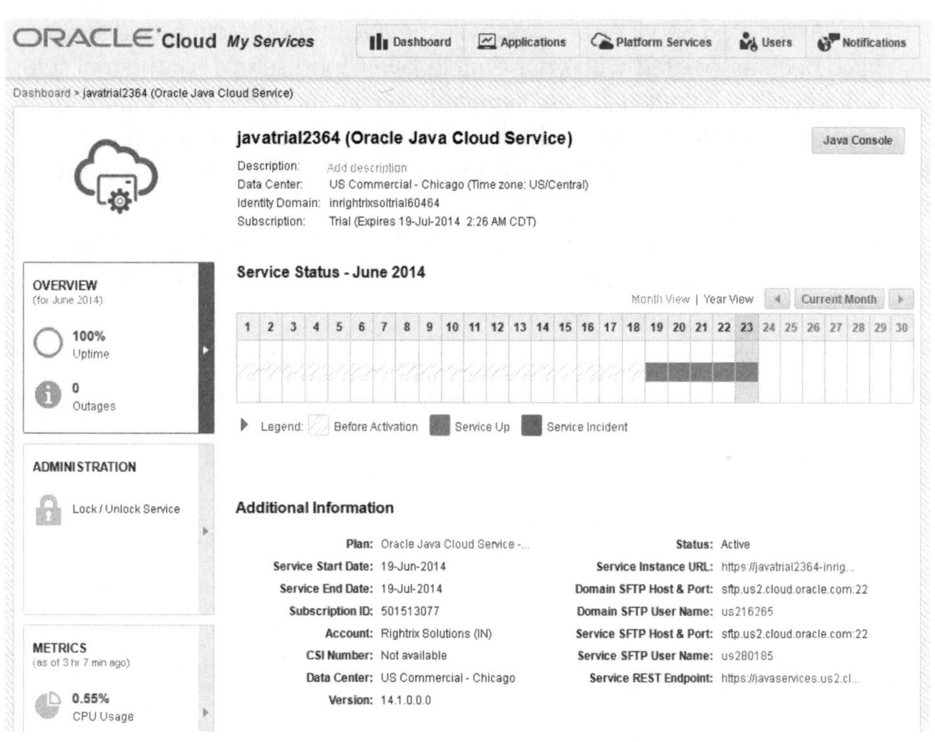

FIGURE 2-4. *Java Cloud Service Dashboard*

Lock / Unlock Service

- Locking this service prevents your users from accessing your applications and cloud service.
- Requests may take time to process.
- Oracle Cloud will send you an email when your lock or unlock operation has completed.

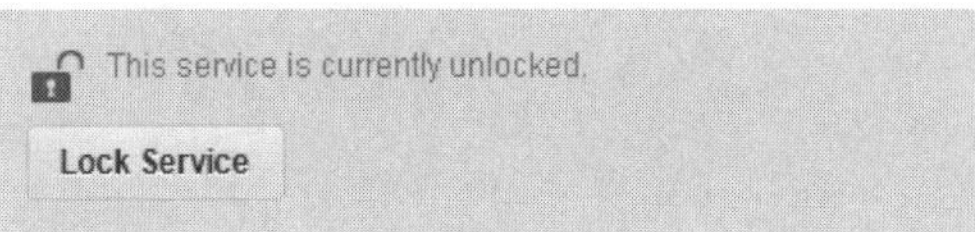

FIGURE 2-5. *Lock/Unlock Service*

Click Administration in the left panel and you will get a screen as shown in Figure 2-5, where you have a button to lock the service, if you so desire.

Click Metrics in the left panel and you will be presented with information such as CPU usage, memory usage, number of applications, and more, as shown in Figure 2-6.

Click Associated Services and you will see any other Oracle Cloud services that have been associated with your Oracle Java Cloud setup. For the trial setup, you would only see your database service listed, as shown in Figure 2-7.

The Java Console button on the top right of Figure 2-4 takes you to the Java Cloud Services Control. We will see more of the Java Cloud Services Control in Chapter 4.

Now that you have your cloud trial up and running, let's integrate it with a popular Java IDE so as to further ease and speed up your use of the Java Cloud.

Latest Usage (as of 3 hr 10 min ago)

CPU Usage	0.55%
Deployed Applications	1
Memory Usage (MB)	335.53
Request Rate (per minute)	0

Historical Usage

No utilization data for last 7 days.

FIGURE 2-6. *Usage Metrics*

FIGURE 2-7. *Associated Services*

IDE Integration

Most Java developers today use some integrated development environment (IDE) for development. Some of the popular Java IDEs are NetBeans, Eclipse, JDeveloper, and IntelliJ IDEA. Although you can choose from a number of available Java development tools, we will use Oracle's officially supported tools for demonstration in this book: NetBeans IDE, Oracle JDeveloper, and OEPE.

Oracle currently offers Oracle Java Cloud integration for NetBeans, JDeveloper, and Eclipse:

- **NetBeans IDE** NetBeans has been around for over a decade and was the flagship Java development tool of Sun Microsystems (later acquired by Oracle). NetBeans continues to thrive under Oracle and is usually the first to support new technologies in Java SE and Java EE. NetBeans' vast feature set and ready to use out of the box state, in my opinion, make it a great choice for beginners as well as advanced Java developers.
- **Oracle JDeveloper** JDeveloper was Oracle's Java IDE prior to the Sun acquisition. In recent years, JDeveloper has moved into a niche as the chosen Java IDE for Oracle developers. It is no longer as popular in pure Java circles, but is the primary Java tool for Oracle application developers. JDeveloper may rarely be a leading topic at a Java-centered conference, but is almost always present at an Oracle conference.
- **Oracle Enterprise Pack for Eclipse (OEPE)** Eclipse has remarkable traction in all kinds of programming, not just Java. Today, numerous companies are shipping products and development tools built on Eclipse. Naturally, there are thousands of developers who are

most comfortable with the Eclipse IDE. Oracle Enterprise Pack for Eclipse is the Eclipse-based Oracle development tool that these developers wanted.

Which IDE is the best? Developers are passionate about their IDE, and each has its merits. In fairness to these leading IDE options, we'll show Java Cloud integration in each one. The integration is quite similar on all IDEs, so none of the three enjoy any edge in regard to the Java Cloud, and you can choose to use whichever you find best for your needs. Before the IDE integrations, you first need to get the Oracle Java Cloud Service SDK.

Oracle Java Cloud Service SDK

Download the Oracle Java Cloud Service SDK, which is freely available for download on the Oracle Technology Network website. Note that the SDK can be used independently of any IDE.

The SDK contains the following tools:

- A command-line interface for interacting with your Oracle Java Cloud Service instances.
- A whitelist tool for checking your application's cloud deployment readiness.
- Ant tasks and Maven plugins for interacting with your Oracle Java Cloud Service instances.
- There's no installation process for the SDK; you simply need to download and unzip the file onto your machine.

NetBeans

Download and install the NetBeans IDE from www.netbeans.org. Ensure that you either download the Java EE Bundle or the All Bundle. Next, install the Oracle Cloud Plugin for NetBeans. Start NetBeans, then choose Tools | Plugins. In the Plugin Manager, select the Available Plugins tab and search for "Oracle Cloud." You should see an Oracle Cloud plugin with the category marked as "Java EE." Select the plugin and install it.

Now choose Tools | Cloud Providers, followed by clicking the Add Cloud button. Select Oracle Cloud on the next screen, and you will see a screen like the one shown in Figure 2-8. Enter your credentials and provide the path to the Oracle Cloud SDK you extracted earlier. You will now see "Oracle Cloud Remote" listed in Cloud Resources, as shown in Figure 2-9. Click Finish.

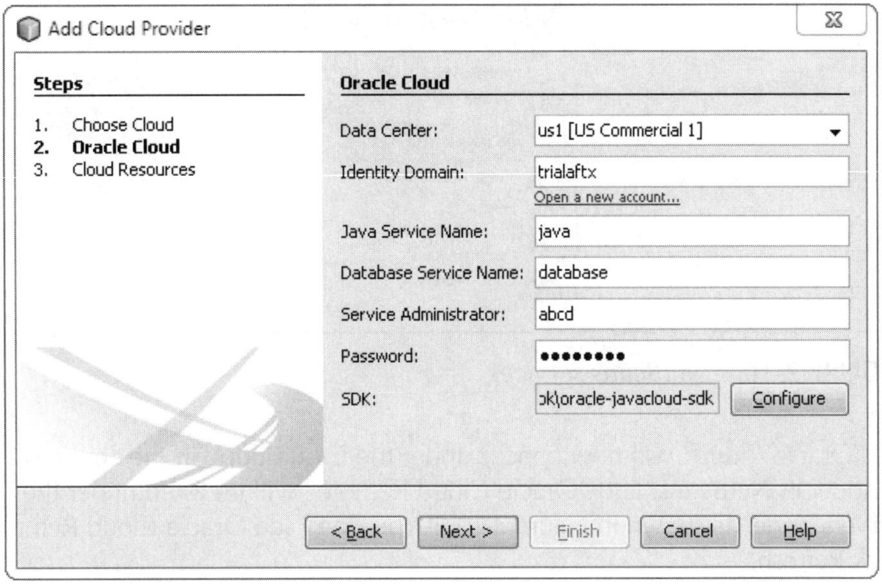

FIGURE 2-8. *Add Cloud Provider*

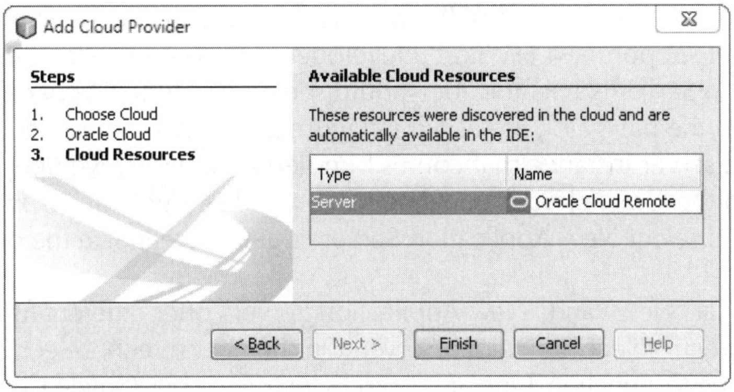

FIGURE 2-9. *Available Cloud Resources*

FIGURE 2-10. *NetBeans services*

"Oracle Cloud" will now appear under the Cloud node in the Services window in NetBeans, and "Oracle Cloud Remote" will be listed under the Servers node, as shown in Figure 2-10. If you don't see Oracle Cloud Remote, click Refresh.

The green arrow beside Oracle Cloud Remote indicates that the server is running. Considering we are using a cloud server, this will always be green. If a local GlassFish server were also running, there would be a similar green arrow beside the GlassFish listing as well.

JDeveloper

Download the latest version of JDeveloper from the OTN. The Studio Edition will support Java EE. Start JDeveloper, followed by selecting View | Application Server Navigator. You should see an IntegratedWebLogicServer instance in the navigator, as shown in Figure 2-11. This represents the WebLogic server instance that comes bundled with the JDeveloper IDE.

To add the Oracle Java Cloud Application Server, right-click Application Servers and select New Application Server to get a screen like the one shown in Figure 2-12.

Note that "New" and "New Application Server" offer different functionality. On this screen, select Standalone Server. On the next screen, select Oracle Cloud as the Connection Type, followed by entering your Oracle Cloud credentials, which naturally are the same across all IDEs.

Once you are done, you will see a second server in the Application Server Navigator. You can now deploy any of your applications to your server on the Oracle Java Cloud.

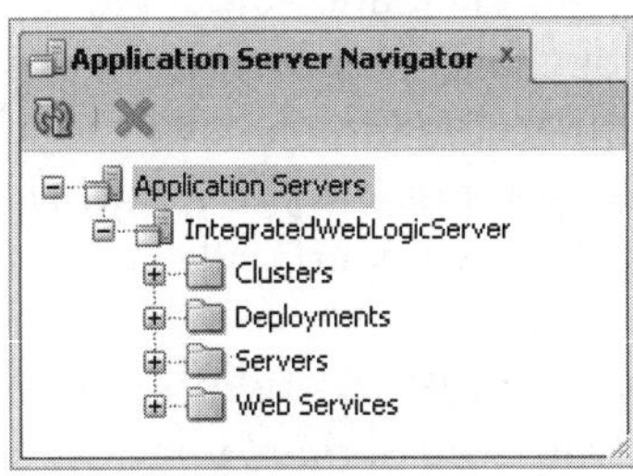

FIGURE 2-11. *JDeveloper Application Server Navigator*

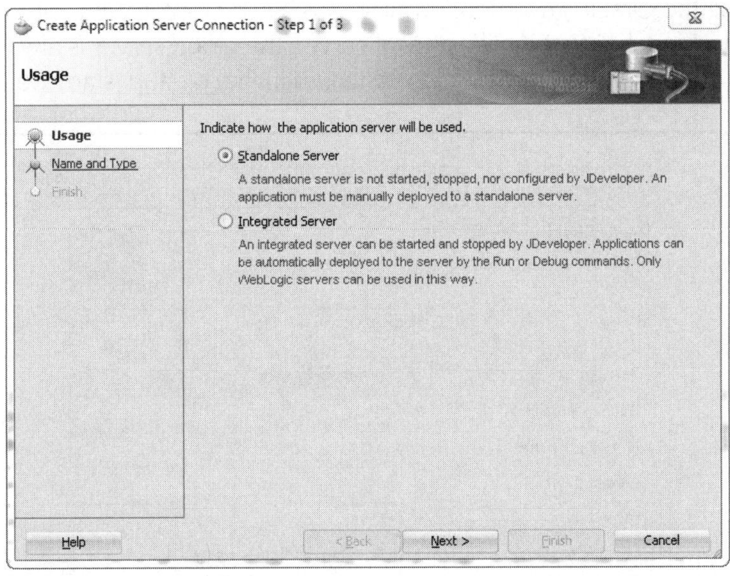

FIGURE 2-12. *Create Application Server Connection screen*

Eclipse

Download the Oracle Enterprise Pack for Eclipse from OTN at www.oracle.com/technetwork/developer-tools/eclipse/. Installation is as straightforward as extracting the zip file. Start Eclipse. You will see a Servers window if you have the Web or Java EE perspective enabled. If this is not enabled by default, you might have to manually open the Servers window. You can also edit servers by selecting Window | Preferences | Server | Runtime Environments.

In the Servers window, right-click and select New | Server. Here, enter your Oracle Java Cloud credentials, as shown in Figure 2-13.

You will also have to point to the Oracle Java Cloud SDK and the Java Runtime Environment. In case you point to JRE 7, you will get the following alert:

> Cloud applications must be developed with Java 6 or earlier. The selected version is "1.7."

In this case, download and install JRE 6 and point to the JRE 6 directory. If your connection is successful, the Servers window will get updated, as shown in Figure 2-14.

As with NetBeans, you will find that Eclipse also shows a green arrow beside a running server, which in this case is the Oracle Java Cloud.

You now have your Oracle Java Cloud set up and integrated with NetBeans, JDeveloper, and Eclipse.

Having the Oracle Java Cloud available as a server integrated with your IDE is also good fun, because unlike a local server, the cloud server is always readily available to you without any need to install, manage, or stop, start, wait....

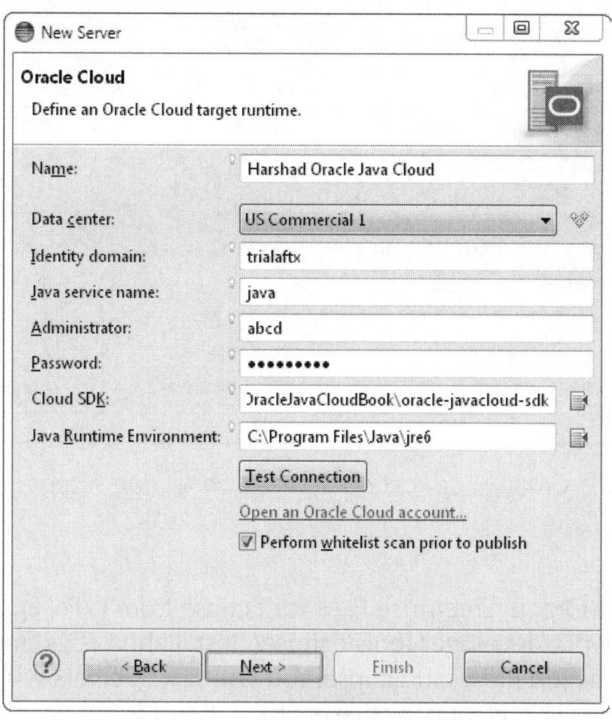

FIGURE 2-13. *Eclipse's New Server window*

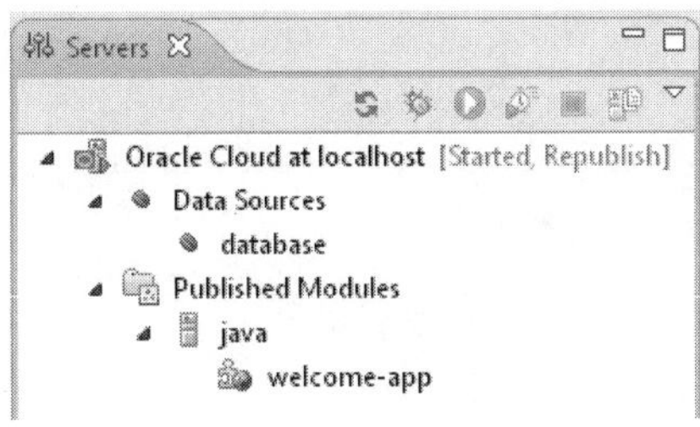

FIGURE 2-14. *Eclipse's Servers window*

Maven and Ant

Maven (http://maven.apache.org/) and Ant (http://ant.apache.org/) are widely used for their project management and build capabilities. Whereas Ant is the old and trusted workhorse build tool, Maven is the relatively newer tool that boasts impressive project management capabilities in addition to its build capabilities.

OJC offers rich integration with both tools via the Cloud SDK. The Maven plugin maven-javacloud.jar and the Ant plugin ant-javacloud.jar can be found in the lib directory of the SDK. With the Maven plugin, commands for the Java Cloud are exposed as Maven goals. Also, there's an Ant task available in the Ant plugin for most of the command-line commands.

If the command is "install," the Maven goal is com.oracle.cloud:javacloud :install, whereas the Ant task is <javacloud:install/>.

The Maven and Ant plugins make it possible for you to integrate any project with the Oracle Java Cloud merely by making a few changes to the Maven or Ant configuration.

Users and Roles

Every Oracle Cloud Service belongs to an Identity Domain that controls the user authentication and authorization for that service. You can share the same identity store among multiple Oracle Cloud Services by placing them in the same Identity Domain.

Click the Users link on the top right of the page, as seen in Figure 2-3 and you will get a screen as shown in Figure 2-15, listing the names, user names, and email for the users in the system. You can use the search box as well as the Show and Sort By drop downs to fetch particular users or type of users.

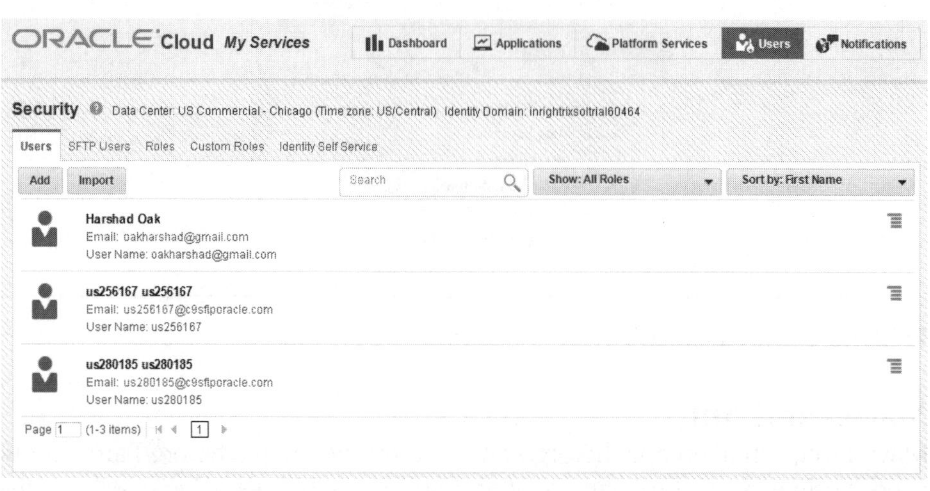

FIGURE 2-15. *Users*

Some not-so-obvious functionality on this screen is that if you click or hover your mouse over the user's name, you get a small popup showing the roles assigned to that user, as shown in Figure 2-16. Also clicking the icon on the extreme right of the listing gets you the option to modify the user's information, reset the password, manage the roles assigned to that user, and to remove the user, as shown in Figure 2-17. The Remove option is disabled for the user with the Identity Domain Administrator role.

FIGURE 2-16. *User Roles*

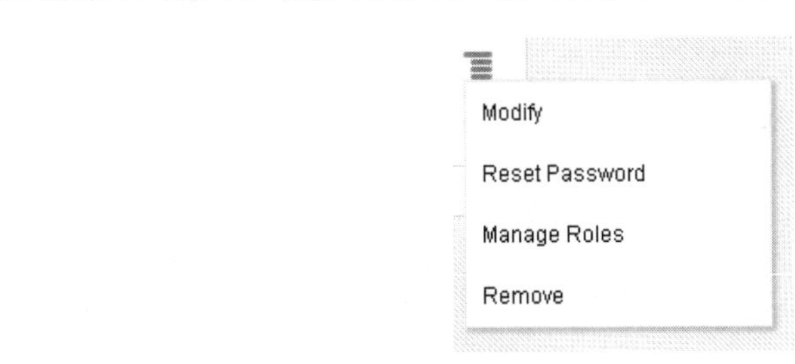

FIGURE 2-17. *Modify User Information*

The user that you used to log in to the Oracle Cloud will also be the Identity Domain Administrator by default. However, you can add and modify users and roles as required.

To add a new user, click the Add button shown in Figure 2-16. You will get a popup as shown in Figure 2-18 where you can add the new user and select the role for that user.

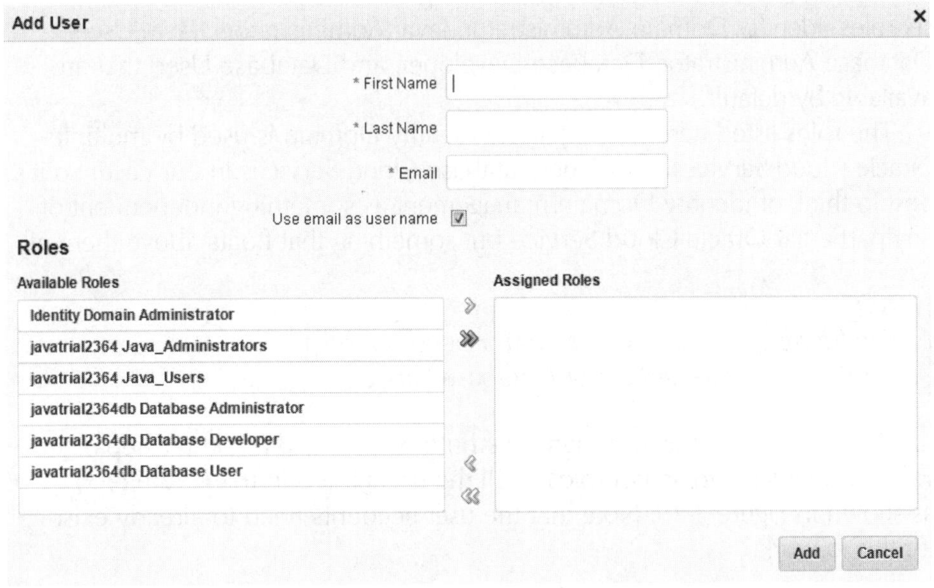

FIGURE 2-18. *Add User*

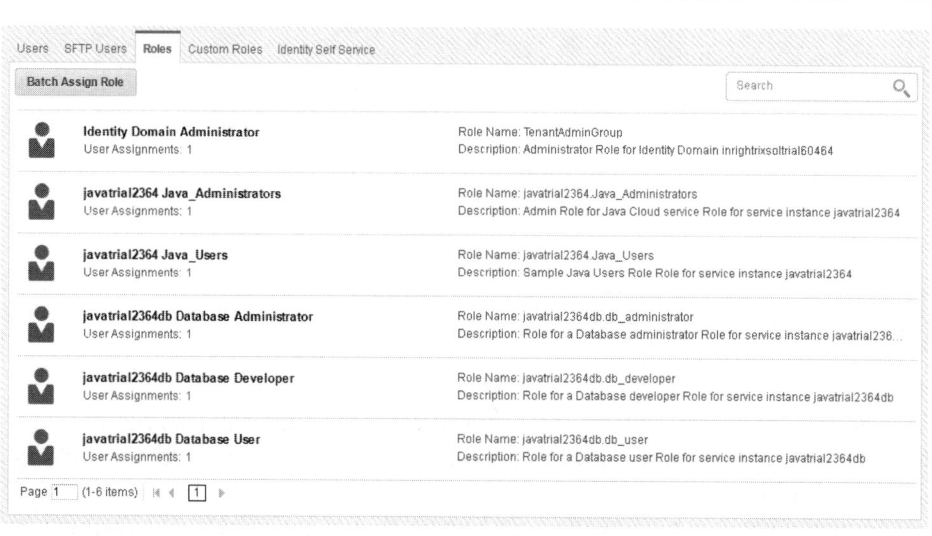

FIGURE 2-19. *Roles*

Click the Roles tab and, as shown in Figure 2-19, you would see the six roles (Identity Domain Administrator, Java_Administrators, Java_Users, Database Administrator, Database Developer, and Database User) that are available by default.

The roles listed here show that the Identity Domain is used by multiple Oracle Cloud Services, Java, and Database Cloud Services in our case. So it's best to think of Identity Domain management as something independent of any particular Oracle Cloud Service but something that floats above them all.

NOTE
The Identity Domain Administrator need not be an administrator for the Java or Database Service.

You can use the Batch Assign Role button to upload a comma-separated values (CSV) file and assign roles to all the users listed in the CSV file, as shown in Figure 2-20. Note that the user accounts need to already exist for this to work.

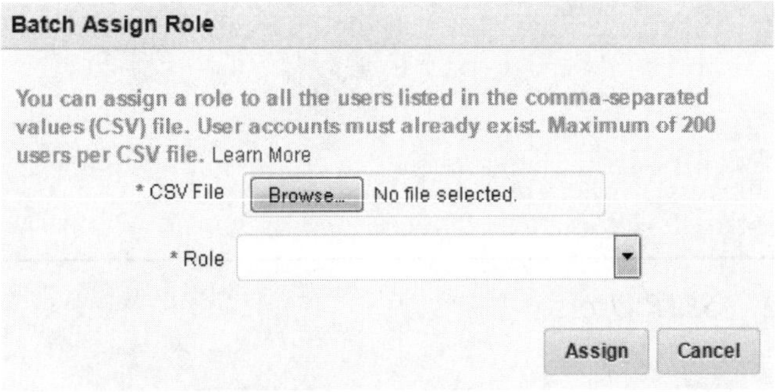

Batch Assign Role

You can assign a role to all the users listed in the comma-separated values (CSV) file. User accounts must already exist. Maximum of 200 users per CSV file. Learn More

* CSV File Browse... No file selected.

* Role

Assign Cancel

FIGURE 2-20. *Batch Assign Roles*

To add a new role, click the Custom Roles tab, followed by clicking the Add button and entering the role information in the Add Role Information popup, as shown in Figure 2-21.

Click the SFTP Users tab to access SFTP user list. Reset Password is the only functionality available for SFTP users, as shown in Figure 2-22.

You can click the Identity Self Service tab to access the forms to change password and challenge questions, as shown in Figure 2-23.

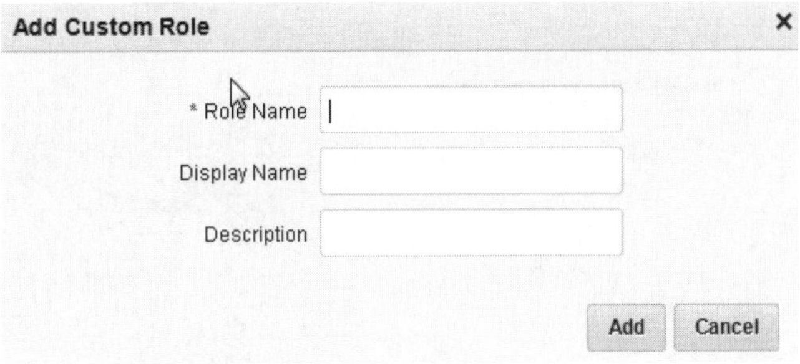

Add Custom Role ×

* Role Name

Display Name

Description

Add Cancel

FIGURE 2-21. *Add Custom Role*

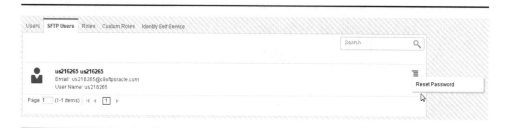

FIGURE 2-22. *SFTP Users*

Users SFTP Users Roles Custom Roles **Identity Self Service**

User Information

Note: First and Last Name cannot be changed via Identity Self Service.

First Name Harshad

Last Name Oak

Email oakharshad@gmail.com

Change Password

Password Policy

* Old Password

* New Password

* Confirm New Password

Submit **Reset**

Change Challenge Questions

* Current Password

* Question 1

* Answer 1

* Question 2

* Answer 2

* Question 3

* Answer 3

Submit **Reset**

FIGURE 2-23. *Identity Self Service*

NOTE
OJC (even the trial setup) does not restrict the number of users or applications deployed. Therefore, it technically supports unlimited users and applications.

Summary

In this chapter, we looked at Oracle's journey into the cloud, followed by specifics on OJC's pricing, features, and trial. We next looked at using the SDK and integrating OJC with an IDE. We closed with a look at the identity management capabilities of Oracle Cloud.

You now have your Oracle Java Cloud ready, set up, and integrated. So let's get going with our Java EE development and start deploying on our Oracle Java Cloud setup.

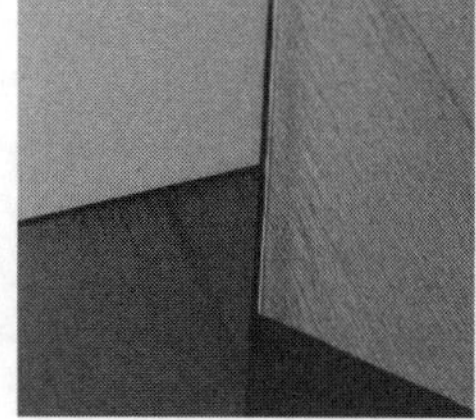

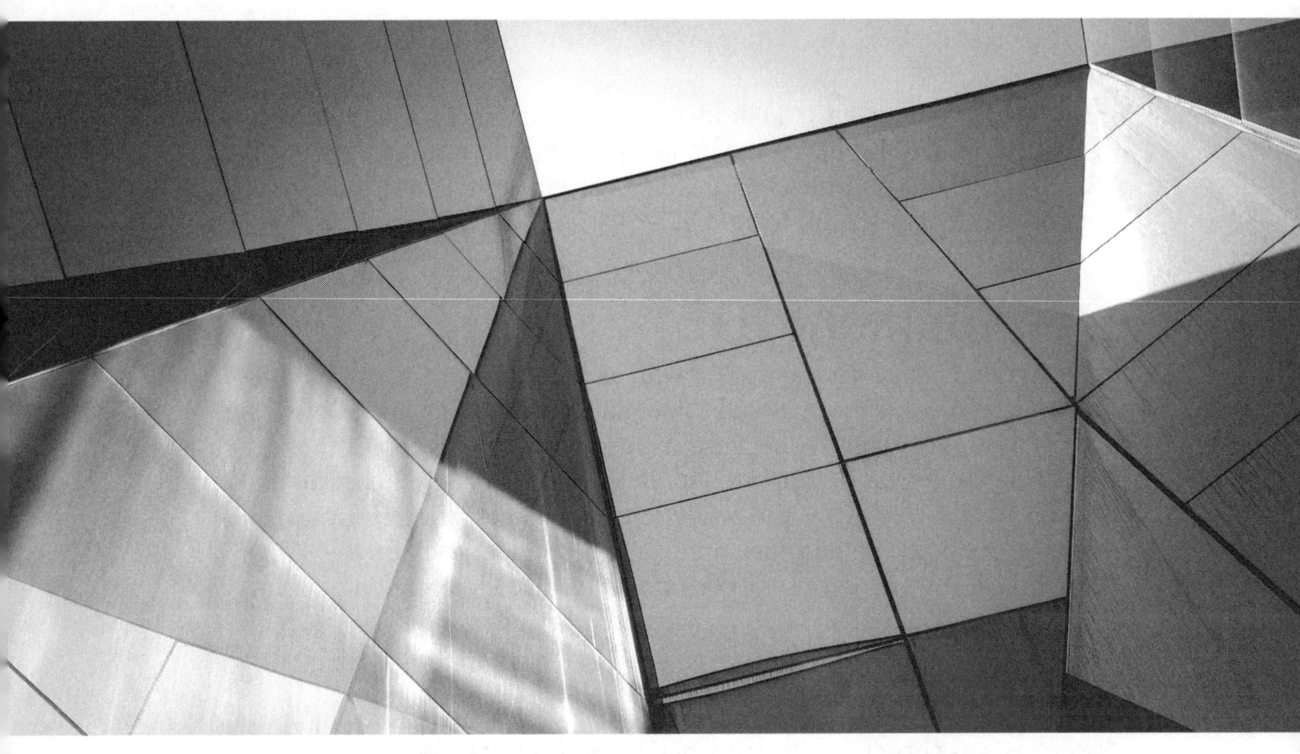

CHAPTER 3

Build and Deploy with NetBeans

Now that we have a fair idea of what Java EE and the Oracle Java Cloud (OJC) have to offer, let's dive in and start building our first Java EE application. We will first select an IDE, and then set up and deploy a basic application to the OJC.

Development IDE

You can build a Java EE application with as little as a text editor, but it is much easier if you choose an IDE. The NetBeans, Eclipse, and JDeveloper IDEs make this even easier because of the natural integration OJC offers with these three Oracle-supported tools. The use of an IDE here will make it easier for you to quickly and easily replicate what's being shown in the book. Before beginning our first application, select and set up the IDE of your choice. For the purposes of this book, we'll build and deploy using the NetBeans IDE, but any IDE you've chosen to use is fine.

Why NetBeans?

NetBeans was chosen as the primary IDE for this book because of its solid reputation, ease of use, and OJC integration. NetBeans is free and Java EE ready "out of the box."

NetBeans is available with dual licenses—Common Development and Distribution License (CDDL) and GNU General Public License (GPL) v2 with Classpath Exception. You can check the licensing FAQ at http://wiki.netbeans.org/NetBeansUserFAQ#License_and_Legal_Questions for details. However, here are the primary takeaways:

- You can use it for commercial work.
- There are no license costs.
- You do not need to open source your code.

NetBeans is also great for the beginner.

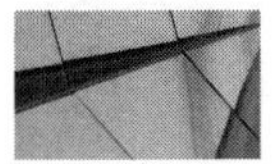

NOTE
Although we are choosing a specific IDE (here, NetBeans) in this book, we will always build applications adhering to the Java EE specification and not write any IDE-specific code.

Building with Java EE Technologies

Let's now start building an application with NetBeans and deploy it on OJC. To begin with, let's focus on building an application and not worry about the micro-level details of each Java EE technology. We will spend future chapters going into more detail on Java EE technologies. For now, it's important to get a view of the whole picture.

TIP
The projects in this book have been written to provide hands-on training. It is important that you try things out firsthand and build your applications alongside the book chapters to gain the full value of these lessons.

NetBeans can be installed on all operating systems that support Java. Therefore, it will install and run the same on Windows, Linux, and Mac OS X systems. We have looked at installing the NetBeans IDE in Chapter 2.

Note that installing even the full version does not mean that all features will be activated right away and start taking up resources. NetBeans has a neat Feature On Demand capability that will enable a technology only when you actually use it.

Therefore, you are likely to get the activation screen when you first start using different technologies in NetBeans.

First NetBeans Project

Once you have NetBeans running, select File | New Project. On this screen, select Java Web | Web Application. Name the project **Ch3WebApplication1**. You do not need to change anything else on this screen. However, do note the text in the Project Location field, so as to be aware of where exactly the project files are being stored on your machine. Click Next.

As shown in Figure 3-1, select Oracle Cloud Remote as your server. The thing to note here is that because OJC as yet does not support Java EE 6, NetBeans will force you to use Java EE 5 so as to prevent you from writing any code that OJC might not be capable of running. NetBeans also recommends that you set the source level to 1.5, as this will stop you from using features from later versions of Java. Also, when the project is compiled, all classes are created with the source level set to 1.5.

TIP
Applications on OJC can use Java SE 6 APIs, so if you intend to use source features in JDK 6, go over to Project Properties | Sources and change the code level to JDK 6. Refer to Appendix C for the list of supported APIs.

OJC's support for Java language and Java EE technology features is meant to be updated as newer versions of Java EE and WebLogic are released.

As mentioned earlier, you can change the source level to JDK 6. But because of the backward compatibility in Java and Java EE, even your Java EE 5 application with Java 5 code will work fine on OJC.

FIGURE 3-1. *Select Oracle Cloud Remote as your server in the Server and Settings section.*

NOTE

Java dropped the Java versioning of 1.5, 1.6, and so on, in favor of Java 5, Java 6, and so on. Therefore, the reference to Java 1.5 here might seem confusing. Please note that 1.5.0 (or 1.5) continues to be used in places that are visible only to developers, or where the version number is parsed by programs, but 1.5.0 refers to exactly the same platform and products numbered 5.0. Therefore, the 1.5 version here is the same Java 5 you might be more familiar with.

Click the Next button seen in Figure 3-1. NetBeans will show a screen like the one in Figure 3-2, asking if you would like to use any additional web frameworks in your project. It lists JavaServer Faces (JSF), Spring Web MVC, Struts, and Hibernate. The JSF framework is part of Java EE, and we will look at it in Chapter 6. The other three are popular third-party, open-source frameworks, but are not part of the Java EE specification as such.

Do not select any of the frameworks. Click Finish. The project should now get created, and the Projects window will show a file structure like in Figure 3-3.

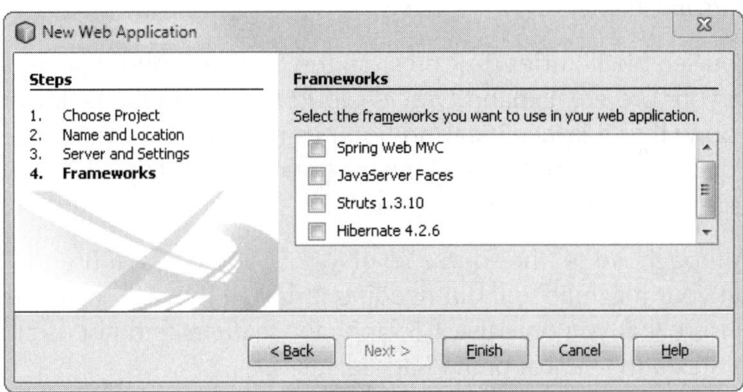

FIGURE 3-2. *Additional web frameworks*

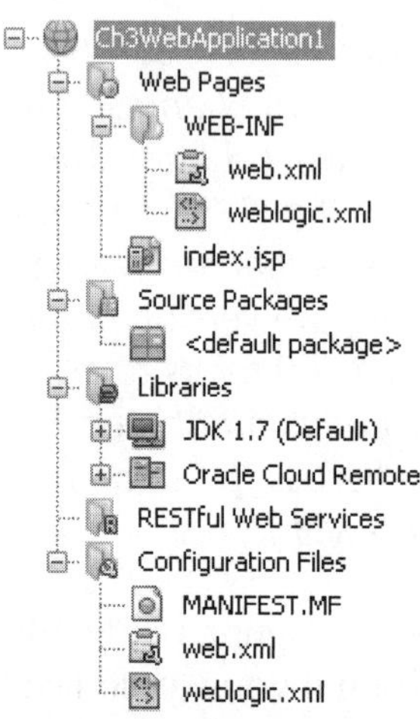

FIGURE 3-3. *The file structure in the Projects window*

Here are a few things to note:

- An index.jsp file is generated by NetBeans. NetBeans does this for all web applications. Although this is a JavaServer Page, you will find that it is pretty much the same as HTML in this case. We will look at JSPs in Chapter 5.
- You see the libraries (JAR files) on the Oracle Cloud that are available to your project. Expand *Oracle Cloud Remote* in the listing and you will find javaee5.jar and libraries required for persistence. Persistence, in most cases, means to talk to a database. We will be using these libraries in Chapter 9.
- Although we set the source level to 1.5, you can still use the JDK 1.7 on your machine without needing to install JDK 1.5. NetBeans will ensure that you only use 1.5 language features and not use the syntax and features of the later releases.
- Because OJC runs on the WebLogic server, a WebLogic configuration file named weblogic.xml file is also generated.

FIGURE 3-4. *The index.jsp from your application deployed on OJC*

If you expect to go through many more steps before you can deploy and run this application on the cloud, you are in for a surprise. All you need to do is right-click the project name and click Run. NetBeans will then compile, package, and deploy your web application on OJC. It will actually go one step further by opening your default browser and pointing you to the index.jsp file in your web application. However, you must sign in to OJC before you can access the page.

- Because you are deploying to a cloud server, you will also require an Internet connection. Also, NetBeans should not be blocked by a proxy or a firewall. Once you complete the login, you should see a Hello World page running from OJC, as shown in Figure 3-4. Congratulations! You built and deployed a Java EE application on the cloud. You are a Cloud Java EE developer!

What Happened?

Now let's look at exactly what happened so you feel that you've earned the title of Cloud Java EE developer. First, let's look at all the work NetBeans did in the background. The easiest way to do this is to go through the NetBeans logs.

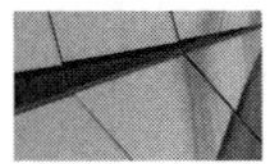

TIP
If you can't see the logs because you closed the log window in NetBeans, reset your NetBeans windows by clicking Windows | Reset Windows.

In NetBeans, you should see your logs in two tabs. The first tab, titled Ch3WebApplication1 (run), lists the actions performed to create the required directories, to compile the code, to package the code, and finally, to deploy the code to OJC. The second tab, Oracle Cloud Remote Deployment, lists the actions performed on OJC. It would be well worth your time to go through these logs. In Listing 3-1, I have trimmed some of the verbose bits, but the logs will give you a sense of what exactly is happening in the background.

Listing 3-1: *Ch3WebApplication1 (Run) Log*

```
ant -f <NPDP>\\Ch3WebApplication1
-Djsp.includes=<NPDP>\\Ch3WebApplication1\\build\\web\\index.jsp
-DforceRedeploy=false -Dclient.urlPart=/index.jsp
-Ddirectory.deployment.supported=false
-Djavac.jsp.includes=org/apache/jsp/index_jsp.java
-Dnb.wait.for.caches=true run
init:
deps-module-jar:
deps-ear-jar:
deps-jar:
Created dir: <NPDP>\Ch3WebApplication1\build\web\WEB-INF\classes
Created dir: <NPDP>\Ch3WebApplication1\build\web\META-INF
Copying 1 file to <NPDP>\Ch3WebApplication1\build\web\META-INF
Copying 3 files to <NPDP>\Ch3WebApplication1\build\web
library-inclusion-in-archive:
library-inclusion-in-manifest:
Created dir: <NPDP>\Ch3WebApplication1\build\empty
compile:
compile-jsps:
Created dir: <NPDP>\Ch3WebApplication1\build\generated\src
Created dir: <NPDP>\Ch3WebApplication1\build\generated\classes
Compiling 1 source file to
<NPDP>\Ch3WebApplication1\build\generated\classes
warning: [options] bootstrap class path not set
in conjunction with -source 1.5
1 warning
Created dir: <NPDP>\Ch3WebApplication1\dist
Building jar: <NPDP>\Ch3WebApplication1\dist\Ch3WebApplication1.war
Distributing
<NPDP>\Ch3WebApplication1\dist\Ch3WebApplication1.war
 to [cloud-deployment]
Uploading...
Deploying...
```

For the sake of brevity, I have replaced <NPDP> in all places where the NetBeans Projects Directory Path appeared in the log. The log in Listing 3-2 shows the various actions performed by NetBeans to build, package, upload, and deploy the application to OJC.

Listing 3-2: *Oracle Cloud Remote Deployment Log*

```
Uploading...
Deploying....
==================== Log file: virusscan====================
<TIME> CDT: Starting action "Virus Scan"
<TIME> CDT: Virus Scan started
<TIME> CDT: ----------------------------------------------
<TIME> CDT: File Scanned: "Ch3WebApplication1.war".
<TIME> CDT: File Size:    "2197".
<TIME> CDT: File Status:  "CLEAN".
<TIME> CDT: ---------------------------------------------
<TIME> CDT: Virus scan passed.
<TIME> CDT: "Virus Scan" complete: status SUCCESS
==================== Log file: whitelist==========================
<TIME> CDT: Starting action "API Whitelist"
<TIME> CDT: API Whitelist started
<TIME> CDT: WARNING  - There are 3 warnings(s)
found for Ch3WebApplication1.war.
...
<TIME> CDT: INFO     - Whitelist validation has completed
 with 0 error(s) and 3 warning(s).
<TIME> CDT: Whitelist validation passed.
<TIME> CDT: "API Whitelist" complete: status SUCCESS

==================== Log file: deploy====================
<TIME> CDT: Starting action "Deploy Application"
<TIME> CDT: Deploy Application started
<TIME> CDT: [Deployer:149194]Operation 'deploy'
on application 'Ch3WebApplication1' has succeeded on 'm0'
<TIME> CDT: WL action state: completed
<TIME> CDT: Application deployment succeeded.
<TIME> CDT: "Deploy Application" complete: status SUCCESS
```

The long timestamp text in the log entry has been replaced with <TIME>. This log is the one returned by OJC and lists actions being performed entirely on the cloud. NetBeans' role is limited to creating, uploading, and deploying the .war file for the application, after which it is up to OJC to scan, verify, and deploy the application. It usually takes a minute or so for the application to be up and running on OJC in the case of a successful deployment.

Files and Directories Generated

The Ch3WebApplication1 (run) log will show that NetBeans has created several directories, followed by building a Ch3WebApplication1.war file that is uploaded and deployed to the cloud. We will talk more about WAR files in the "We Are at WAR" section later in this chapter.

Figure 3-3 showed how NetBeans organizes your project files. However, this can be confusing because the way files are organized in NetBeans is meant to ease development—it does not quite map to the actual directory structure on your computer. To better understand this, open Windows Explorer or a similar tool on your operating system and look at the directory structure created. It should be identical to the one shown in Figure 3-5.

Although you can get this same view within NetBeans in the Files window, it's often easier to understand NetBeans' work when you can relate it to your familiar OS directories. It is important to have a clear understanding of what NetBeans is doing in the background; otherwise, it can seem like NetBeans is performing some magic to make your application go.

Directories such as WEB-INF are created as required by the Java EE specification. However, others (such as build, src, and dist) are only created as per common developer conventions—for example, keeping source files in the src directory, build files in the build directory, and the distribution .war files

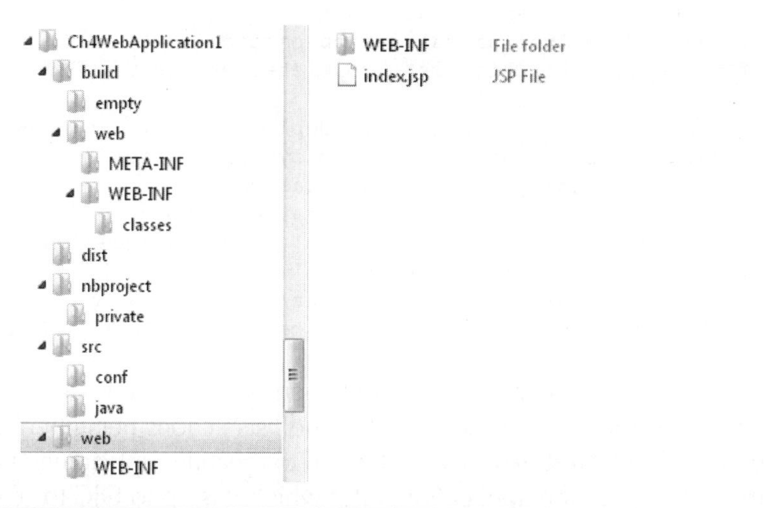

FIGURE 3-5. *Project directories*

in the dist directory. The nbproject directory is for NetBeans configuration information and scripts.

The Cloud Deployment

The second log file, Oracle Cloud Remote Deployment, provides insights into what exactly happens once NetBeans uploads your application to OJC. The first section is marked "virus-scan." Once the virus scan is cleared, next is the "whitelist." A whitelist is a list of those technologies and APIs that fulfill the technical and security requirements of a software/service and have been approved to run on it. The whitelist log in Listing 3-2 shows three warnings and zero errors.

You will find that the warnings are more recommendations for changes in the XML. You would get these warnings with all IDEs because none of them, by default, generate the XML expected.

Because there are no errors in the whitelist scan, OJC moves to the next task of deploying the application. Only after this log says

```
"Deploy Application" complete: status SUCCESS
```

is the application actually deployed. The last line in the log says

```
Deployment was successful. Application is being opened at https://
java-trialaftx.java.us1.oraclecloudapps.com/Ch3WebApplication1
```

followed by your default browser opening. The actual URL would vary in each case based on the Identity Domain and which data center is linked to your account. In this example, trialaftx is the Identity Domain and us1 represents the U.S. data center. Therefore, the format is

> https://<*CloudServiceName*>-<*IdentityDomain*>.java.<*DataCenter*>
> .oraclecloudapps.com/<*ApplicationName*>

The first warning displayed in the log is

```
Recommended child element "login-config" missing under element.
If you want to make your application public, you can have empty
<login-config/> in your web.xml. If you need authentication then
you must have <login-config> and its child <auth-method> element
in web.xml. Without this element(<login-config>), users may be
challenged by SSO.
```

You need not worry about what a web.xml file is at this point in time, but if you do not want the Single Sign On (SSO) page to come up, just add the <login-config/> tag to the web.xml file.

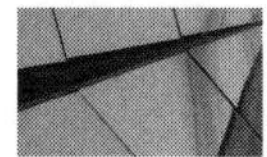

NOTE
OJC will force you to sign in for every web application that does not have the <login-config> tag in the web.xml file. This is true for all web applications that NetBeans creates for us in this book.

You will find that the other two warnings also talk of missing XML tags. Whitelist warnings are not showstoppers, however. As long as you don't get any errors, your application will deploy. However, in most cases, it would be wise to heed to these warnings from OJC and make the necessary changes.

Clean and Build, Verify

Let's look at a couple of useful features in NetBeans and their integration with OJC. If you right-click the project name in the Projects window, you will see a context menu that provides many options, including the following:

- **Clean and Build** NetBeans will delete any previously compiled files, build outputs, and then recompile and package your application.
- **Verify** If you wish to verify your application against the OJC whitelist, you need not upload and verify it online. You can click Verify and use the Cloud SDK on your machine to verify your application against the whitelist.
- The other IDEs (Eclipse and JDeveloper) offer similar capability; however, the placement and naming of these options is a bit different.
- Let's now delve further into the structure of the web application.

Web Application Structure

Java EE is focused on structures, standards, and conventions. There is almost always a definitive way of doing things, and if you comply with that way, the Java EE platform software will do most of the heavy lifting for you. This is especially important when building an application. If you are building a Java EE application, for the application server to do its magic, you need to follow the standards, part of which is placing your files in a certain place and packaging your application in a certain way.

Directories

Figure 3-5 showed the directory structure for our application, whereas Figure 3-6 shows the key files and directories in a Java EE application. Note that this is not an exhaustive list. Only the most important files and directories are highlighted here.

As shown in Figure 3-6, the WEB-INF directory is at the root of the application, along with your HTML, XHTML, JSP, and other files. However, whereas these files are publicly available, WEB-INF is a special private directory, and the server will ensure that the contents of that directory cannot be accessed directly. So although you are able to access an HTML file placed at the root with a URL, such as example.com/apage.html, you cannot use example.com/WEB-INF/apage.html if you were to place that same HTML file within the WEB-INF directory.

Within the WEB-INF directory is the web.xml file, which is the web deployment descriptor that holds all the configuration information for the web application.

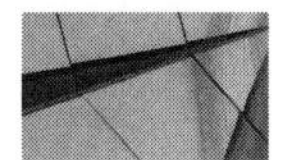

NOTE
OJC runs a mix of Java EE 5 and 6 technologies. Whereas web.xml is optional in EE 6, this file is mandatory with EE 5 and, therefore, is always required while deploying applications to OJC.

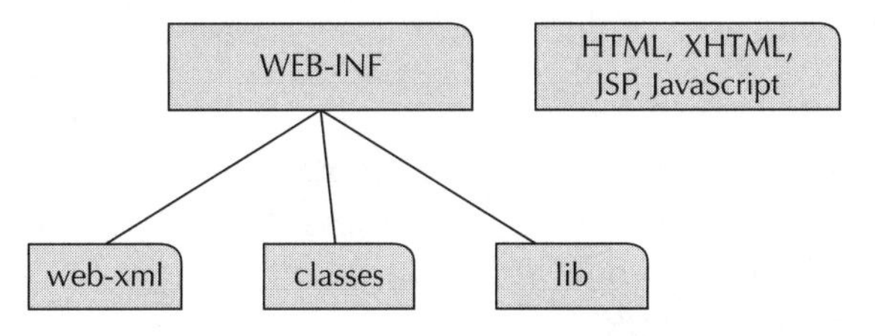

FIGURE 3-6. *Key files and directories in a web application*

The classes directory is where your Java classes should be placed. Create a directory structure within the classes directory based on your Java package names. The class file for com.example.User.java will be at /WEB-INF/classes/com/example/User.class.

The lib directory is where any libraries (your own or third party) should be placed. The libraries are JAR files that the application server will load to make available to the application. Now that we have looked at the directory structure for a web application, let's move on to how your Java EE application is packaged.

Packaging the Application

If you have a local Java EE application server running on your machine, you usually have the option of just copying your application to a certain directory, and the server will deploy the application. However, with cloud providers such as OJC, you are expected to package your application in the standard Java EE format and upload the packaged file to the server.

We Are at WAR

Throughout the earlier logs, you may have noticed references to the Ch3WebApplication1.war file. The Java EE web application you created has been packaged into that file by NetBeans. In all probability, you would have encountered Java Archives (JAR) files earlier with Java development, but if the JAR file contains a web application, you should name the file as a .war file. Here, WAR stands for "web archive," and it is essentially a JAR file but with the file extension set to .war, so as to convey that it is a web application. All Java EE–compatible application servers (either local or on the cloud) will have an option to deploy a WAR file. There's another kind of JAR file, known as an Enterprise Archive (EAR) file, that we will encounter later in the book.

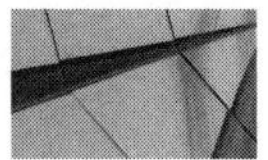

TIP

JAR, WAR, and EAR are all built with the ZIP file format. Therefore, you can open, compress, and extract these files using any ZIP software you already might have installed.

In the Ch3WebApplication1 (run) log, you will see the following lines:

```
Created dir: ...\Ch3WebApplication1\dist
Building jar: ...Ch3WebApplication1\dist\Ch3WebApplication1.war
```

As briefly mentioned earlier, the dist directory that NetBeans has created is not mandated by the Java EE specification, but it is convention to name your directory with the distribution files as dist. If you open the dist directory, you will find the file Ch3WebApplication1.war.

Note that this Ch3WebApplication1.war file is the *only* file that NetBeans actually uploaded to OJC and deployed on the cloud. You can open this WAR file using a Java JAR tool and even with a ZIP tool such as WinZip or 7-Zip. Take a look at exactly what has been uploaded. Irrespective of which developer tool or IDE you use and how the tool displays the files in the UI, the WAR file will always be in the structure dictated by the specification.

When you open this file, you will find it to be as per the structure shown in Figure 3-5. The lib directory is missing only because our application isn't using any additional libraries and does not require a lib directory.

Notice that in our application, we have a web.xml file and a weblogic.xml file. The web.xml file is the web deployment descriptor and has all the configuration information specific to our web application. The weblogic.xml file is the runtime deployment descriptor and is used for WebLogic-specific configuration parameters.

In Chapter 7, we will look at packaging a WAR file along with a JAR file. This is achieved using a second kind of Java EE application packaging known as an EAR (Enterprise Archive) file, as we'll discuss in detail.

Summary

In this chapter, we developed an application using NetBeans and then deployed it to OJC. We also had a look at the structure of a Java EE web application and how you package a Java EE application. In the next chapter, we will take our application further and add functionality to it using Servlets technology.

CHAPTER 4

Servlets, Filters, and Listeners

In the previous chapter, we created a basic web application using NetBeans and discussed the structure and packaging of a Java EE application. In this chapter, we'll look at Servlets, a Java EE technology that has been integral to Java EE application building from day one. We'll also look at the key files for Servlet-based Java EE applications, sharing data, session management, filters, and listeners. Finally, we'll deploy applications using these features onto the Oracle Java Cloud (OJC).

Servlets

Servlets have been around since the late 1990s and, amazingly enough, continue to be a key foundation technology even today. In a sense, the Java EE story began with Servlets. Java Servlet Development Kit was a precursor to Java 2 Platform, Enterprise Edition (J2EE) that was introduced in 1999 (http://oracle.com.edgesuite.net/timeline/java/). Servlets were launched at a time when Java itself was pretty new and Java applets were still cool and widely used.

Servlets back then were aimed at leveraging the power of Java to help developers extend the functionality of a web server. I distinctly remember that, while I was preparing for campus placements during my master's degree, the standard answer for "What is a Servlet?" was "It's an applet that runs on the server." No one quite knew what that meant, but Servlets was still a buzzing technology, and this answer did help many of us land good jobs.

Servlets today are anything but "applets on the server." Applets themselves have faded out of the Java mainstream. The basic structure and code for Servlets have not changed much over the years. However, Servlets today are more a foundation technology that most other Java EE technologies either utilize or build over. The Oracle Java Cloud (OJC) supports the Servlet 2.5 specification.

In previous chapters, we have talked of application servers, where the server receives a request for a resource and sends back a response in reply. What if you wanted this same request/response process to do more and to have the smarts to perform action X if some condition Y was fulfilled? Enter Servlets, which give you the ability to generate dynamic content while leveraging the many Java libraries and features.

Servlet Interface

A Servlet is an implementation of the javax.servlet.Servlet interface. The Servlet interface defines lifecycle methods to initialize a Servlet, process requests, and destroy a Servlet. However, the usual way to use the Servlet interface is not by directly implementing the interface, but by subclassing an abstract implementation of the Servlet interface.

It could either be javax.servlet.GenericServlet or javax.servlet.http.HttpServlet, which extends GenericServlet. Both GenericServlet and HttpServlet are abstract classes that simplify writing Servlets because they provide a basic framework for your Servlet, as well as provide implementations of the Servlet lifecycle methods. Because these are abstract classes, the Servlet developer needs to extend them and override at least one method.

Therefore, instead of having to write your class as

```
public class YourServlet implements Servlet
```

and then be forced to implement all the methods in the interface, you have the simpler option of either

```
public class YourServlet extends HttpServlet
```

or

```
public class YourServlet extends GenericServlet
```

HttpServlet

Whereas GenericServlet is protocol independent, HttpServlet is meant specifically for use over the HTTP and HTTPS protocols and is the one that's commonly used.

If you are building a web application, you would be talking over HTTP and have to use HttpServlet, which provides methods for the various HTTP request methods. So, there's a doGet method to handle GET requests, a doPost method to handle POST requests, and so on. The other methods in HttpServlet meant specifically to handle the various HTTP methods are doDelete, doGet, doHead, doOptions, doPut, and doTrace.

TIP
HTTP request methods (GET, POST, OPTIONS, PUT, DELETE, TRACE, and CONNECT) are part of the HTTP specification (www.w3.org/Protocols/rfc2616/rfc2616.html) and are just as relevant across technologies. HttpServlet only facilitates handling of the various HTTP requests by providing corresponding methods for each, which are automatically called by the server based on the type of HTTP method request.

GET and POST are the most commonly used HTTP requests. GET is used to request a resource. So every time you enter a URL in your browser, you are essentially firing a GET request. POST is mostly used for HTML form submissions. The other HTTP request methods are rarely used. So in most cases, your Servlet will override the doGet and the doPost methods from HttpServlet.

TIP
Leveraging HTTP request methods in your application has had a rebirth of sorts due to the RESTful way of building distributed applications. REST stands for Representational State Transfer, but that usually only adds to the confusion. We will look at REST in Chapter 8.

Servlet One

Let's build our first Servlet using NetBeans and then deploy and run it on OJC. Note that the way in which the Servlet will be packaged in a WAR file and deployed to the cloud is similar to what was discussed in the previous chapter. Here are the steps to follow:

1. Start up NetBeans.
2. Select File | New Project.
3. On the resulting screen, select Java Web | Web Application.

4. Name the project **Ch4Servlet1**. As in the previous chapter, make sure you select Oracle Cloud Remote as your server.
5. Click Finish.

Select the project Ch4Servlet1 in the Projects window. You can now either select File | New File from the menu bar or right-click and select New | Servlet from the context menu. You should now see the New Servlet window, as shown in Figure 4-1.

Here, enter **servlets** for the package name and **Hello** for the class name. Click Next. On the next screen, shown in Figure 4-2, note that you are providing the Servlet a name that can be distinct from the class name and a URL pattern that can be used to access the Servlet.

NOTE
Although NetBeans, by default, will use the class name as the Servlet name and the URL pattern, that need not be the case. You can very well have a Servlet whose class name is A, Servlet name is B, and URL pattern to access the Servlet is C.

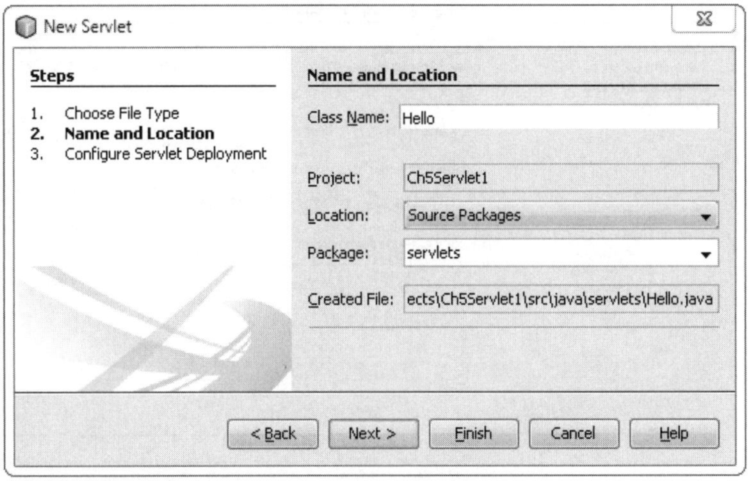

FIGURE 4-1. *New Servlet window*

It is a good practice to not tie your class name with the Servlet name and the URL patterns. The URL patterns are representative of the application flow and functionality, whereas the class and Servlet names depend on how you organize your code.

You even have the option of declaring multiple Servlet names, all of which point to the same class. Therefore, you can have one class with multiple Servlet names declared, where each Servlet name can have multiple URL patterns.

Now change the Servlet Name field to **HelloServletName** and the URL Pattern(s) field to **/HelloUrl, /MyServlet**, as shown in Figure 4-2, so as to make the difference in the names and their usage obvious. Note that we have specified two URL patterns for the Servlet, telling the server to run our Servlet whenever it gets a request with the URL pattern /HelloUrl as well as /MyServlet. Multiple URL patterns are useful because you often want to access the same Servlet functionality through different flows in your application.

You can use the asterisk (*) wildcard in the URL pattern so as to map a wide range of URL patterns to a servlet. Thus, you can have the URL pattern *.abc, which will mean that all requests in the form <*anything*>.abc will be directed to the Servlet. Or you can have the URL pattern /abc/*, which will direct all requests in the form /abc/<*anything*> to the Servlet.

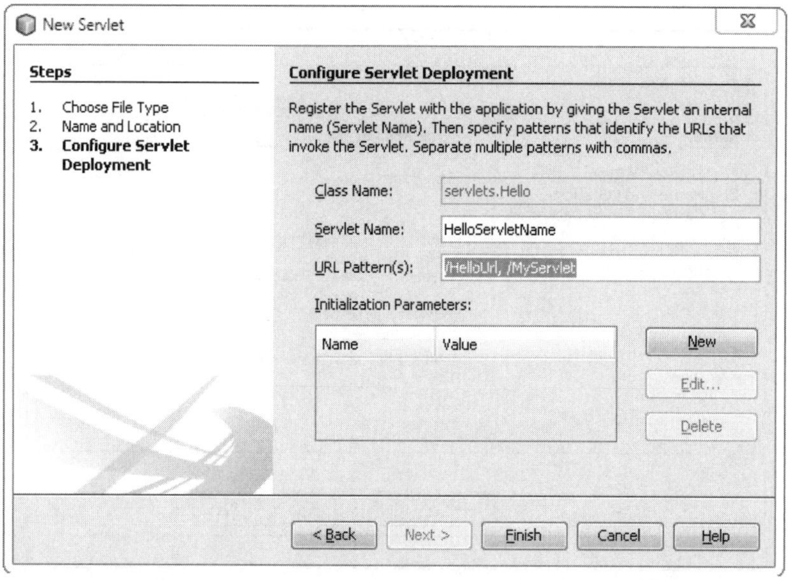

FIGURE 4-2. *Configuring the Servlet*

This capability is commonly used where you want a central Servlet/framework to manage your application. You will see this capability being used in Chapter 6.

TIP

*The * wildcard here is not used as liberally as you might have seen with regular expressions. This wildcard can be placed either at the start of the URL pattern or before or after the slash (/). You cannot end a URL pattern with a slash. Therefore, you do not have the tens of usage combinations for this wildcard that the usage in regular expressions might offer.*

Click Finish. NetBeans now opens two files for you: the Servlet Java class named Hello.java and the web.xml file.

Now right-click anywhere within the Servlet file Hello.java and click Run File. You could also get the same Run option by right-clicking the Hello.java listing in the NetBeans Projects window. You will see the window shown in Figure 4-3, which asks for the Servlet execution URI. You need not change this; however, as you can see in the example shown in the figure, you can use this screen to pass additional query parameters to your Servlet. Click OK.

Now, the same steps as discussed in the previous chapter will be repeated, as can be seen from the log. The NetBeans Output window will show two tabs: one with a log of the steps being carried out on your machine and the second (the Oracle Cloud Remote Deployment log) listing what's being sent to OJC and the response. The logs application will state the details of the packaging and deployment on OJC. Next, your default web browser will open up and point to your Servlet, as shown in Figure 4-4.

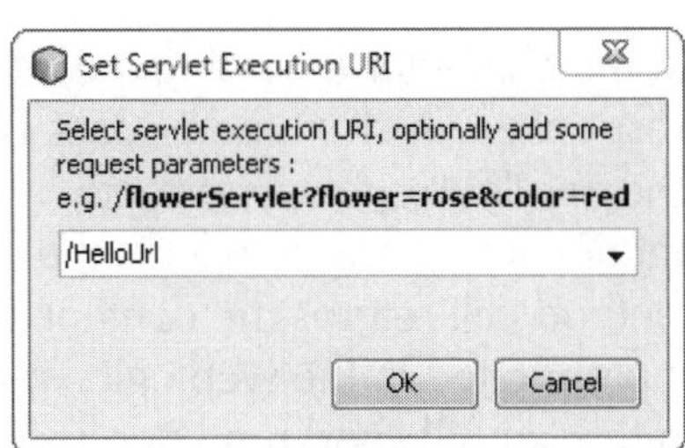

FIGURE 4-3. *Selecting a Servlet execution URI*

FIGURE 4-4. *Servlet running in the browser*

Servlet Class

Now that we have deployed the Servlet to the OJC, let's discuss the actual Servlet code and its capabilities. Our Servlet class extends the HttpServlet class and overrides the methods doGet and doPost. You will find that NetBeans has added a method, processRequest, that is being called from both doGet and doPost. Note that processRequest is not something dictated by the Java EE standard; NetBeans introduces this method so as to avoid duplicating code in doGet and doPost.

If you look at the code in the processRequest, you will find that most of it is generating static HTML through out.println method calls. These out.println calls are made on a PrintWriter object and generate the HTML for the entire page.

We also set the context type (via setContentType) for the response by specifying the Multipurpose Internet Mail Extensions (MIME) type of the content. The default is text/plain, but because we want an HTML web page, we set it to text/html. Other commonly used MIME types are text/xml, image/jpeg, and application/pdf. A web search should easily get you a list of additional MIME types. We have also set the character encoding to UTF-8 in the same method call. You could have also achieved this via a separate call to setCharacterEncoding.

The content type and the character encoding are vital information for the recipient of the Servlet response (which in most cases is a web browser) to be able to process/display the Servlet response correctly.

The only dynamic functionality in this Servlet is the call to request .getContextPath(). This method call returns the content path for our application. You will find the context path stated in the weblogic.xml configuration file. You can edit the value in the .xml file and run your application with a different context root. Note that the application content root is not dependent on the name of your project or the name of the WAR file.

Let's now take a closer look at HttpServletRequest and HttpServletResponse, the two objects that bring in most of the power and functionality in a Servlet, followed by a look at the role of the configuration .xml files.

HttpServletRequest

Your Servlet can know everything there is to know about the request via an object of HttpServletRequest. Note that HttpServletRequest is an interface. The Servlet container creates an implementation of HttpServletRequest with loads of information about the request and then passes it to the Servlet. Through the HttpServletRequest methods, we can retrieve information such as the request path, host, port, request protocol, request parameters, cookies, request URI, and more. Some of these methods are inherited from its super interface ServletRequest.

HttpServletResponse

You can work with the response you are sending from your Servlet using an object of HttpServletResponse. Again, HttpServletResponse is an interface, and it is the Servlet container that creates an implementation of HttpServletResponse. In the code, you have already seen how you can use the HttpServletResponse object to set the content type and get a PrintWriter to generate the output. You can also use HttpServletResponse to redirect, add a cookie, add headers, encode the URL, set the locale, and more. Methods such as setLocale and setCharacterEncoding, which are not specific to HTTP, are inherited from its super interface ServletResponse. HttpServletResponse adds HTTP-specific functionality methods such as addCookie, encodeURL, and others.

Let's now look at the configuration XML files you need to set up for your application on OJC.

web.xml

The web.xml file is the web deployment descriptor—the file where you state the configuration and deployment information for your application. Double-click web.xml in the Projects window. NetBeans, by default, will open the

GUI tool for editing the XML. Click the Source tab and you will find XML, as shown in Listing 4-1.

Listing 4-1: *web.xml*

```
<?xml version="1.0" encoding="UTF-8"?>
<web-app version="2.5" xmlns="http://java.sun.com/xml/ns/javaee"
xmlns:xsi="http://www.w3.org/2001/XMLSchema-instance"
xsi:schemaLocation="http://java.sun.com/xml/ns/javaee
http://java.sun.com/xml/ns/javaee/web-app_2_5.xsd">
    <servlet>
        <servlet-name>HelloServletName</servlet-name>
        <servlet-class>servlets.Hello</servlet-class>
    </servlet>
    <servlet-mapping>
        <servlet-name>HelloServletName</servlet-name>
        <url-pattern>/HelloUrl</url-pattern>
    </servlet-mapping>
    <servlet-mapping>
        <servlet-name>HelloServletName</servlet-name>
        <url-pattern>/MyServlet</url-pattern>
    </servlet-mapping>
    <session-config>
        <session-timeout>
            30
        </session-timeout>
    </session-config>
    <welcome-file-list>
        <welcome-file>index.jsp</welcome-file>
    </welcome-file-list>
</web-app>
```

First up is the <servlet> tag, where the Servlet name and class are stated. This is followed by <servlet-mapping>, where you find the URL patterns we provided to the NetBeans wizard while creating our Servlet. Do note that the <servlet-name> tag is what correlates the two tags. Therefore, if you were to change <servlet-name> in the <servlet> tag, you would have to update it in the <servlet-mapping> tag as well.

The <session-timeout> tag is used to define the timeout duration for a session. We will talk more about sessions in the "Session Management" section later in this chapter. Lastly, the <welcome-file-list> tag states the welcome page for your application. In the case of our current application, if you run the project instead of the individual Servlet, your browser will point to https://.../Ch4Servlet1/, which will actually invoke https://.../Ch4Servlet1/ index.jsp, because index.jsp is the welcome file stated in web.xml.

You can have multiple welcome files declared, and the server will look for them in the order in which they are declared. If no welcome file is specified, the server will look for index.html or index.jsp, in that order.

weblogic.xml

The weblogic.xml file is a WebLogic-specific deployment descriptor XML file that contains the WebLogic-specific configuration for an application. If an application does not contain a weblogic.xml deployment descriptor, WebLogic uses the default values for the many WebLogic deployment descriptor elements. Each of these elements provides some additional WebLogic-specific configuration capability for your application. Because we do not intend to take up any WebLogic configuration here and plan to stay clear of using any server-specific features/configuration, you do not need to add the file here.

You can try removing the weblogic.xml file from your project, and then right-click your project and select Verify. The whitelist tool will issue the warning

Recommended resource "WEB-INF/weblogic.xml" missing

but this is not an error and your application will continue to work. OJC does not require you to use any WebLogic features or APIs or expect you to have any WebLogic-specific configuration files in your application.

Sharing Data

Now that we have had a close look at the structure of a Servlet and the various elements that get it working, let's move on to a very commonly required functionality in a web application—that of sharing some data between different components in the application. You can achieve this data sharing by using attributes. The three types of attributes available in a Servlet are ServletContext, HttpSession, and ServletRequest, as shown in Figure 4-5. Here, ServletRequest has the smallest scope, whereas ServletContext is the widest.

The attributes in the ServletRequest scope are accessible for the duration of the current request. So once a request is completed, all the ServletRequest attributes are lost. The HttpSession attributes are accessible as long as the session is active. We will have a closer look at sessions in a later section, but for the time being, a session can be thought of as the same user accessing multiple Servlets or pages from your application. The ServletContext scope is

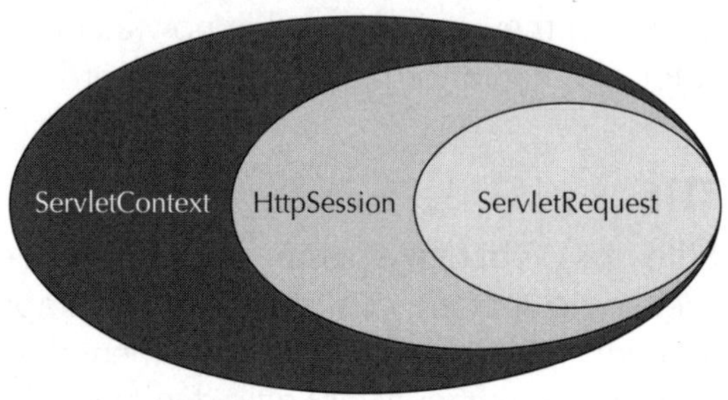

FIGURE 4-5. *Attribute scopes*

the largest scope, and ServletContext attributes are accessible as long as your application is running.

Based on the need, you can use the getAttribute and setAttribute methods of ServletContext, HttpSession, or ServletRequest. In each case, you name the attribute and pass an object of java.lang.Object as the attribute value. As you will have realized, java.lang.Object essentially means any object. You can remove the object by calling the removeAttribute method.

Let's try this out by creating a new web project named Ch4Attributes. Along similar lines as the previous examples, select Oracle Cloud Remote as the server for the new web project you create in NetBeans. In this new project, create two Servlets named SetAttributes and GetAttributes. Now, edit the processRequest method in SetAttributes, as shown in Listing 4-2

Listing 4-2: *The processRequest Method in the SetAttributes Servlet*

```
protected void processRequest(HttpServletRequest request
        , HttpServletResponse response)
        throws ServletException, IOException {
    response.setContentType("text/html;charset=UTF-8");
    PrintWriter out = response.getWriter();
    try {
          out.println("<h1>Set Attributes</h1>");
          request.setAttribute("Request Attribute", "REQ");
          request.getSession()
                   .setAttribute("Session Attribute", "SES");
          getServletContext()
                   .setAttribute("ServletContext Attribute", "CON");
```

```
    } finally {
        out.close();
    }
}
```

Next, edit the processRequest method in GetAttributes, as shown in Listing 4-3.

Listing 4-3: *The processRequest Method in the GetAttributes Servlet*

```
protected void processRequest(HttpServletRequest request
           , HttpServletResponse response)
           throws ServletException, IOException {
    response.setContentType("text/html;charset=UTF-8");
    PrintWriter out = response.getWriter();
    try {
           out.println("<h1>Get Attributes</h1>");
           out.println("<h1> Request Attribute Value = "
                       + request.getAttribute("Request Attribute")
                       + "</h1>");

           out.println("<h1> Session Attribute Value = "
                       + request.getSession()
                       .getAttribute("Session Attribute")
                       + "</h1>");

           out.println("<h1> ServletContext Attribute Value = "
                       + getServletContext()
                       .getAttribute("ServletContext Attribute")
                       + "</h1>");
    } finally {
           out.close();
    }
}
```

Note that both methods omit all the basic HTML tags such as <html> and <body> so as to cut down on the code and clutter and to make the code easier to understand. Removing these tags is not proper web programming technique; however, all modern browsers will display the web content even without these basic tags. For the purpose of this example, removing these tags helps us focus on the essentials of the code without the clutter of numerous tags.

Now, run the SetAttributes Servlet so that the various attribute values get set. Next, run the GetAttributes Servlet. You will see the page shown in Figure 4-6. You can see that the request attribute value is null, the session attribute value SES is displayed, and so is the ServletContext attribute value CON.

The reason for this is that the request to GetAttributes is distinct from the request to SetAttributes, so the request attributes set in the SetAttributes Servlet are not available to the GetAttributes Servlet. However, the HttpSession and ServletContext attributes are available because this is still the same session and the same application.

Note that to get this result, both Servlets need to be invoked from the same browser, and cookies should not be disabled on the browser in order for the session attribute values to be retained and visible. The next section talks about the role of cookies in session management.

Now copy the URL for GetAttributes and try running it in another browser. In other words, if your default browser is Firefox, try it in Chrome or Internet Explorer. You will find that only the Servlet Context Attribute value will still be displayed and that both the request attribute and session attribute values will be null. This is because although you are still running the same application, the session has changed.

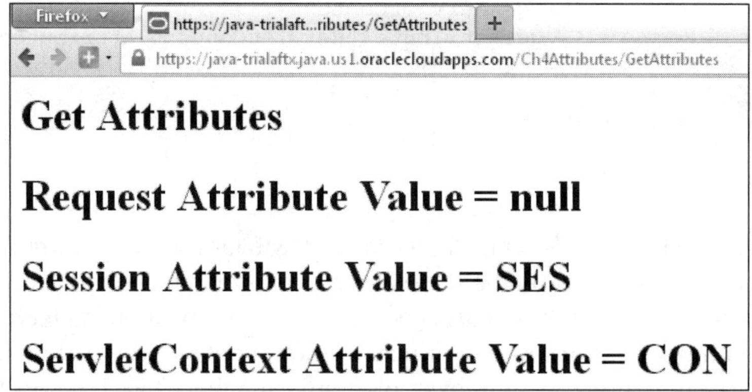

FIGURE 4-6. *The Get attributes displayed*

Session Management

One of the most common capabilities in a web application is tracking the user across multiple pages and providing a login functionality so as to provide user-specific pages and content. Unfortunately, the HTTP protocol has no capability to recall state, so it is up to the web application to save and manage state and be able to figure out that it is the same user accessing multiple pages. Considering that this is a commonly required feature for a web application, most web development platforms provide session management capability out of the box. HttpSession in Java EE provides the session management capability required.

HttpSession

The server creates an implementation of the HttpSession interface, which helps us track a user across multiple pages and also store information about the user. As seen in Listing 4-1 and Listing 4-2, you get the HttpSession object by calling the getSession method of the HttpServletRequest, which will return the current session for that request. If there is no such session, it will create a new session.

In the previous example, we looked at how you can use the session to add and retrieve attributes. But how is it that the server knows that it is the same session and the same user coming back? The answer lies in something called the session ID, which is a unique identifier that gets passed back and forth between the client and the server.

The default mode to achieve this is by using browser cookies. So when you accessed the SetAttributes Servlet, a cookie with a unique identifier was set on your browser. Next, when you accessed GetAttributes Servlet, the server figured that you were the same user because this request had the same unique identifier in the browser cookie as had been set when you accessed SetAttributes. Once it figured that this was part of the same session, the session attribute value was made available to the GetAttributes Servlet. Open up your browser's privacy setting, and you will find a cookie there with the URL for OJC and a cookie name of JSESSIONID. Note that for the browser, this JSESSIONID cookie is no different from other cookies. The JSESSIONID is simply a text value that's the unique identifier (session ID).

The only requisite for session management by the application server is that the unique identifier (session ID) keeps being sent back. Very rarely are cookies disabled on browsers, but if they are, you now have to find a way to send the unique identifier in each request. Your choices are as follows:

- Encode the URL using the response.encodeURL method. The encodeURL method adds the session ID in the URL when it finds that cookies have been disabled. Therefore, if not via a cookie, the ID continues to be sent back to the server as a request parameter.
- Pass the session ID as a hidden form field. This way, when a user submits a form, the session ID is also sent to the server as a hidden form field.

As long the session ID is going back and forth, you will be able to leverage the capabilities of HttpSession. Note that because attributes are taking up memory on your server—especially with the HttpSession and ServletContext attributes, which stay in memory for a long time—you need to use attributes with caution.

TIP
Most modern web development frameworks will default to using cookies, but have a fallback option of using encodeURL or hidden form fields in case cookies are disabled. Cookies being disabled is not as much a concern if you are using a framework as compared to custom-building your application.

RequestDispatcher

In the earlier example, regardless of what you do, the request attribute is always null, because the request to SetAttributes and GetAttributes is always distinct. So is there a way in which Servlets can collaborate and share data using request attributes? Can you forward a request to another Servlet or include the output of one Servlet into the output of another?

The RequestDispatcher can get us the desired result. As the name suggests, the RequestDispatcher will dispatch a request to another resource in your application. Add the lines in Listing 4-4 at the end of the **try** block in the processRequest method in the SetAttributes Servlet.

Listing 4-4: *RequestDispatcher*

```
RequestDispatcher rd1 = request.getRequestDispatcher("GetAttribu
tes");
//RequestDispatcher rd = getServletContext().
getRequestDispatcher("/GetAttributes");
if (rd1 != null) {
      //rd1.forward(request, response);
      rd1.include(request, response);
}
```

The first two lines in the code show the two ways in which you can get the RequestDispatcher. The difference between the two methods is that whereas the getRequestDispatcher of the ServletRequest takes a relative path, the getRequestDispatcher method of ServletContext takes an absolute path and therefore begins with a slash.

Next, we check for null. After that is a commented call to **forward** and next to **include**. As the names suggest, **forward** will forward the request to the GetAttributes Servlet, whereas **include** will include the output of GetAttributes in the output generated by SetAttributes. Upon running the updated code, you will get the page shown in Figure 4-7. The first line is the output of the SetAttributes Servlet, whereas the rest is generated by the GetAttributes Servlet.

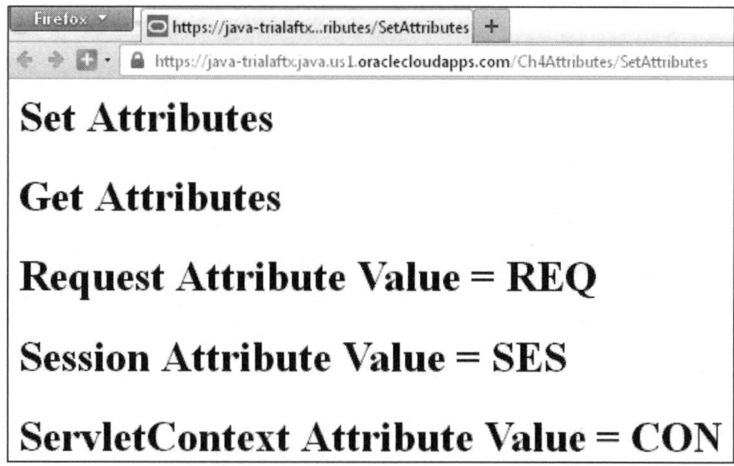

FIGURE 4-7. *A request dispatched to Get attributes*

Thus, we can use the RequestDispatcher for multiple Servlets to collaborate, delegate, and share. We can create a real web application using many such Servlets working together. That's actually what Java EE web applications in the earlier days of enterprise Java looked like.

WebLogic-Specific Servlet Capabilities on OJC

The Oracle Java Cloud supports several WebLogic-specific APIs, one of which is the weblogic.servlet.annotation.* package. This package provides the WLFilter, WLInitParam, and the WLServlet annotation, which can enable you to use annotations to provide metadata right within the Servlet class, eliminating the need to declare the servlets in the web.xml descriptor we looked at earlier.

The support for WebLogic APIs is useful and something to be aware of if you are looking to move existing WebLogic applications to the cloud. However, I would not recommend using these WebLogic-specific APIs for new applications. These annotations are not part of the Java EE specification, so not only would they lock your application into WebLogic, but similar annotations offering the same features have been introduced in the newer versions of Java EE and the Servlet API.

Supported public WebLogic Server 10.3.6 APIs are listed here:

- weblogic.logging.*
- weblogic.jsp.*
- weblogic.cache.*
- weblogic.application.*
- weblogic.i18n.*
- weblogic.i18ntools.*
- weblogic.jndi.*
- weblogic.jws.*
- weblogic.servlet.*
- weblogic.transaction.*

Unless there's a pressing need for it, you would not want to use vendor-specific code in your Java EE application. We have discussed the reasons in Chapter 1.

Let's now look at filters and listeners, whose capabilities are often required for well-rounded Java EE applications. Filters and listeners can be used within all the Java EE web applications we build in the book, regardless of whether or not we use Servlets.

Filters

When you think of the word "filter," you tend to think of passing something (say, water) through a filter, removing the impurities and getting pure filtered water. However, a filter in Java EE is capable of doing much more with the request and the response. It can a) filter out things from the request, b) edit/add to the request or simply log the contents of the request, c) filter the response, or d) edit/add to the response or simply log the contents of the response. Therefore, a filter is more of a request pre-processor and a response post-processor.

Filters are usually used where multiple servlets and any other Java EE web components require some common functionality, such as authentication, logging, and encryption. It makes sense to have one or more filters working together in a chain delivering the expected functionality for the Java Servlets or other Java EE components.

Let's add a simple filter to the Ch4Servlet1 project we created earlier in this chapter. Right-click Ch4Servlet1 and select New | Other. On this screen, select the Web category and the Filter file type. Click Next. On the next screen, specify the filter name as **LogFilter** and the package as **filters**. Click Next. You should now get a Configure Filter Deployment screen, as shown in Figure 4-8. Note the filter mapping here says that the filter LogFilter applies to /*. As with URL patterns discussed earlier in the chapter, * here is a wildcard, so /* means that the filter will apply to all requests. Click Next.

Click Next, and you will get a screen where you can set configuration values at filter initialization. We do not need to set these here, so click Finish. NetBeans will now generate LogFilter.java. The web.xml file for the project would also now have the addition shown in Listing 4-5.

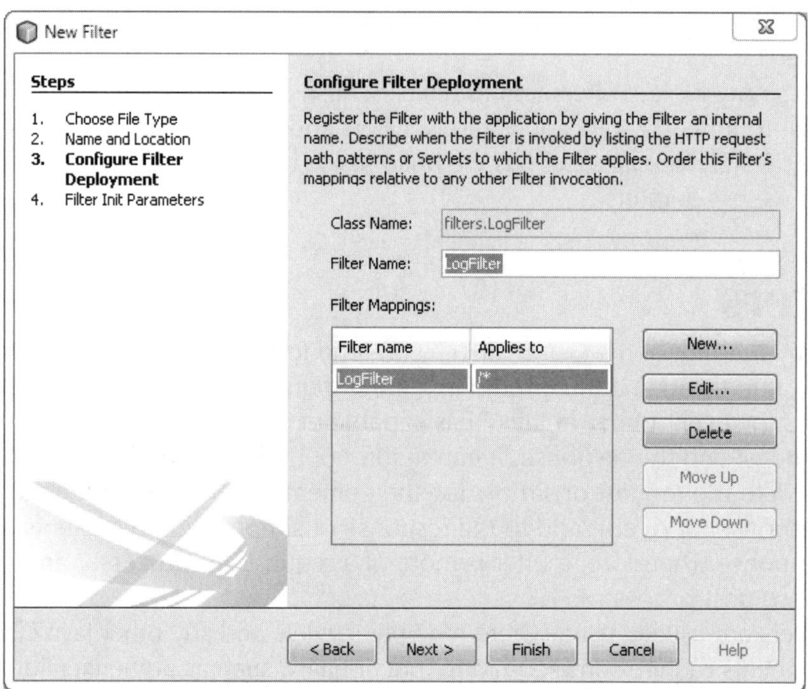

FIGURE 4-8. *The Configure Filter Deployment screen's filter mappings*

Listing 4-5: *Filter Tags in web.xml*

```
<filter>
    <filter-name>LogFilter</filter-name>
    <filter-class>filters.LogFilter</filter-class>
</filter>
<filter-mapping>
    <filter-name>LogFilter</filter-name>
    <url-pattern>/*</url-pattern>
</filter-mapping>
```

You will notice that these tags are similar to the Servlet tags in Listing 4-1. In both cases, you declare a Servlet/filter and then map it to a URL pattern.

The LogFilter.java code generated by NetBeans is feature rich; however, it is also rather intimidating for beginners. Therefore, Listing 4-6 shows my simplified, cleaned-up version.

Listing 4-6: *LogFilter.java*

```
package filters;

import java.io.*;
import java.util.logging.*;
import javax.servlet.Filter;
import javax.servlet.*;

public class LogFilter implements Filter {

    private final static Logger LOGGER
            = Logger.getLogger(LogFilter.class.getName());

    public void doFilter(ServletRequest request
            , ServletResponse response, FilterChain chain)
            throws IOException, ServletException {

        long timeRequest = new java.util.Date().getTime();

        LOGGER.log(Level.INFO, "Request Protocol: {0}"
                , request.getProtocol());
        LOGGER.log(Level.INFO, "Request Received At:{0}"
                , new java.util.Date());

        chain.doFilter(request, response);

        long timeResponse = new java.util.Date().getTime();

        LOGGER.log(Level.INFO
                , "Response Sent In : {0} milliseconds"
                , timeResponse - timeRequest);
    }

    public void init(FilterConfig fc) throws ServletException {
    }

    public void destroy() {
    }
}
```

The LogFilter class implements the Filter interface and therefore has to implement the methods in the interface. The doFilter method is what the server will call when a request matches the filter mapping we have declared.

In this code we are using the Java Logging API to log information about the request and the response.

Filters cannot be directly run by the user, but are meant to get invoked automatically whenever the filter mapping applies. Therefore, in our case, we won't try to run LogFilter but rather run Hello.java. When we send a request to the Servlet that we created earlier with Hello.java, the following should happen:

1. The request will get pre-processed by LogFilter.
2. It will then be processed by the Hello.java Servlet, which will generate a response.
3. The Servlet response will again go through the filter, where it can be processed again.

The output after the filter's post-processing is what will be sent back to the client.

The following log output, generated by LogFilter, shows the results of these three steps:

```
Request Protocol: HTTP/1.1
Request Received At:<Date Time>
Response Sent In : 2 milliseconds
```

Because viewing the logs is something useful throughout the application, and not just in Servlets or filters, we will see how and where you can view logs on OJC in "View Java Logs," later in the chapter. You can quickly jump over to that section now and then return when you're done.

In this example, we looked at a single filter; however, you can very well create a series/chain of filters. The filters are executed in the order in which they are declared in the web.xml file.

Listeners

Java EE provides the capability for you to track key events in your application using event listeners. The methods in these listeners are called by the server whenever the corresponding lifecycle event occurs.

When you add a listener to your application, you need to a) write a class that implements the appropriate listener interface and b) declare the listener in the web deployment listener. Listeners are generally used in cases where you want to execute some actions or load some data/configuration on application startup, or to open and close database connections on occurrence of an event and to perform any actions on the application being shut down.

The listener interfaces are as follows:

Listener	Description
javax.servlet.ServletContextListener	Notified when ServletContext is created and when the ServletContext is destroyed.
javax.servlet.ServletContextAttributeListener	Notified when the ServletContext attribute changes, new attributes are added, or existing attributes are removed or replaced.
javax.servlet.http.HttpSessionListener	Notified when session lifecycle changes such as creation, invalidation, and timeout occur.
javax.servlet.http.HttpSessionAttributeListener	Notified when the HttpSession attribute changes, new attributes are added, or existing attributes are removed or replaced.
javax.servlet.ServletRequestListener	Notified when a ServletRequest is initialized or destroyed.
javax.servlet.ServletRequestAttributeListener	Notified when the ServletRequest attribute changes, new attributes are added, or existing attributes are removed or replaced.

You can choose to have a separate class for each listener implementation or a single class implementing multiple listeners. Each interface we implement will force us to implement the event-handling methods in that interface. These

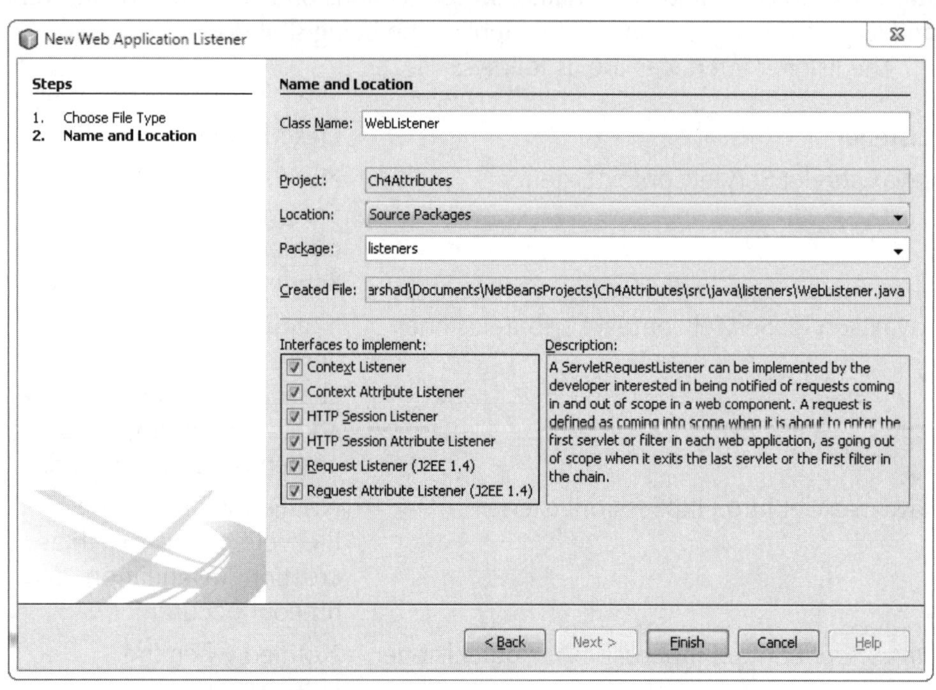

FIGURE 4-9. *New web application listener*

method implementations we provide are the ones that would be called by the server on occurrence of the corresponding event.

Let's add a listener class to the Ch4Attributes project we created earlier. The attributes being set in the project will lead to the corresponding listeners being triggered.

Right-click Ch4Servlet1 in the Projects window. Then click New | Other and select the Web category and Web Application Listener file type. In the next screen, shown in Figure 4-9, add **WebListener** in the Class Name field and **listeners** in the Package field.

Select all the interfaces under Interfaces to Implement. This way, we will have one class that implements six listeners. We will update the code to log the call to each method, as shown in Listing 4-7.

Listing 4-7: *WebListener*

```
package listeners;

import java.util.logging.*;
import javax.servlet.*;
import javax.servlet.http.*;

public class WebListener implements ServletContextListener
, ServletContextAttributeListener, HttpSessionListener
, HttpSessionAttributeListener, ServletRequestListener
, ServletRequestAttributeListener {

    private final static Logger LOGGER =
            Logger.getLogger(WebListener.class.getName());

    public void contextInitialized(ServletContextEvent sce) {
        LOGGER.log(Level.INFO, "contextInitialized: {0}"
                , sce.getServletContext());
    }

    public void contextDestroyed(ServletContextEvent sce) {
        LOGGER.log(Level.INFO, "contextDestroyed: {0}"
                , sce.getServletContext());
    }

    public void attributeAdded(ServletContextAttributeEvent scae){
        LOGGER.log(Level.INFO, "attributeAdded: {0}"
                , scae.getName());
    }

    public void attributeRemoved
        (ServletContextAttributeEvent scae) {
        LOGGER.log(Level.INFO, "attributeRemoved: {0}"
                , scae.getName());
    }

    public void attributeReplaced
        (ServletContextAttributeEvent scae) {
        LOGGER.log(Level.INFO, "attributeReplaced: {0}"
                , scae.getName());
    }

    public void sessionCreated(HttpSessionEvent hse) {
        LOGGER.log(Level.INFO, "sessionCreated: {0}"
                , hse.getSession());
    }

    public void sessionDestroyed(HttpSessionEvent hse) {
        LOGGER.log(Level.INFO, "sessionDestroyed: {0}"
```

```
                , hse.getSession());
    }

    public void attributeAdded(HttpSessionBindingEvent hsbe) {
        LOGGER.log(Level.INFO, "attributeAdded: {0}"
                , hsbe.getName());
    }

    public void attributeRemoved(HttpSessionBindingEvent hsbe) {
        LOGGER.log(Level.INFO, "attributeRemoved: {0}"
                , hsbe.getName());
    }

    public void attributeReplaced(HttpSessionBindingEvent hsbe) {
        LOGGER.log(Level.INFO, "attributeReplaced: {0}"
                , hsbe.getName());
    }

    public void requestDestroyed(ServletRequestEvent sre) {
        LOGGER.log(Level.INFO, "requestDestroyed: {0}"
                , sre.getServletRequest());
    }

    public void requestInitialized(ServletRequestEvent sre) {
        LOGGER.log(Level.INFO, "requestInitialized: {0}"
                , sre.getServletRequest());
    }

    public void attributeAdded
        (ServletRequestAttributeEvent srae) {
        LOGGER.log(Level.INFO
                , "ServletRequest attributeAdded: {0}"
                , srae.getName());
    }

    public void attributeRemoved
        (ServletRequestAttributeEvent srae) {
        LOGGER.log(Level.INFO
                , "ServletRequest attributeRemoved: {0}"
                , srae.getName());
    }

    public void attributeReplaced
        (ServletRequestAttributeEvent srae) {
        LOGGER.log(Level.INFO
                , "ServletRequest attributeReplaced: {0}"
                , srae.getName());
    }
}
```

Apart from the code in the listener class, one other thing that needs to be done is to tell the server that this is the listener class whose methods it is supposed to call. Therefore, the listener tag is added to the web.xml file. If you open the web.xml file, you will find that a new xml block, as shown in Listing 4-8, has been added to the file.

Listing 4-8: *Listener Tags in web.xml*

```
<listener>
    <description>
         ServletContextListener,
         ServletContextAttributeListener, HttpSessionListener,
         HttpSessionAttributeListener, RequestListener,
         RequestAttributeListener
    </description>
    <listener-class>listeners.WebListener</listener-class>
</listener>
```

The value of the <listener-class> is what's important for the server. The description tag can be safely edited to any text you prefer. You do not need to tell the server which listeners you are implementing because the server can figure that out based on the interfaces your class has implemented.

Now, run the SetAttributes Servlet we created earlier in the chapter. Although the Servlet will run exactly the same way as earlier, the log will now show the output logged by the various listeners that were triggered by the actions in the SetAttributes Servlet.

View Java Logs

It is likely that while trying out the applications in this chapter, you didn't get the desired results and are wondering what went wrong. Also, in the examples for filters and listeners, we need to look at the application logs to be able to understand the functioning.

Checking the application and the server logs is a simple task with a local setup or a dedicated server. However, on the cloud, where you don't even know exactly what the infrastructure is that's running your application, your access to the logs is limited to what access the cloud vendor provides.

You can access the OJC logs in multiple ways. Let's first look at the accessing the logs from the Java Cloud Services Control.

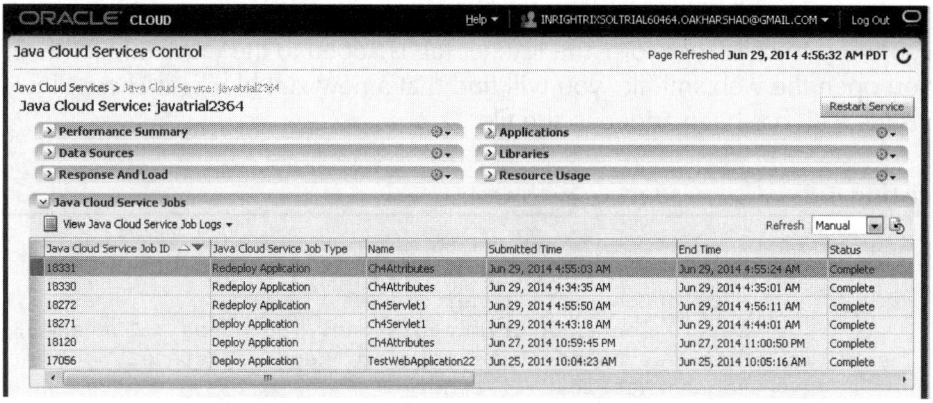

FIGURE 4-10. *Java Cloud Service Job logs*

The Java Cloud Service Jobs log is shown in Figure 4-10. This log shows the steps followed during the deployment, the whitelist validation, and the virus scan, as well as whether any errors or warnings occurred. You can click the drop-down list highlighted in Figure 4-10 to select which log you wish to view. On the right is the option to auto-refresh the log every few minutes. The default setting is Manual.

If you view the Java Cloud Service Jobs log, you realize that these are the same log entries you see in the Oracle Cloud log from within NetBeans, or for that matter, any IDE. We took a close look at these log entries in the previous chapter.

The second log is the one that's useful once you have your application running. This is the one that has the entries logged from the application. To access this log, click View Log Messages in the Performance Summary, as shown in Figure 4-11. You will now get a search screen where you can choose exactly which log messages you wish to view.

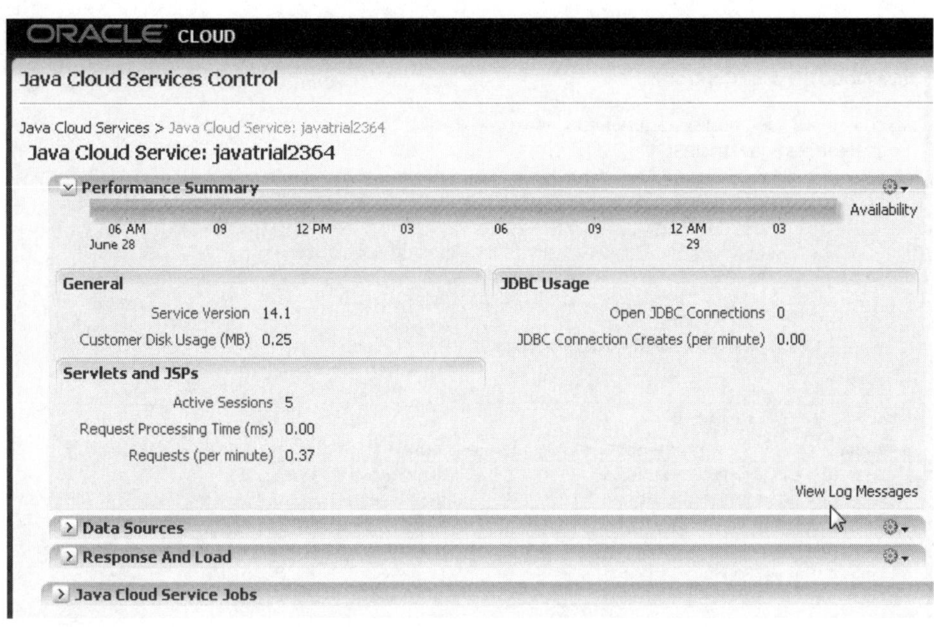

FIGURE 4-11. *View Log Messages in the Performance Summary*

You can specify a date range or select the exact date duration and then select the kind of message types you wish to view. You will get a screen like the one shown in Figure 4-12.

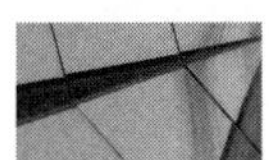

TIP

This log shows the messages you have logged using Java's built-in Logging API, Log4J, and System logs. "System log" here refers to the System.out .print kind of logging that developers often use, but it is not recommended. Using Java's built-in Logging API, as used in the examples in this chapter, is what I would recommend.

You can export the log messages to a .txt, .csv, or .xml file by choosing that option after clicking the Export Messages to File button shown in the figure.

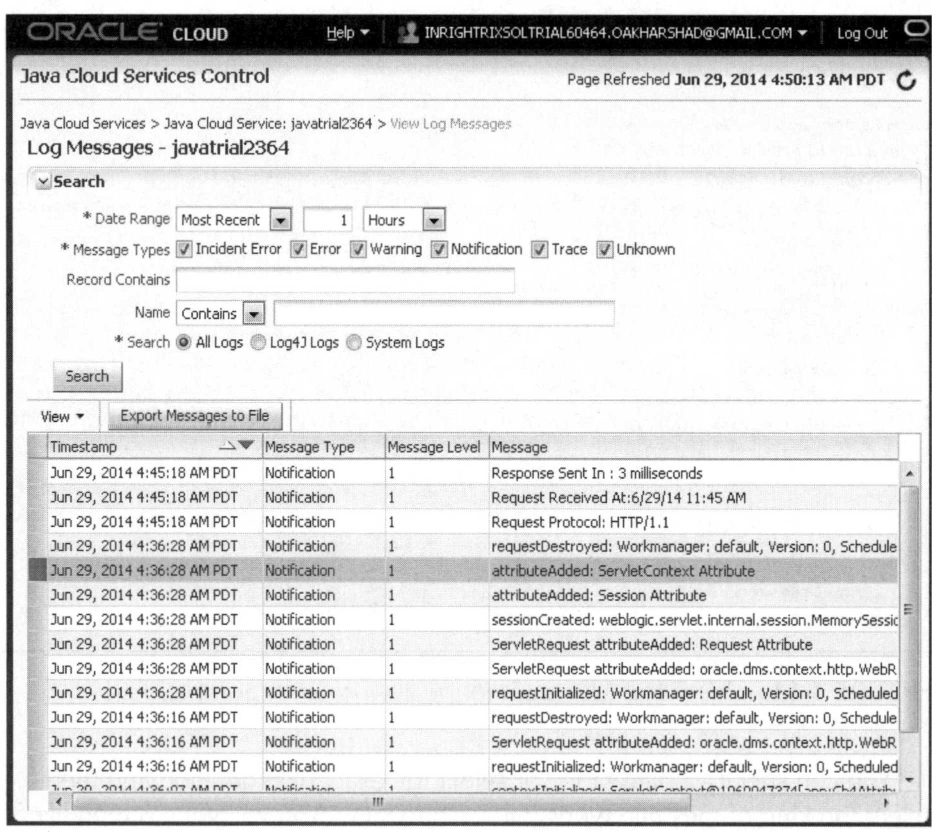

FIGURE 4-12. *The Log Messages screen*

TIP

A delay may occur before the messages appear in the log. You might have to wait for a while or click the Search button again.

You also have the choice of using the Oracle Cloud SDK or the Ant and Maven plugins to access the logs. To access the logs using the SDK, you can execute the command **query-service-logs** from the command prompt. The command requires you to pass the arguments **user**, **serviceinstance**, **identitydomain**, and **datacenter**:

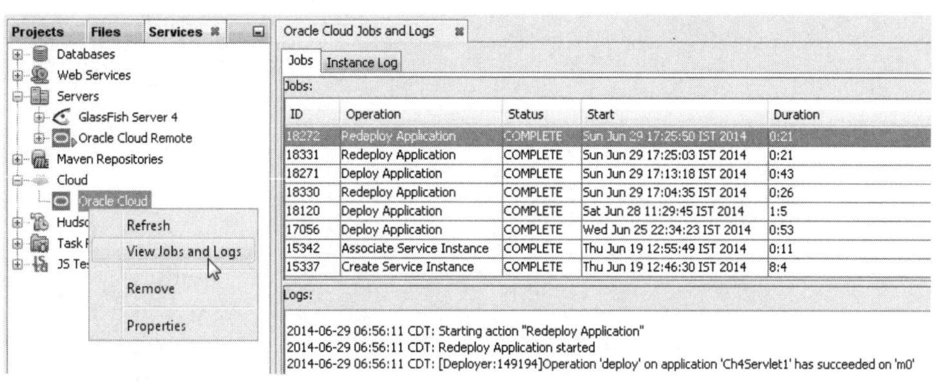

FIGURE 4-13. *Oracle Cloud Jobs and Logs*

```
java -jar javacloud.jar query-service-logs -user username
 -serviceinstance java -identitydomain yourindentitydomain
 -datacenter yourdatacenter
```

The **query-service-logs** method takes many arguments, so you can customize the output to get precisely the log messages you desire. You can either refer to the SDK documentation for the entire list of arguments or just fire the command

```
java -jar javacloud.jar query-service-logs -help
```

and all the arguments will be listed on-screen.

You can also access the logs from within NetBeans. As shown in Figure 4-13, open the Services window, right-click Oracle Cloud that's listed under the Cloud category, and select View Jobs and Logs.

You will notice that the logs window has two tabs within it. One tab shows the log for the jobs executed and the other tab shows your WebLogic instance log. It's better to access the instance log as shown in Figure 4-12, as you get a tabular display that you can sort, filter, and export to a file if required.

Summary

In this chapter, we looked at Servlets, sharing data, session management, filters, and listeners. We also looked at how to access your application logs on OJC. In the next chapter, we will look at JavaServer Pages as we move toward producing more feature-rich web applications for the browser.

CHAPTER 5

JavaServer Pages, JSTL, and Expression Language

In the previous chapter, we built applications using Servlets, filters, and listeners and deployed them on the Oracle Java Cloud Service. You likely noticed that building applications using Servlets can be rather tedious and involves a lot of Java coding, even when what is being generated is static HTML code. To address this issue, JavaServer Pages (JSP) emerged. JSP lets you embed snippets of Java code into your HTML. The functionality is similar to Servlets, but JSP drastically reduced the amount of Java code that has to be written, leading to more streamlined, efficient coding and increased developer productivity. Although JSPs can be used to generate any text-based format, it is most commonly used for HTML.

The Origin of JSP

Like Servlets, JSP has been around from the early days of enterprise Java. Version 1.0 was released in 1999, and JSP (version 2.3) is very much a part of Java EE 7. JSP also continues to be used in all kinds of applications, including those deployed on the cloud.

Even when JavaServer Faces (JSF) was introduced as a framework for building component-based user interfaces, JSP continued to be the view technology for JSF. Only with JSF 2.0 was JSP deprecated as a view technology for JSF and replaced by Facelets. "View technology" here refers to that part of the JSF framework that is responsible for generating the view for an application. We will take a closer look at JSF in the next chapter. So the point to note is that JSP is very much around. It has *not* been deprecated as a whole, but only as the view technology for JSF 2.0 and above.

TIP

Deprecation is meant to indicate to developers that a technology is still available but the creators suggest that you avoid using it. This is usually because that technology might be removed/replaced in a future version.

JSP enhancements have been sluggish over the past few years. However, JSP is very much an integral part of almost all Java EE applications built over the past decade and continues to be widely used even today, despite most books and blogs recommending JSF over JSP. This is not only because JSP is easy to use and good for rapid development, but also because JSP skills are easy to find. Also, many developers used to building with JSP find that it serves them very well and are not that keen on switching.

What's more, JSP, with its simple request-response model, is often a good-enough backend for applications and even JavaScript clients that only require that basic functionality. The newer JSF comes with more complex lifecycle management by the web container, which can seem like overkill in some cases.

Due to backward compatibility, even the latest JSP versions support usage syntax from the early days of JSP. In many cases, this means there are multiple ways to do the same thing. In this chapter, we will mostly look at the newer and more elegant ways, using tag libraries and expression language.

JSP on the Oracle Java Cloud

The Oracle Java Cloud currently supports JSP version 2.1, which is the version included in Java EE 5. JSP version 2.1 was a significant release because it introduced a unified expression language for JSP and JSF. OJC does not impose any JSP-specific restrictions or limitations. A widget marked Servlets and JSPs on the Java Cloud Services Control page, shown in Figure 5-1, shows the number of active sessions, the average request processing time for Servlets and JSPs in the past five minutes, and the number of requests per minute in the past five minutes.

TIP

All "per minute" statistics shown on the Java Cloud Service Control are "per minute" in the last five minutes.

Although the values in Figure 5-1 are for your entire Java Cloud instance, you can see values for a particular application in the Applications table and also on the Java Cloud Control page for that application. Although we will look at what custom tags are later in the chapter, this is a good place to note that OJC also supports custom WebLogic Server–specific tags in weblogic.jsp.*.

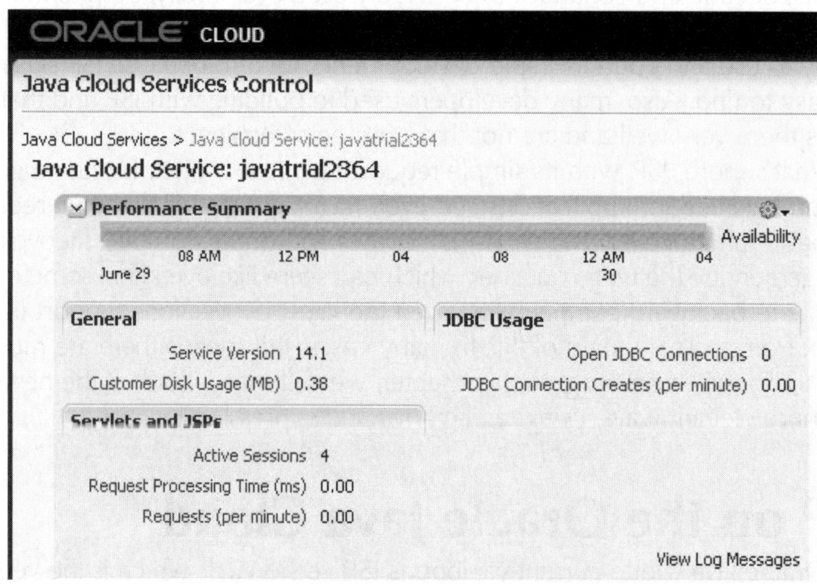

FIGURE 5-1. *The Servlets and JSPs widget under Performance Summary*

JSP Internals

A JSP is text document—in most cases, an HTML file—that has some JSP-specific tags and at times some Java code in it. The recommended file extension is .jsp. A JSP file can be either in XML form, such that it can be parsed and used by any XML parser, or in a standard syntax, which is less verbose but is not well-formed XML.

JSP in XML form never quite caught on with developers; writing a JSP with standard syntax was just simpler. Unless there's a need to parse the JSP using APIs for XML, most developers tend to use the standard syntax. We will be using the standard syntax for the code in this chapter; however, we will look at the corresponding XML tags as well.

JSP Lifecycle

The key to understanding a JSP is in understanding Servlets, because when one runs a JSP, what actually runs is a Servlet. When the server receives the first request for the JSP, it translates the JSP into a Servlet class, followed by compiling that class. After that, on every request, the server runs the Servlet class until it finds that the JSP file has been updated, in which case it will again translate and compile the new JSP.

The biggest performance hit from a JSP page is at the time when it is being compiled, so it is a best practice to precompile your JSPs so that your Servlet is in place when the first request from a user is received. Although there are multiple ways to precompile your JSPs, the easiest way, in our case, is to add the <precompile>true</precompile> tag within the <jsp-descriptor> tag in the weblogic.xml configuration file of the application so that the XML is as shown in Listing 5-1.

Listing 5-1: *Precompile JSP*

```
<jsp-descriptor>
  <precompile>true</precompile>
</jsp-descriptor>
```

Servlet Code

The best way to understand the working of a JSP is to look at the JSP page and analyze and understand the corresponding Servlet generated. Let's begin by creating a new web application named **Ch5JavaServerPages1** in NetBeans along exactly the same lines as the applications we created in the previous chapter. As in the previous cases, follow these steps:

1. Select Oracle Cloud as the server on the Server and Setting screen.
2. Do not choose any framework on the Frameworks screen.

NetBeans, by default, creates an index.jsp file, as shown in Listing 5-2, in every web application that it generates.

Listing 5-2: *NetBeans-Generated index.jsp*

```
<%@page contentType="text/html" pageEncoding="UTF-8"%>
<!DOCTYPE html>
<html>
    <head>
        <meta http-equiv="Content-Type" content="text/html;
 charset=UTF-8">
        <title>JSP Page</title>
```

```
    </head>
    <body>
        <h1>Hello World!</h1>
    </body>
</html>
```

You will notice that except for the first line, which begins with **<%@**, this JSP is exactly the same as an HTML file.

TIP
You can rename any plain .html file as .jsp and it would work just the same, as long as the HTML does not include any tags or characters that have a special meaning in JSP.

NetBeans has a useful feature where you can simply right-click a JSP file and click View Servlet, as shown in Figure 5-2. This shows the translated Servlet code for a JSP after it has been run at least once. However, because we have configured our project to run on the Oracle Cloud, the View Servlet option does not work even after you run the JSP and it gets deployed on the Oracle Cloud. This is because the process of translating the JSP is being carried out on the WebLogic Server running on the cloud, to which we only have limited access. There's currently no way in which we can look at the actual Servlet being generated on the WebLogic Server on OJC.

For the sake of understanding the JSP, a workaround is available. Instead of using the WebLogic on the cloud, you could install a local WebLogic server or use the GlassFish server that's bundled with NetBeans.

Right-click the .jsp file in the Projects window and select the option Compile File. NetBeans will now create an src directory at

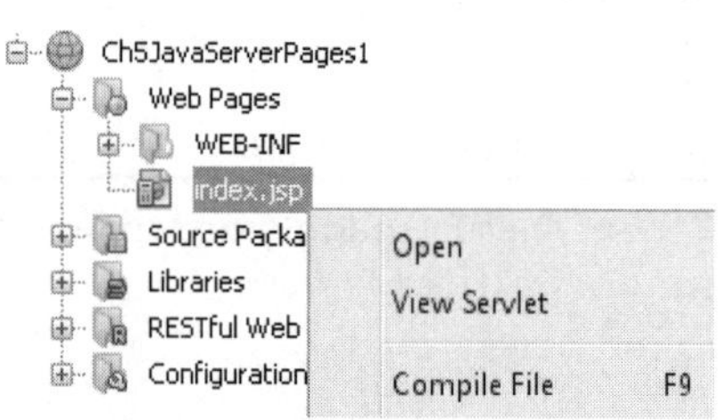

FIGURE 5-2. *The View Servlet option*

<NetBeansProjectsDirectory>\Ch5JavaServerPages1\build\generated\, where <NetBeansProjectsDirectory> is the location for your NetBeans projects on your machine.

You will find the directory creation line listed in the log in the output window. Within the *generated* directory, if you are using GlassFish, you will find an \org\apache\jsp directory hierarchy within which you will find the file index_jsp.java, shown in Listing 5-3.

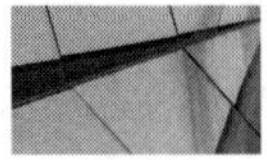

TIP

It's okay even if you do not have a local server installed or are unable to get the Compile option working. Just take a look at Listing 5-3 because it shows the syntax and conveys the core point about how JSPs are translated to Servlets.

Listing 5-3: *Translated Servlet for index.jsp*

```
package org.apache.jsp;
import javax.servlet.*;
import javax.servlet.http.*;
import javax.servlet.jsp.*;
public final class index_jsp extends org.apache.jasper.runtime.
HttpJspBase
    implements org.apache.jasper.runtime.JspSourceDependent {
  private static final JspFactory _jspxFactory = JspFactory.
getDefaultFactory();
  private static java.util.List<String> _jspx_dependants;
  private org.glassfish.jsp.api.ResourceInjector _jspx_
resourceInjector;
  public java.util.List<String> getDependants() {
    return _jspx_dependants;
  }
public void _jspService(HttpServletRequest request,
HttpServletResponse response)
        throws java.io.IOException, ServletException {
    PageContext pageContext = null;
    HttpSession session = null;
    ServletContext application = null;
    ServletConfig config = null;
    JspWriter out = null;
    Object page = this;
    JspWriter _jspx_out = null;
```

```
    PageContext _jspx_page_context = null;
    try {
      response.setContentType("text/html;charset=UTF-8");
      pageContext = _jspxFactory.getPageContext(this, request,
response,
                        null, true, 8192, true);
      _jspx_page_context = pageContext;
      application = pageContext.getServletContext();
      config = pageContext.getServletConfig();
      session = pageContext.getSession();
      out = pageContext.getOut();
      _jspx_out = out;
      _jspx_resourceInjector = (org.glassfish.jsp.api.
ResourceInjector) application.getAttribute("com.sun.appserv.jsp.
resource.injector");
      out.write("\n");
      out.write("<!DOCTYPE html>\n");
      out.write("<html>\n");
      out.write("    <head>\n");
      out.write("        <meta http-equiv=\"Content-Type\"
content=\"text/html; charset=UTF-8\">\n");
      out.write("        <title>JSP Page</title>\n");
      out.write("    </head>\n");
      out.write("    <body>\n");
      out.write("        <h1>Hello World!</h1>\n");
      out.write("    </body>\n");
      out.write("</html>\n");
    } catch (Throwable t) {
      if (!(t instanceof SkipPageException)){
        out = _jspx_out;
        if (out != null && out.getBufferSize() != 0)
          out.clearBuffer();
        if (_jspx_page_context != null) _jspx_page_context.
handlePageException(t);
        else throw new ServletException(t);
      }
    } finally {
      _jspxFactory.releasePageContext(_jspx_page_context);
    }
  }
}
```

The JSP-translated Servlet is not identical on all servers; the class and package name depend on which servlet-jsp container is being used by the server. Because GlassFish uses a derivative of Apache Tomcat, the package name org.apache.jsp is being used.

In the Servlet code, note the instance variables created and where the HTML code ends up. This class is very much a Servlet, but it extends org.apache.jasper.runtime.HttpJspBase in this case, which in turn extends HttpServlet, which we discussed in the previous chapter. So all the things we discussed in the previous chapter for Servlets work exactly the same way for a JSP; you just need to be aware and understand where your JSP code is appearing in the Servlet.

You can open this code file in NetBeans (or any code editor); we will keep coming back to it to see how the changes we make to the JSP are being reflected in the Servlet.

Let's now look at the various JSP elements that provide dynamic content generation and also the ability to write Java code as required.

JSP Directives

Directives provide page information to the JSP engine, affecting the translated Servlet code. The three types of directives are page, include, and taglib.

Page Directive

The page directive provides information about the page. The first line in Listing 5-2 is a page directive that says that the content generated by the page is HTML and the encoding is UTF-8:

```
<%@page contentType="text/html" pageEncoding="UTF-8"%>
```

In Listing 5-3, you will notice that this directive gets translated to the line

```
response.setContentType("text/html;charset=UTF-8");
```

The page directive supports many attributes apart from contentType and pageEncoding. You can press CTRL-SPACE in NetBeans and you will get a popup showing the directive attributes (see Figure 5-3).

TIP

NetBeans provides autocomplete capability even for JSP attributes where you either have a true/false option or you have to choose from a set list of choices. CTRL-SPACE is what gets you the autocomplete options.

```
<%@page contentType="text/html" pageEncoding="UTF-8" %>
<!DOCTYPE html>
<html>
    <head>
        <meta http-equiv="Content-Type" content="te
        <title>JSP Page</title>
    </head>
    <body>
        <h1>Hello World!</h1>
    </body>
</html>
```

```
autoFlush
buffer
errorPage
extends
import
info
isELIgnored
isErrorPage
isThreadSafe
language
session
```

FIGURE 5-3. *Directive attributes*

Include Directive

The include directive is used to include a file at JSP translation time so that the contents of the two files are merged into the generated Servlet:

```
<%@ include file="footer.html" %>
```

Be careful while using the include directive and merging JSP files because it can lead to surprising errors in certain cases, such as when the same variable names are used in multiple files.

Taglib Directive

The taglib directive conveys that a tag library is being used in the JSP. The usage syntax is as follows:

```
<%@ taglib prefix="test" uri="taglib.tld" %>
```

We will discuss tag libraries in a separate section later in the chapter. For now, just note that to use a tag library, we use the tag library directive.

JSP Directives as XML

In the previous sections, we have looked at the shorter syntax for directives; however, if you need to use well-formed XML, the XML syntax for JSP directives is

```
<jsp:directive.___ attribute= "value" />
```

Replace the ___ with page, include, or taglib, based on which directive you wish to use.

JSP Declaration

JSP declarations are used to declare variables and methods in a JSP, which you could utilize in the rest of the page. Let's first add a declaration and see where it ends up in the translated Servlet code (see Listing 5-4).

Listing 5-4: *JSP Declaration*

```
<%! int count = 0;%>
<%!
String welcomeMsg(String name){
      return "Welcome " + name;
}
%>
```

Because no output is being generated by this block of code, where you place the code in the JSP is immaterial. Now, again, right-click and choose Compile File and have a look at the generated Servlet code. You will find that **count** is an instance variable and **welcomeMsg** is a new method in the Servlet. This is where any variable and methods you add to a JSP end up.

JSP Scriptlets

JSP scriptlets are Java code fragments embedded in the JSP page. Scriptlets are arguably the most used and abused feature of JSP. If used judiciously, scriptlets can save a lot of time and effort, but if used too much, the JSP can end up being a nightmare for anyone except the person who wrote the code. Java code snippets all over the JSP make debugging and maintaining the JSP a tough task.

Let's add the scriptlet in Listing 5-5 to index.jsp. Note that you will need to add this within the HTML body tags for the output to be displayed in the browser. Also note that we already declared a **count** variable in the declaration, so we are adding a second **count** variable in a scriptlet here.

Listing 5-5: *JSP Scriptlet*

```
<% int count = 0;%>
<h1>Count In Declaration = <% out.print(this.count);%></h1>
<h1>Count In Scriptlet = <% out.print(count);%></h1>
<% this.count++;%>
<% count++;%>
```

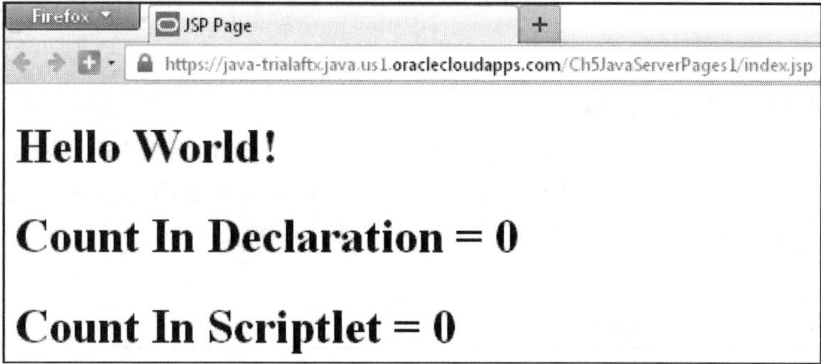

FIGURE 5-4. *Declaration and scriptlet count*

Again, run the index.jsp file and you will get a screen like the one shown in Figure 5-4, where the **count** is 0 for the declaration and the scriptlet.

The curious part is where you refresh the page in the browser. You will find that the **count** for the declaration keeps rising while the **count** for the scriptlet stays zero throughout, despite the scriptlet in Listing 5-5 explicitly incrementing both **count** variables.

The answer to this mystery again lies in the Servlet code. You will find that all the code in the scriptlets has been translated into corresponding Java code in the _jspService method. So whereas the **count** variable in the JSP declaration became an instance variable, the **count** variable in the scriptlet is a local variable in the _jspService method. Every time you refresh your page, the same Servlet instance is being accessed, so the value keeps getting incremented. However, in the case of the local variable **count**, the *int count = 0* line is part of the _jspService method and will get executed for each request. So the local variable **count** keeps getting reset to zero.

JSP Expressions

JSP expressions are in the form

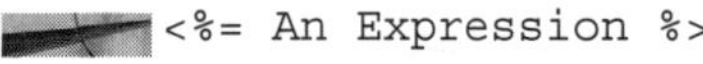

```
<%= An Expression %>
```

and provide a shortcut to print values in the output. Therefore, the line <% out.print(count);%> in Listing 5-5 could be replaced with <%= count %>

and get you the same output. Add the line to the JSP, and in the translated Servlet code, you will find that all you state in the expression essentially goes into an out.print in the Servlet code.

Implicit Objects

Scriplets and expressions are powerful and useful because code in the scriptlet ends up in the _jspService method and has access to not only the HttpServletRequest and HttpServletResponse objects, but also to the other objects such as Session and ServletContext that you will find declared at the top of the _jspService method. These are known as JSP implicit objects because instead of the developer having to go to the trouble of creating them, the JSP in its translated Servlet code creates them and makes them available to the developer for use.

We looked at using attributes and sharing data as well session management in the previous chapter. If you wish to achieve the same in a JSP, you will save some time and effort because you do not have to create the requisite objects, but can directly use the implicit objects.

The following table lists the various implicit objects, the class/interface to which they refer, and their common usage.

Object	Class/Interface	Usage
application (interface javax.servlet .ServletContext)	Refers to the web application's environment.	Used to get ServletContext attributes and information.
session (interface javax .servlet.http.HttpSession)	Refers to the user's session.	Used to retrieve session information.
request (interface javax.servlet.http .HttpServletRequest)	Refers to the current request to the page.	Used to retrieve query parameters, request parameters, and attributes.
response (interface javax.servlet.http .HttpServletResponse)	Refers to the response to be sent.	Used to set header information, set response content type, redirect responses, and add cookies.

(continued)

Object	Class/Interface	Usage
out (class javax.servlet .jsp.JspWriter)	Refers to the output stream for the page.	Used to output content for the response.
page (class java.lang .Object)	Refers to the page's Servlet instance.	Used to refer to the instance of the Servlet generated for that JSP. It's the same as using **this**.
pageContext (class javax .servlet.jsp.PageContext)	Refers to the page's environment.	Used to get and set attributes in different scopes because it holds references to other implicit objects.
config (interface javax .servlet.ServletConfig)	Refers to the Servlet's configuration.	Used to get initialization parameters.
exception (class java.lang .Throwable)	Refers to the exception occurred.	Used for error handling to generate the appropriate response. It contains any exception thrown by previous page.

JSP Comments

Comments are used throughout programming as a best practice to communicate your ideas or as an approach to addressing a particular issue within the code. In JSP, you have three choices for how you want to use comments—JSP Comment, Java Comment, and HTML Comment (see Listing 5-6).

Listing 5-6: *JSP Comments*

```
<%-- JSP Comment --%>
<% //Java Comment %>
<!-- HTML Comment -->
```

The difference between these three is that the JSP Comment appears only in the JSP and not even in the translated Servlet code. The Java Comment appears in the JSP and the Servlet code, whereas HTML Comment is the only one that will make it to the response (usually HTML) and can be viewed if the user selects View Source in the web browser.

None of the styles of comments will affect the output of the JSP page, but understanding where the comments appear is vital for you to be able to use the right kind of comment at the right place. If the comment is meant only for the JSP developers, you should use the <%-- JSP Comment --%> style of commenting. The <!-- HTML Comment --> style should be used only if you want the comment to appear in the HTML response. Although it's true that the <!-- HTML Comment --> comments are visible only if someone checks the source in the browser, you would still be moving a lot of unnecessary data to the client and also reveal developer-specific information.

The <% //Java Comment %> comment type is the one that Java developers are comfortable with and often end up using. However, it has no real benefit over the JSP Comment, because including the comment in the translated Servlet usually does not serve much purpose. So in most cases, JSP Comment will be the one to use.

In this section, we looked at the working of the JSP, the basic syntax, and usage of directives, scriptlets, expressions, and comments. Let's now look at how you can use tags to make your JSPs fast to build and easy to maintain.

Tags and Expressions

We have so far seen how you can use scripting in a JSP to add dynamic content to HTML. However, the problem with JSP scripting wasn't with JSPs as such, but in the way it was being used by web developers. Developers created large and complex JSPs using procedural code and a ton of functionality packed into them. So within no time, the page became difficult to manage and interpret for anyone but the original developer. Also, the idea of JSP was to separate HTML and Java, but that wasn't being achieved because most JSP files ended up having Java all over the place.

To tackle this, custom tags (and later the JSP Standard Tag Library, or JSTL) and expressions were introduced. Custom tags provide a way to build your own tag outright. JSTL, as the name suggests, is a standard set of tags with commonly required functionality. The expression language provides a way to achieve complex functionality without the need to write Java code.

JSTL combined with expression language can ensure that your JSP pages are feature-rich and yet clean and easy to understand and maintain.

Custom Tags

With custom tags, you can create new tags that have the meaning and functionality you desire. For example, using a <p> tag in HTML leads to a new paragraph being created because the browser knows that's what is intended wherever it sees a <p> tag in the HTML.

Similarly, with custom tags, you can use a tag named a2z in your JSP, and then tell the server that it is to print the alphabet from A to Z wherever it sees that tag.

Creating your own custom tags is possible, and many did attempt doing so in the early days of custom tags. However, with JSTL and many other third-party tag libraries available, most developers now prefer to use tried-and-tested tags from these libraries instead of creating their own tags. In most cases, it's best to stick to JSTL.

Although we will not get into the specifics of building a new custom tag from scratch, do note that building a new tag involves the following steps:

1. Writing the code for the functionality that the tag is supposed to provide, also known as the *tag handler*.
2. Writing the description for what that tags are supposed to achieve, also known as the *tag library descriptor* (TLD).
3. Packaging the tags into a JAR file, which is the tag library.
4. To use a tag in a JSP, you need a taglib directive to convey which tag and prefix you wish to use. You will see this in action in examples later in the chapter.

OJC supports custom WebLogic Server–specific tags at weblogic.jsp.*. These tags have been around before BEA was acquired by Oracle. As mentioned in the previous chapter, as much as possible, you do not want to use server-specific tags and limit the portability of your application. However, the tag support will be useful for those looking to move a WebLogic deployment to the cloud.

Before we get into the specifics of JSTL and expressions, Listing 5-7 shows a simple example to whet your appetite.

Listing 5-7: *JSTL and Expressions*

```
<c:forEach var="i" begin="1" end="5">
          <p>Item <c:out value="${i}"/></p>
     </c:forEach>
```

Can you figure out what we have achieved with the code in Listing 5-7? We have used a tag called **foreach** to iterate over a list from 1 to 5. We hold each value in the variable **i** and then print out the current value using the **out** tag. And within the **out** tag, we use the expression **${i}**.

So, as you can see, we have packed quite a lot of functionality into an easy-to-understand-and-maintain format that's free of any Java code. Let's look at expressions followed by JSTL and then try using them together to deliver greater functionality in our JSPs.

Expression Language

The unified expression language introduced in JSP 2.1 provides a common expression language for JSP and JSF. With the expression language, you can write simple expressions to access content from beans and perform arithmetic and logical operations.

Expressions are in the form **${*expression*}** in case of immediate evaluation of the expression, which is what you would use with JSP. However, with frameworks such as JSF where deferred evaluation is required, the **$** in the expression is replaced by a **#** sign and the expression is in the form **#{}**. With deferred evaluation, the framework can evaluate the expression at different stages in the lifecycle of the page. We will be using only immediate evaluation expressions in this chapter, but in Chapter 6 on JSF, you will see using both kinds of expressions.

The expression language also introduced additional implicit objects, listed in the following table, that you can use within an expression to access key data related to the page and the application.

Object	**Function**
param	Maps the request parameter name to a value
paramValues	Maps all request parameter names to an array of all request parameter values
header	Maps the request header name to a value

(continued)

Object	Function
headerValues	Maps all request header names to an array of all request header values
cookie	Maps the cookie name to a cookie
initParam	Maps the context initialization parameter name to a value

In the previous chapter, you saw the various scopes that can be used for sharing data. Here are the implicit objects that provide access to the scoped variables:

- pageScope
- requestScope
- sessionScope
- applicationScope

The implicit objects can be used in expressions, which can be used within JSTL tags or on their own.

JSTL Libraries

JSR 52 for JSTL states the following: "The original expert group that designed the JavaServer Pages 1.0 and JavaServer Pages 1.1 specifications wanted to include a list of standard tags as part of those specifications. Unfortunately, time pressures and the dangers of standardizing on not fully understood functionality forced the removal of any but a few very basic standard tags from these specifications."

So by the time the JSTL was introduced, JSPs packed with Java code had become the norm. Tag libraries were being developed—some open source, some proprietary—but there was no standardization happening. So if you were to use a tag, you were forced to also ship the tag library JAR file along with your application.

It was by this time quite obvious as to the kind of things that developers were looking to achieve in their JSP pages. Therefore, the expert group for JSR 52 came up with commonly used functionality that warranted having a standard tag.

JSTL has multiple tag libraries, each with a unique URI and consisting of many different tags:

- **Core** http://java.sun.com/jsp/jstl/core
- **XML** http://java.sun.com/jsp/jstl/xml
- **Formatting** http://java.sun.com/jsp/jstl/fmt
- **SQL** http://java.sun.com/jsp/jstl/sql
- **Functions** http://java.sun.com/jsp/jstl/functions

Taglib Directive

Before we use any of the tag libraries, we need to first use a taglib directive to state which libraries we are using and their prefix. The prefix and the URI are important so as to avoid any conflict between tags with the same name but in different libraries.

The taglib directives for the JSTL tag libraries are shown in Listing 5-8.

Listing 5-8: *JSTL Taglib Directives*

```
<%@ taglib prefix="c" uri="http://java.sun.com/jsp/jstl/core" %>
<%@ taglib prefix="sql" uri="http://java.sun.com/jsp/jstl/sql" %>
<%@ taglib prefix="x" uri="http://java.sun.com/jsp/jstl/xml" %>
<%@ taglib prefix="fn"
 uri="http://java.sun.com/jsp/jstl/functions" %>
<%@ taglib prefix="fmt" uri="http://java.sun.com/jsp/jstl/fmt" %>
```

TIP

Note that the prefixes used are per convention, but you can change the prefix being used. Also, the URI is only being used here as a unique identifier for the library. It does not suggest that page has to communicate with that URI and retrieve anything.

Core Tag Library

The core tag library consists of the tags you would need to use most often. It provides functionality for setting variables, running a loop, and producing output when a logical condition is fulfilled.

The directive for the core tag library is

```
<%@ taglib prefix="c" uri="#http://java.sun.com/jsp#/jstl/core" %>
```

The tags in the library are listed in the following table:

Tag	Function
<c:out>	Evaluates an expression and outputs the result of the evaluation to the current JspWriter object
<c:set>	Sets the value of a scoped variable or a property of a target object
<c:remove>	Removes a scoped variable
<c:catch>	Catches a java.lang.Throwable thrown by any of its nested actions
<c:if>	Evaluates its body content if the expression specified with the test attribute is true
<c:choose>	Provides the context for mutually exclusive conditional execution
<c:when>	Represents an alternative within a <c:choose> action
<c:otherwise>	Represents the last alternative within a <c:choose> action
<c:forEach>	Repeats its nested body content over a collection of objects, or repeats it a fixed number of times
<c:forTokens>	Iterates over tokens, separated by the supplied delimiters
<c:import>	Imports the content of a URL-based resource
<c:url>	Builds a URL with the proper rewriting rules applied
<c:redirect>	Sends an HTTP redirect to the client
<c:param>	Adds request parameters to a URL

Source: http://jcp.org/en/jsr/detail?id=052

XML Tag Library

The XML tag library is useful for working with XML. The directive for the XML tag library is

```
<%@ taglib prefix="x" uri="http://java.sun.com/jsp/jstl/xml" %>
```

You can parse, transform XML, and control flow using the tags listed in the following table:

Tag	Function
<x:parse>	Parses an XML document.
<x:out>	Evaluates an XPath expression and outputs the result of the evaluation to the current JspWriter object.
<x:set>	Evaluates an XPath expression and stores the result in a scoped variable.
<x:if>	Evaluates the XPath expression specified in the select attribute and renders its body content if the expression evaluates to true.
<x:choose>	Provides the context for mutually exclusive conditional execution.
<x:when>	Represents an alternative within an <x:choose> action.
<x:otherwise>	Represents the last alternative within an <x:choose> action.
<x:forEach>	Evaluates the given XPath expression and repeats its nested body content over the result, setting the context node to each element in the iteration.
<x:transform>	Applies an XSLT stylesheet transformation to an XML document.
<x:param>	Sets transformation parameters. Nested action of <x:transform>.

Source: http://jcp.org/en/jsr/detail?id=052

Formatting Tag Library

Formatting tags are used to format text, dates, time, and numbers as well as for internationalization. The directive for the formatting library is

```
<%@ taglib prefix="fmt" uri="http://java.sun.com/jsp/jstl/fmt" %>
```

and the tags are listed in the following table.

Tag	Function
<fmt:setLocale>	Stores the specified locale in the javax.servlet .jsp.jstl.fmt.locale configuration variable
<fmt:bundle>	Creates an i18n localization context to be used by its body content
<fmt:setBundle>	Creates an i18n localization context and stores it in the scoped variable or the javax.servlet .jsp.jstl.fmt.localization context-configuration variable
<fmt:message>	Looks up a localized message in a resource bundle
<fmt:param>	Supplies a single parameter for parametric replacement
<fmt:requestEncoding>	Sets the request's character encoding

SQL Tag Library

The SQL tag library contains tags for interacting with databases. Most applications tend to avoid talking to the database directly from a JSP and instead have a Java layer in between using Servlets or technologies such as managed beans or EJBs, which we will look at later in Chapters 6 and 7. However, if you are building a small application and need to talk to a database from a JSP, it can be easily achieved using the SQL tags.

The directive for the SQL tag library is

```
<%@ taglib prefix="sql" uri="http://java.sun.com/jsp/jstl/sql" %>
```

and the tags are as follows:

Tag	Function
<sql:query>	Queries a database.
<sql:update>	Executes a SQL INSERT, UPDATE, or DELETE statement.
<sql:transaction>	Establishes a transaction context for <sql:query> and <sql:update> subtags.
<sql:setDataSource>	Exports a data source either as a scoped variable or as the data source configuration variable (javax.servlet.jsp.jstl.sql.dataSource).

Tag	**Function**
<sql:param>	Sets the values of parameter markers ("?") in a SQL statement. It's a subtag of SQLExecutionTag actions such as <sql:query> and <sql:update>.
<sql:dateParam>	Sets the values of parameter markers ("?") in a SQL statement for values of type java.util.Date.

Functions Tag Library

This library includes handy string-related manipulation and check functions. Note that these are not tags, but functions that can be used in expressions or in expressions within tag attributes. The directive for the Functions tag library is

```
<%@ taglib prefix="fn"
 uri="http://java.sun.com/jsp/jstl/functions" %>
```

and the tags are as follows:

Tag	**Function**
fn:contains	Tests whether a string contains the specified substring
fn:containsIgnoreCase	Tests whether a string contains the specified substring in a case-insensitive way
fn:endsWith	Tests whether a string ends with the specified suffix
fn:escapeXml	Escapes characters that could be interpreted as XML markup
fn:indexOf	Returns the index within a string of the first occurrence of a specified substring
fn:join	Joins all elements of an array into a string
fn:length	Returns the number of items in a collection, or the number of characters in a string
fn:replace	Returns a string resulting from replacing all occurrences of a string with another string
fn:split	Splits a string into an array of substrings
fn:startsWith	Tests whether a string starts with the specified prefix

(continued)

Tag	Function
fn:substring	Returns a subset of a string
fn:substringAfter	Returns a subset of a string following a specific substring
fn:substringBefore	Returns a subset of a string before a specific substring
fn:toLowerCase	Converts all the characters of a string to lowercase
fn:toUpperCase	Converts all the characters of a string to uppercase
fn:trim	Removes whitespace from both ends of a string

Using Tags in a JSP

Now that we have looked at the various tags, let's look at how to use them in a JSP. To use JSTL in our application, we need to refer to the JSTL library in the weblogic.xml file, as shown in Listing 5-9. You will find the exact specification and implementation version listed in the Libraries widget on the Cloud Services Control, as shown in Figure 5-5. The shared Libraries widget lists the various

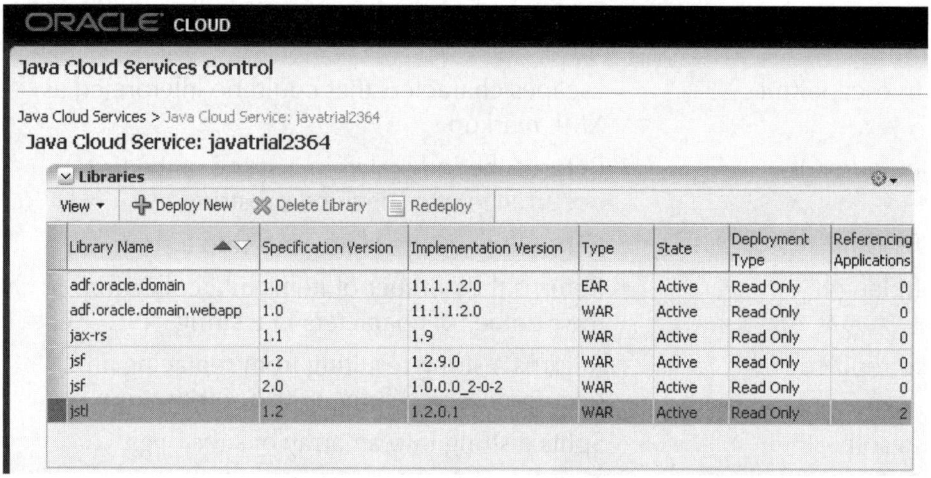

ORACLE CLOUD

Java Cloud Services Control

Java Cloud Services > Java Cloud Service: javatrial2364

Java Cloud Service: javatrial2364

Libraries

View ▾ Deploy New Delete Library Redeploy

Library Name	Specification Version	Implementation Version	Type	State	Deployment Type	Referencing Applications
adf.oracle.domain	1.0	11.1.1.2.0	EAR	Active	Read Only	0
adf.oracle.domain.webapp	1.0	11.1.1.2.0	WAR	Active	Read Only	0
jax-rs	1.1	1.9	WAR	Active	Read Only	0
jsf	1.2	1.2.9.0	WAR	Active	Read Only	0
jsf	2.0	1.0.0.0_2-0-2	WAR	Active	Read Only	0
jstl	1.2	1.2.0.1	WAR	Active	Read Only	2

FIGURE 5-5. *Shared Libraries - JSTL*

libraries available to you. You can add a new library using the Deploy New button. OJC will check the library for compliance with Oracle standards before it is made available to your application. We do not need to add the JSTL library in our case, as JSTL 1.2 is already deployed and available.

I have dragged the Libraries widget to the left of the page for the sake of the Figure 5-5 screen capture, however by default you will find it on the right of the page.

Listing 5-9: *Refer to the JSTL library*

```
<library-ref>
  <library-name>jstl</library-name>
  <specification-version>1.2</specification-version>
  <implementation-version>1.2.0.1</implementation-version>
  <exact-match>false</exact-match>
</library-ref>
```

Next, create a new JSP named jstl1.jsp. In this JSP, add the code shown in Listing 5-10.

Listing 5-10: *Using Expressions with JSTL Tags Set, Choose When*

```
<%@page contentType="text/html" pageEncoding="UTF-8"%>
<%@taglib prefix="c" uri="http://java.sun.com/jsp/jstl/core" %>
<%@taglib prefix="fmt" uri="http://java.sun.com/jsp/jstl/fmt" %>

<!DOCTYPE html>
<html>
    <head>
        <meta http-equiv="Content-Type" content="text/html;
charset=UTF-8">
        <title>JSP Page</title>
    </head>
    <body>

        <%--Expression Language With JSTL--%>

        <%--Set a request attribute--%>
        <c:set var="amount" scope="request" value="500" />

        <%--Multiple ways to access the attribute--%>
        <ul>
            <li>Amount = ${requestScope.amount}</li>
            <li>Amount = ${requestScope["amount"]}</li>
```

```
            <li>Amount = ${amount}</li>
        </ul>

        <%--Choose When --%>

        <c:choose>
            <c:when test="${requestScope.amount < 1000 }">
                <p>Access Restricted!</p>
                <p>Your amount was
                    <fmt:formatNumber minFractionDigits="2"
                    value="${amount}"/>
                </p>
            </c:when>
            <c:otherwise>
                <p>Welcome!</p>
            </c:otherwise>
        </c:choose>
    </body>
</html>
```

Although the taglib directives (first two lines) will work fine, regardless of where you place them in the JSP, it is recommended that you place them at the top of the JSP, below the page directive. The rest of the non-HTML code goes into the <body> tag because we want to get the output displayed in the browser. Now, run the JSP and you will get the output shown in Figure 5-6.

In this example, we are setting a request attribute named **amount** with the value 500. Note that here we are benefiting from the automatic type conversion capability of JSTL. We are passing 500 as a string but later working with it as if it is an integer.

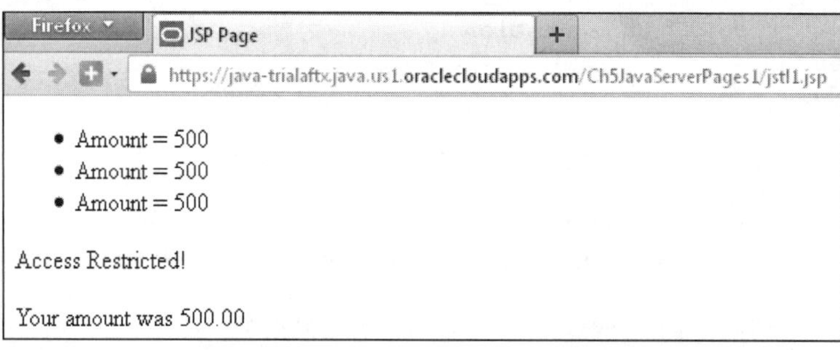

FIGURE 5-6. *Output using JSTL and expressions*

Next, we see how we can access the **amount** attribute in multiple ways provided by the expression. In the case where we just say **${amount}**, the server will look for the **amount** variable from the narrowest scope to the widest. Therefore, if there's a possibility that you might have attributes with the same name in multiple scopes, you should always state the scope as well.

Next, we use the <choose> tag, which contains the <when> tag, where we test whether the amount is less than 1000. If it is less than 1000, we use the formatting tag and format the number such that we have at least two digits after the decimal.

Now let's try out another example, where we deal with a commonly required use case of iterating over many items. These items that we wish to iterate over could be a list of inputs from a user or, at times, a list of items retrieved from a database. Create a new JSP called Jstl2.jsp. In this JSP, add the code shown in Listing 5-11.

Listing 5-11: *JSTL forEach*

```
<%@taglib prefix="c" uri="http://java.sun.com/jsp/jstl/core" %>
<%@taglib prefix="fn"
 uri="http://java.sun.com/jsp/jstl/functions" %>
<%@page contentType="text/html" pageEncoding="UTF-8"%>
<!DOCTYPE html>
<html>
    <head>
        <meta http-equiv="Content-Type"
        content="text/html; charset=UTF-8">
        <title>JSP Page</title>
    </head>
    <body>
<%@taglib prefix="c" uri="http://java.sun.com/jsp/jstl/core" %>
<%@taglib prefix="fn"
 uri="http://java.sun.com/jsp/jstl/functions" %>
        <h1>List Technologies</h1>
        <c:forEach items="${paramValues.tech}" var="technology">
          <p>
          <c:if test="${fn:containsIgnoreCase(technology,'java')}">
              *
          </c:if>
          ${technology}
          </p>
        </c:forEach>
    </body>
</html>
```

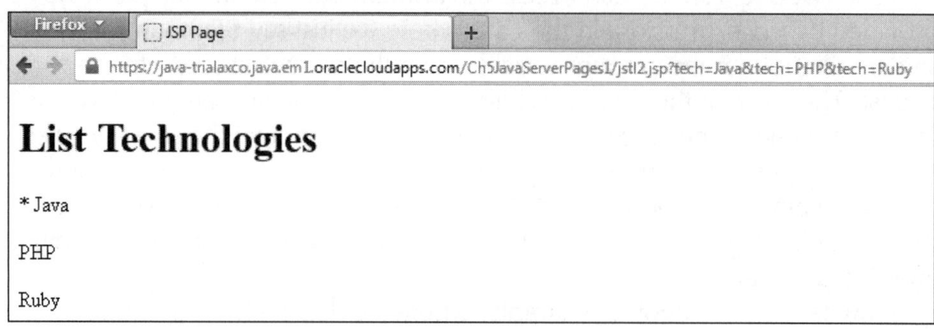

FIGURE 5-7. *Output using JSTL forEach*

Run the JSP. You will initially not get the desired output because we are not passing any parameters to the JSP. Modify the query string in the browser to the following:

```
/Ch5JavaServerPages1/jstl2.jsp?tech=Java&tech=PHP&tech=Ruby
```

By doing this, we are simulating the submission of three values from a check box. You should now get the output shown in Figure 5-7.

Note that we are using the implicit object paramValues mentioned in the "Expression Language" section, earlier in the chapter. Let's create another JSP, called Jstl3.jsp, to see how you can further leverage expressions and the implicit objects provided (see Listing 5-12).

Listing 5-12: *Expressions and Implicit Objects*

```
<%@page contentType="text/html" pageEncoding="UTF-8"%>
<!DOCTYPE html>
<html>
    <head>
        <meta http-equiv="Content-Type" content="text/html;
charset=UTF-8">
        <title>JSP Page</title>
    </head>
    <body>
        <%--Expression Language Usage--%>
        <p>Cookie = ${cookie.JSESSIONID.value}</p>
        <p>Host = ${header.host}</p>

        <p>2 + 3 = ${ 2 + 3 }</p>
```

```
        <p>Mod 10/4 = ${ 10 mod 4 }</p>
        <p>Mod 10/4 = ${ 10 % 4 }</p>

        <p>10/5 = ${ 10 div 5 }</p>
        <p>10/5 = ${ 10/5 }</p>

        <p>10 is greater than or equal to 5 = ${ 10 ge 5 }</p>
        <p>10 is greater than or equal to 5 = ${ 10 >= 5 }</p>

        <p>z > a = ${'z' > 'a'}</p>
        <p>Example param exists = ${!empty param.Example}</p>
    </body>
</html>
```

Upon running the JSP, you will get the output shown in Figure 5-8. As you can see, a lot can be achieved using expressions. Note that because we are only using expressions and no tags, the taglib directive is not required in this case. Also, note that the values for **cookie** and **host** will vary based on your setup.

FIGURE 5-8. *Output using various expressions*

In these examples, we have looked at commonly encountered scenarios—how you can produce dynamic content in a JSP using JSTL and expression language (EL) and without writing any Java code. The key to using JSTL and EL well is to be aware of all the tags we have covered, to understand the range of expressions possible, and to use them as and when appropriate.

Going through all the many tags would not be appropriate here, but do note that the format is pretty much the same in all cases—most tags have multiple attributes to provide for various possibilities, and these attributes in many cases accept expressions to make the tags even more capable.

Summary

JSP has been around for a long time and yet continues to be a good, quick option for building Java EE applications. Using JSP, along with JSTL and EL, enables you to build rich applications while still having clean code. JSP skills are easily available, and JSP continues to be an important part of even the latest versions of Java EE. OJC runs your JSP files as well as any local server, and there are no JSP-specific restrictions on your development.

Do not discount JSP and take up the more complex frameworks only because JSP is no longer fashionable. If you don't find the tags you need in the libraries we've discussed here, explore some of the many open-source tag libraries available for niche requirements.

In the next chapter, we will look at JavaServer Faces (JSF), which is a feature-rich web framework and the framework of choice for most new Java EE web applications.

CHAPTER 6

JavaServer Faces

In the previous chapter, we looked at JavaServer Pages (JSP), which continues to be a popular technology for building web applications, but suffers from some major drawbacks of being rather unstructured, prone to chaotic coding, and difficult to maintain. So in this chapter, we will look at JavaServer Faces (JSF), which is the preferred web technology for Java EE applications today. It offers a neat and feature-rich way of building server-side web applications. The key capabilities of JSF are the UI component model, event handling, validation framework, structured page navigation, and internationalization.

From JSP to Struts to JSF

With JSP, we think of a web page as a collection of scripts, tags, and HTML; however, with JSF we think of a web page as a set of components placed on a page. We tweak and customize the working of each component. The components, in most cases, are tied to backend Java code that further enhances their capability.

JSF is a framework for building web applications, so it goes beyond just a web page view and looks at how an entire application should be designed and managed. It provides a definite structure and development paradigm for building a web application. So whereas JSP is a view technology, JSF is much more than that.

Until JSF version 2.0, JSP was the view technology for JSF. JSF 2.0 and later use Facelets as the primary view technology; however, JSP continues to be supported and used.

Having said that, the origins of JSF lie not just in the limitations of JSP, but also in a popular web framework from the early 2000s named Struts. Although Struts is still around (http://struts.apache.org/), it is no longer as popular.

Struts provided an open-source framework for building web applications based on the Model-View-Controller (MVC) design paradigm. MVC is a design pattern where the Model represents the business logic, the View the page, and the Controller the application navigation. Struts was tailor-made for HTTP web applications and provided rich capabilities for common web functionality such as request response handling and form submissions. The decoupling of the Controller and the View brought in great value for web applications, which at the time were getting too large and complex to manage using just JSPs.

Java EE has always excelled at adopting good ideas. The Struts creator, Craig McClanahan, was also the co-specification lead for JSF 1.0. Therefore, JSF's backend code and the navigation-handling capability are pretty similar to those of Struts. The Facelets UI component part of JSF has adopted ideas from frameworks such as Apache Tapestry and Tiles. Earlier, Tiles was part of Struts, but is now a separate project known as Apache Tiles.

JSF on the Oracle Java Cloud

As mentioned in previous chapters, OJC supports a mix of Java EE 5 and Java EE 6 technologies, so even in the case of JSF, OJC supports JSF release 1.2 as well as release 2.0, which was introduced in Java EE 6. The support for JSF 2.0 is important because Facelets, the preferred view technology for JSF today, was introduced only in JSF 2.0. "View technology" here essentially means the code that generates the web page view. Having said that, JSP continues to be supported even with the latest JSF versions, but Facelets is the recommended view technology. If you are building a new application, it's best to avoid JSP and use Facelets instead.

Another important change with JSF 2.0 was the support for annotations. So until JSF 1.x, all the configuration was in a configuration file named faces-config.xml; however, with version 2.0 you can use annotations. We could not use annotations in Chapter 4 on Servlets because the Servlet version supported on OJC does not support annotations. However, because OJC supports JSF 2.0, which supports annotations, we can use annotations in this chapter.

TIP

An annotation is metadata that has no direct effect on the operation of the code but is used for configuration or to provide additional information to the compiler or other development/deployment tools.

Facelets

Facelets are a part of the JSF specification. It provides a page declaration language and templating capability, and is suited for building component-based pages. Facelets bring in performance improvement along with the option for developers to easily plug in new components as required.

Facelets' component-based model has also given vendors the option to ship component libraries that can be easily plugged in to any application. There are many such free, open-source, and commercial component libraries available. The creators of those libraries usually just ship a .jar file with their bunch of components built as per the Facelets and JSF norms.

The component-based model of Facelets has also led to the creation of tools that can efficiently add and edit components. Facelets also provides tag libraries in addition to the JSTL we discussed in the previous chapter.

From the look of it, Facelets vary from JSPs due to the use of XHTML and the different tags and components used. However, Facelets also support expression language capabilities beyond JSP. So in the previous chapter, we only looked at expressions that are evaluated immediately using the **${}** syntax. However, with JSF and Facelets, we can also leverage the deferred evaluation capability using the #{} syntax so that expressions are evaluated only at an appropriate point in the lifecycle of a component.

Let's now build a JSF application and try to better understand JSF with reference to our sample application.

Select Java Web | Web Application to create a new project in NetBeans. Name the project **Ch6JSF1**. Along similar lines to projects in previous chapters, use the Oracle Cloud Remote server. In the next step, shown in Figure 6-1, select JavaServer Faces in the list of frameworks. You now need to set the server library for your JSF application. Because we will be running the application on OJC, our library options are limited to JSF 2.0 and JSF 1.2, which are listed in the Server Library drop-down. Select JSF 2.0.

Next, click the Configuration tab. As shown in Figure 6-2, the JSF Servlet URL Pattern field is set to /faces/*. This means that all requests received by your web application that match the URL pattern /faces/* will be handled by the JSF framework. Here, * is the wildcard character, which implies that you can have Servlets and JSPs like the ones in the previous chapter running alongside JSF. If the request URL does not match /faces/*, the JSF framework will not get involved and your Servlet/JSP can work independently.

Next, we need to select the preferred page language. The choices here are Facelets and JSP. In case you only see the JSP option (no Facelets), check whether you have selected JSF 2.0 in the Server Library drop-down, as shown in Figure 6-1. Select Facelets.

Next, select the Components tab. You will see the screen shown in Figure 6-3. Listed are popular JSF suites (PrimeFaces, ICEFaces, and RichFaces) that bring in their own set of rich components. Although JSF itself has many

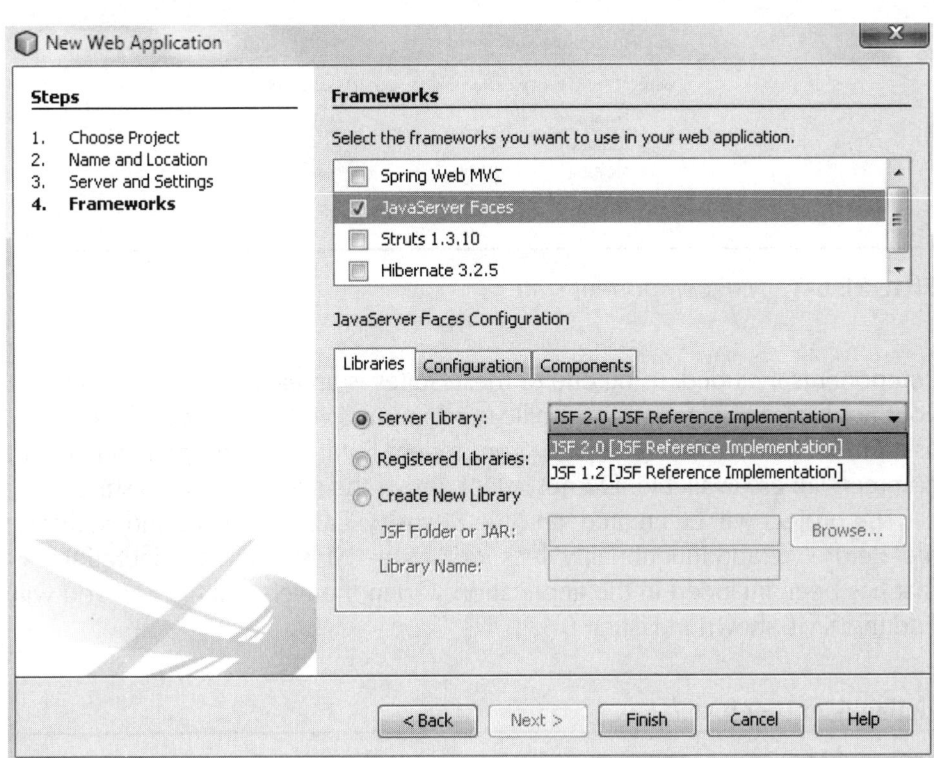

FIGURE 6-1. *Selecting the JSF library*

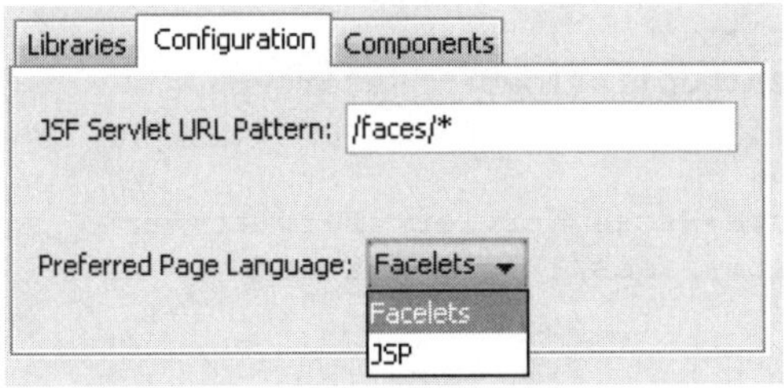

Libraries | Configuration | Components

JSF Servlet URL Pattern: /faces/*

Preferred Page Language: Facelets

Facelets

JSP

FIGURE 6-2. *The Configuration tab*

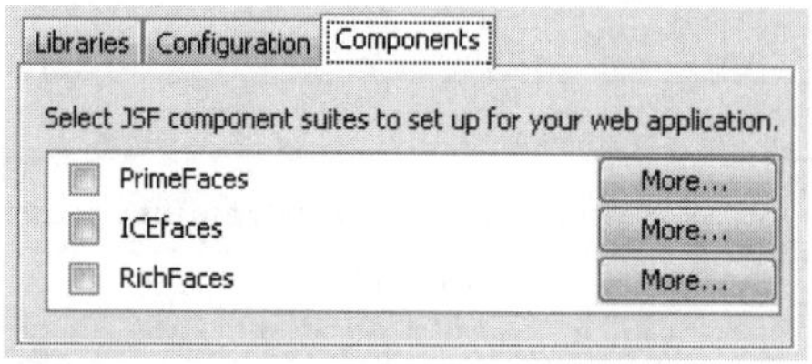

FIGURE 6-3. *JSF component suites*

components included, using one of these suites is an easy way to jazz up your application with more capability and impressive UIs. Besides the ones listed here, many other third-party component libraries, both open source and commercial, are available. Do not select any of the suites. Click Finish.

The project will be created, and NetBeans will also create an index.xhtml file. Before we add functionality, let's look at the JSF-specific configuration that has been included in the application. Open the web.xml file and you will find the XML shown in Listing 6-1.

Listing 6-1: *web.xml*

```
<context-param>
      <param-name>javax.faces.PROJECT_STAGE</param-name>
      <param-value>Development</param-value>
</context-param>
<servlet>
      <servlet-name>Faces Servlet</servlet-name>
      <servlet-class>
         javax.faces.webapp.FacesServlet
      </servlet-class>
      <load-on-startup>1</load-on-startup>
</servlet>
<servlet-mapping>
      <servlet-name>Faces Servlet</servlet-name>
      <url-pattern>/faces/*</url-pattern>
</servlet-mapping>
```

First up is the parameter javax.faces.PROJECT_STAGE, which is set to Development, but can also take the value Production, SystemTest, or UnitTest. Based on this value, the JSF implementation can optimize its behavior, as well as modify the verbosity of development-time diagnostics, error messages, and debugging information.

Next, notice that the value we set in Figure 6-2 has led to a new Servlet being declared, with all /faces/* requests being mapped to it. Note that /faces/* is the pattern we provided in the wizard. We could have very well used some other pattern.

Now let's look at the index.xhtml file, which has the code shown in Listing 6-2.

Listing 6-2: *index.xhtml*

```
<?xml version='1.0' encoding='UTF-8' ?>
<!DOCTYPE html PUBLIC "-//W3C//DTD XHTML 1.0 Transitional//EN"
"http://www.w3.org/TR/xhtml1/DTD/xhtml1-transitional.dtd">
<html xmlns="http://www.w3.org/1999/xhtml"
      xmlns:h="http://java.sun.com/jsf/html">
    <h:head>
        <title>Facelet Title</title>
    </h:head>
    <h:body>
        Hello from Facelets
    </h:body>
</html>
```

Although this is a bare-bones .xhtml file, it still has enough in it for us to discuss the foundation of a Facelets-based .xhtml file.

XHTML is HTML that is also XML. Therefore, all the hacks and shortcuts you can get away with in an HTML file will not work in XHTML. XHTML brings in the following conditions: **doctype** is a must; all elements have to be nested, closed, and in lowercase; the document must have one root element; all attributes must be in lowercase; attributes must be quoted; and more. Apart from leading to nice, readable code, the other important benefit is that XHTML can be parsed using an XML parser, which is an important capability if you want tools and editors to use and modify the file.

TIP

One of the most common HTML tag issues involves the <br> tag. For it to be valid, well-formed XML, the tag has to be <br /> and not <br>.

Next, you will find that apart from the xmlns="http://www.w3.org/1999/xhtml namespace declaration, there's also xmlns:h="http://java.sun.com/jsf/html", which is the namespace declaration for all the tags we are using with the prefix **h**. Therefore, the tags h:head and h:body are not part of the basic XHTML, but rather, a part of the additional tag library introduced by Facelets. Although the h:head and h:body tags here only generate the corresponding <head> and <body> tags, we have the choice of using the various attributes of these tags to get them to do more than generate just the HTML tags.

CAUTION

JSF 2.2 introduced new namespaces that start with http://xmlns.jcp.org instead of http://java.sun.com. Therefore, a lot of the tools, as well as many new online samples, use the new namespace. However, note that OJC supports JSF 2.0 and the http://java.sun.com namespaces.

The tag libraries supported by Facelets in JSF 2.0 are listed here:

Tag Library	URI	Prefix
Facelets	http://java.sun.com/jsf/facelets	ui:
HTML	http://java.sun.com/jsf/html	h:
Core	http://java.sun.com/jsf/core	f:
Composite	http://java.sun.com/jsf/composite	composite:
JSTL Core	http://java.sun.com/jsp/jstl/core	c:
JSTL Functions	http://java.sun.com/jsp/jstl/functions	fn:

We looked at some of the JSTL tags in Chapter 5, and will look at some of the key tags in the other libraries in later examples in this chapter.

JSF Managed Beans

JSF managed beans are Plain Old Java Objects (POJOs) that are managed by JSF. All that it takes to make a Java class a managed bean is to add the annotation @ManagedBean to the code or the appropriate XML configuration.

The managed bean is usually used to process HTML form values and is the place where you add Java code you want bound to UI components.

The managed bean at times even includes the actual business logic of the application; however, moving the business logic code to a dedicated business logic class or an EJB is considered to be a better practice.

TIP

The term managed bean was once used almost exclusively for JSF managed beans. However, with newer specifications such as Contexts and Dependency Injection (CDI), the term lately tends to be used for any Java class that is being managed by the server, and is no longer a JSF-specific usage. You can read more about CDI managed beans at http://docs.oracle.com/javaee/6/tutorial/doc/gjfzi.html. CDI is not supported on OJC, so any managed bean usage in this chapter refers to JSF managed beans.

So let's add a managed bean to our application with a single String property, yourname. We will then bind this property in the bean to a text box in the UI .xhtml file.

To add a managed bean, right-click the project in the Projects window and then select New | Other | JavaServer Faces | JSF Managed Bean. You will get the screen shown in Figure 6-4. The class is WelcomeBean, and the package is managedbeans.

You should now have WelcomeBean.java open up in your editor window. You can either manually add the code for the yourname property or use the NetBeans wizard. To add using NetBeans, right-click within the class body in the code editor and select Insert Code | Add Property. Name the property **yourname** and set the type as String. You can have NetBeans generate Javadoc comments by checking the Generate Javadoc box. Uncheck the box to keep the code brief. Click OK. You should now have the code shown in Listing 6-3.

Listing 6-3: *WelcomeBean*

```
package managedbeans;
import javax.faces.bean.ManagedBean;
import javax.faces.bean.RequestScoped;
```

```
@ManagedBean(name = "welcome")
@RequestScoped
public class WelcomeBean {
    private String yourname;
    public WelcomeBean(){
    }
    public String getYourname() {
        return yourname;
    }
    public void setYourname(String yourname) {
        this.yourname = yourname;
    }
```

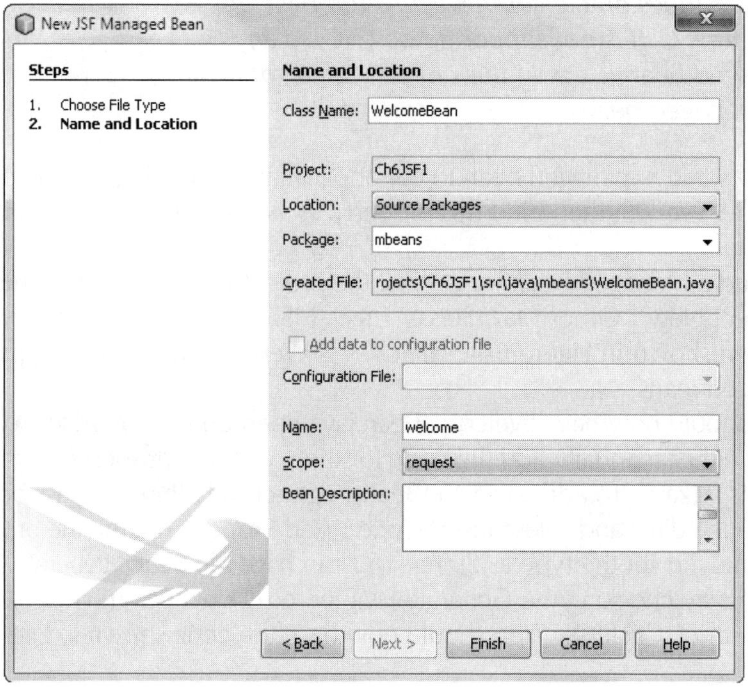

FIGURE 6-4. *The new JSF managed bean*

Although the Java code is pretty simple, the things to note are the annotations @ManagedBean(name = "welcome") and @RequestScoped.

Now that we have our bean ready, let's add a text box to our .xhtml and bind it to the property yourname in the bean. The index.xhtml file is shown in Listing 6-4.

Listing 6-4: *Form in index.xhtml*

```
<?xml version='1.0' encoding='UTF-8' ?>
<!DOCTYPE html PUBLIC "-//W3C//DTD XHTML 1.0 Transitional//EN"
"http://www.w3.org/TR/xhtml1/DTD/xhtml1-transitional.dtd">
<html xmlns="http://www.w3.org/1999/xhtml"
      xmlns:h="http://java.sun.com/jsf/html">
    <h:head>
        <title>Welcome JSF</title>
    </h:head>
    <h:body>
       <h:form>
         <h:inputText label="Name" id="yourname"
          value="#{welcome.yourname}" >
         </h:inputText>
         <h:commandButton action="welcomepage" value="Go!"/>
       </h:form>
    </h:body>
</html>
```

Note that an enclosing HTML form is required for your button to work and submit the value entered in the text box.

In this code, the inputText tag generates a text box and the command button generates a submit button with the text "Go!" However, what's special about this code is the **value** attribute that is being bound to the property in the managed bean. The most obvious benefit of this binding is that it would be the framework's job to call the getter and setter methods as and when the property value is to be fetched or processed. The developer is freed of the mundane task of fetching request parameters.

Note that we are using **#{** in the expression, which means that it's a deferred evaluation. Therefore, the JSF framework can decide when the expressions are evaluated at appropriate points in the lifecycle of a component. JSF mostly uses deferred evaluation expressions.

Within the expression **#{welcome.yourname}, welcome** is the name of the managed bean, as stated in the @ManagedBean annotation in Listing 6-3, and **yourname** is the property. The **yourname** property value will get set based on what's being entered. Note that we have written our accessor methods (get and set methods, also known as "getter-setter methods") in Listing 6-3 as per the JavaBeans specification, and they are also being invoked as specified. Therefore, the setYourName method is invoked by the JSF implementation to *set* the yourname value, and the getYourName method is invoked to *get* the yourname value.

Next, you can see that the action attribute in the h:commandButton tag has the value welcomepage, which currently has no meaning within the JSF application. Therefore, create a new JSF page named welcomepage.xhtml. Right-click the project and select New | JSF Page. In the next screen, shown in Figure 6-5, select the Facelets option and click Finish. Now update the page as shown in Listing 6-5.

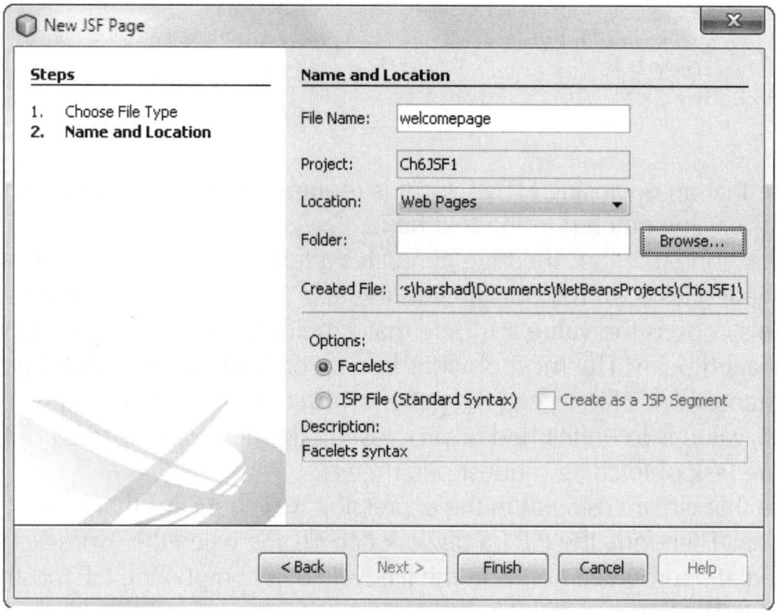

FIGURE 6-5. *The new JSF page*

Listing 6-5: *Welcome Page*

```
<?xml version='1.0' encoding='UTF-8' ?>
<!DOCTYPE html PUBLIC "-//W3C//DTD XHTML 1.0 Transitional//EN"
"http://www.w3.org/TR/xhtml1/DTD/xhtml1-transitional.dtd">
<html xmlns="http://www.w3.org/1999/xhtml"
      xmlns:h="http://java.sun.com/jsf/html">

    <h:head>
        <title>Welcome Page</title>
    </h:head>
    <h:body>
        Welcome #{welcome.yourname}
    </h:body>
</html>
```

Next, right-click and run the index.xhtml file. Along similar lines to all applications in previous chapters, the project will get packaged and deployed on OJC, and upon accessing the page from your browser, you will get the page shown in Figure 6-6.

Enter some text in the text box and either press ENTER or click the Go! button. JSF will take you to the welcomepage.xhtml page, where you will see the message "Welcome *<the value you entered>*." So what has happened here is that the yourname value was set in the WelcomeBean property when you submitted the form, and we retrieved the value from the bean in the welcomepage.xhtml page. Considering how often you need to accept and process form submissions in a web application, JSF's form-handling capability is especially useful.

With form submissions, it is often the case that you need to decide page flow based on the values submitted. In Listing 6-6, we check the value of *yourname* and return *welcomepage* if it is *java* and *notwelcomepage* if it is anything else.

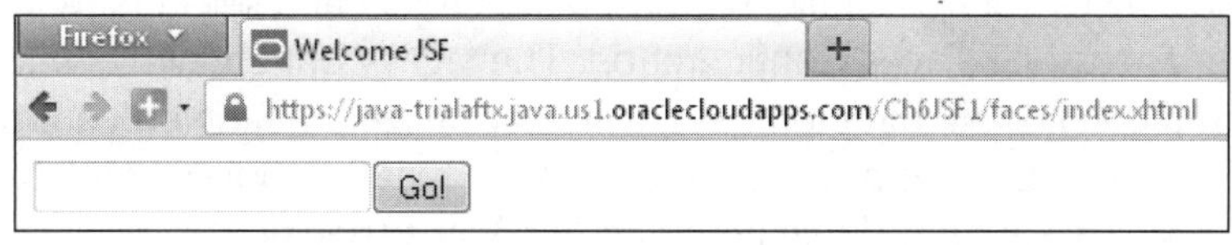

FIGURE 6-6. *index.xhtml in the browser*

Listing 6-6: *The checkedWelcome Method in WelcomeBean*

```
public String checkedWelcome() {
      if (yourname.equalsIgnoreCase("java")) {
            return "welcomepage";
      } else {
            return "notwelcomepage";
      }
}
```

Next we need to edit the command button tag in index.xhtml as follows:

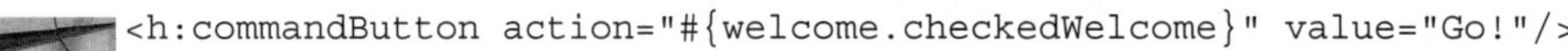

```
<h:commandButton action="#{welcome.checkedWelcome}" value="Go!"/>
```

Also, add a new JSF page named notwelcomepage.xhtml to handle the **else** condition. Keep the page exactly the same as the *welcomepage* in Listing 6-5; just change the word **Welcome** to **NotWelcome**, except in the expression where we are referring to the managed bean.

Again, run index.xhtml. You will find that based on whether you enter the word **java** in the text box, you are forwarded to either welcomepage or notwelcomepage. We have so far hard-coded the page-names, which is neither advisable nor feasible in real applications. Therefore, we will now enhance the navigation capability by introducing the JSF Faces Configuration file (faces-config.xml), which is a configuration file that can be used to define page-navigation rules and configure beans.

TIP

JSF, by default, looks for a configuration file named faces-config.xml in the WEB-INF directory, but you can use a different name or split the configuration into multiple files. You just need to add a context parameter named javax.faces.CONFIG_FILES in your web.xml.

To add a faces-config.xml file, right-click the project and select New | Other | JavaServer Faces | JSF Faces Configuration. The faces-config.xml file will be created in the WEB-INF directory. We will now utilize a neat NetBeans tool that facilitates creating the navigation rules. Note that the tool only generates the requisite XML; we are not doing anything NetBeans specific.

In the faces-config.xml editor window, click the PageFlow tab. Our three xhtml pages are shown in three boxes. Click and drag the dot on the

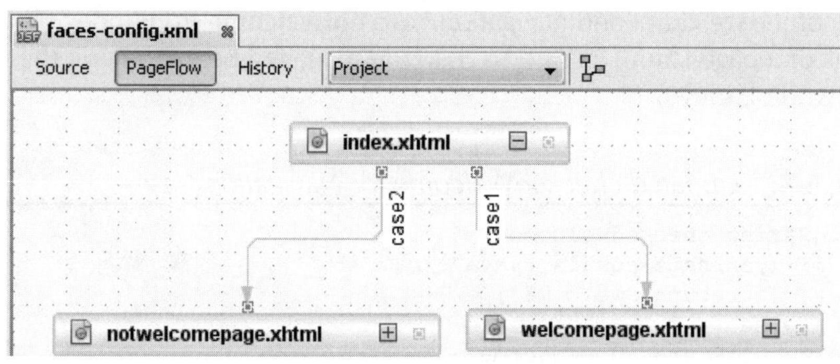

FIGURE 6-7. *JSF Faces Configuration visual editor*

right of the index.xhtml box and drag it to welcomepage.xhtml and then to notwelcomepage.xhtml. You will get the screen shown in Figure 6-7.

NetBeans, by default, will name the page-flows case1 and case2, respectively. We will update them to the more relevant names welcome and notwelcome, respectively. Now click the Source tab, and you will see that the visual editor has generated the XML shown in Listing 6-7.

Listing 6-7: *faces-config.xml*

```
<?xml version='1.0' encoding='UTF-8'?>
<faces-config version="2.1"
    xmlns="http://java.sun.com/xml/ns/javaee"
    xmlns:xsi="http://www.w3.org/2001/XMLSchema-instance"
    xsi:schemaLocation="http://java.sun.com/xml/ns/javaee
"http://java.sun.com/xml/ns/javaee/web-facesconfig_2_1.xsd">
    <navigation-rule>
        <from-view-id>/index.xhtml</from-view-id>
        <navigation-case>
            <from-outcome>welcome</from-outcome>
            <to-view-id>/welcomepage.xhtml</to-view-id>
        </navigation-case>
        <navigation-case>
            <from-outcome>notwelcome</from-outcome>
            <to-view-id>/notwelcomepage.xhtml</to-view-id>
        </navigation-case>
    </navigation-rule>
</faces-config>
```

Now that we have defined the navigation case **welcome** from index.xhtml to welcomepage.xhtml and navigation case **notwelcome** from index.xhtml to notwelcomepage.xhtml, let's go back to the managed bean and edit the code as shown in Listing 6-8.

Listing 6-8: *Updated checkedWelcome for Navigation Cases*

```
public String checkedWelcome() {
      if (yourname.equals("java")) {
            return "welcome";
      } else {
            return "notwelcome";
      }
}
```

Now, based on the value of the text box input, we can decide the navigation of our application. We have kept our navigation flexible by declaring it in an XML file and not hard-coding it into our code.

Validation

Validating user input is one of the most common tasks in a web application. Prior to JSF, you either had to write the validation code or plug in a separate validation framework. However, with JSF's rich validation capability, you can easily validate user input and generate messages accordingly. JSF provides multiple validators along with the validator tags in the JSF core tag library. The tags are detailed in the following table:

Tag	Function
validateLength	Checks whether the length is within range.
validateLongRange	Checks whether the value is within range. The value should be numeric or a string that can be converted to the type long.
validateDoubleRange	Checks whether the value is within range. The value should be numeric or a string that can be converted to floating-point.
validateRegEx	Checks the value against a regular expression from java.util.regex.

Tag	Function
validateRequired	Checks that the value is not empty. Used to mark a form field as required.
validateBean	Used to register a separate bean validator.

Let's go back to our code and validate the name input in the text box in index.xhtml. For that, we need to first declare the core tag library usage in the html tag, as shown in Listing 6-9.

Listing 6-9: *Tag Library Declaration*

```
<html xmlns="http://www.w3.org/1999/xhtml"
        xmlns:h="http://java.sun.com/jsf/html"
        xmlns:f="http://java.sun.com/jsf/core">
```

Next, we edit the h:inputText tag, as shown in Listing 6-10.

Listing 6-10: *Validate Length*

```
<h:inputText label="Name" id="yourname"
 value="#{welcome.yourname}" >
      <f:validateLength maximum="10" />
      <f:validateRequired/>
</h:inputText>
```

TIP
Use CTRL-SPACE *in the NetBeans editor for tag autocomplete and documentation.*

The field is a required field, with a maximum length of 10. Now run index.xhtml, followed by entering any length of text greater than 10. You will get a screen similar to the one in Figure 6-8. We currently do not have any element on the page that is meant to handle and display the validation messages. Therefore, by default, the messages appear in red and at the bottom of the page, the javax.faces.PROJECT_STAGE value in web.xml is set to Development. We discussed javax.faces.PROJECT_STAGE values earlier in this chapter.

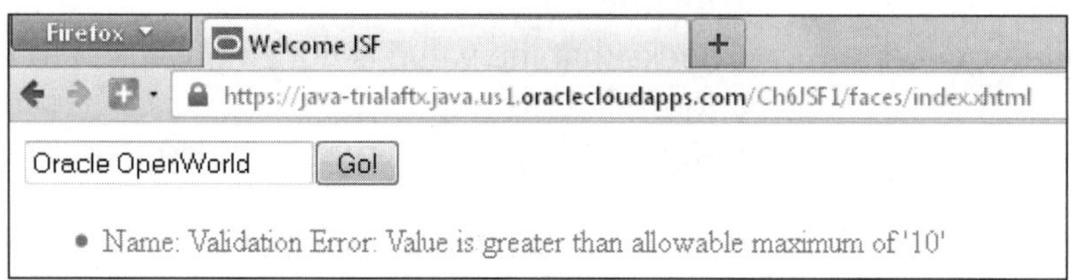

FIGURE 6-8. *Validation message*

TIP

Take note of the benefit of using a deferred evaluation expression in the form #{}. Even though there's a validation error that leads to a postback and the same page being reloaded, the value that was entered is not lost.

You can control the positioning of all the validation messages in one go by placing the tag <h:messages /> in your page, or you can provide a particular position and style for validation messages for individual fields using the <h:message /> tag. Edit the code as shown in Listing 6-11.

Listing 6-11: *Validation Messages*

```
<h:messages />
<h:form>
      <h:inputText label="Name" id="yourname"
       value="#{welcome.yourname}" >
            <f:validateLength maximum="10" />
            <f:validateRequired/>
      </h:inputText>
      <h:commandButton action="#{welcome.checkedWelcome}"
       value="Go!"/>
</h:form>
<h:message for="yourname" style="color:blue" />
```

In this case, we are using both options: <h:messages /> will show all validation messages, whereas <h:message /> will show the validation messages for the yourname text field in the color blue.

Ajax

Ajax was all the rage a few years back and has now become the norm for most rich UI applications. A plethora of third-party Ajax frameworks are available; however, JSF comes with built-in support for the basic Ajax functionality.

Let's look at a simple example where you use Ajax to refresh the time upon a click and avoid a page reload. In order to do this, first create a new JSF named ajaxtime.xhtml, as shown in Listing 6-12.

Listing 6-12: *Ajax Time*

```
<?xml version='1.0' encoding='UTF-8' ?>
<!DOCTYPE html PUBLIC "-//W3C//DTD XHTML 1.0 Transitional//EN"
"http://www.w3.org/TR/xhtml1/DTD/xhtml1-transitional.dtd">
<html xmlns="http://www.w3.org/1999/xhtml"
      xmlns:h="http://java.sun.com/jsf/html"
      xmlns:f="http://java.sun.com/jsf/core">
    <h:head>
        <title>Ajax Time</title>
    </h:head>
    <h:body>
        <p>Time: <h:outputText value="#{welcome.time}"
      id="timetext" /></p>
        <p>
            <h:link value="Refresh Time" >
                <f:ajax render="timetext"/>
            </h:link>
        </p>
    </h:body>
</html>
```

Here, we are getting the value of the property **time** using the expression **#{welcome.time}**, which will lead to a call to getTime in the managed bean WelcomeBean. Add the property and the method as shown in Listing 6-13.

Listing 6-13: *The getTime Method in the Managed Bean*

```
private String time;
public String getTime() {
    return new java.util.Date().toString();
}
```

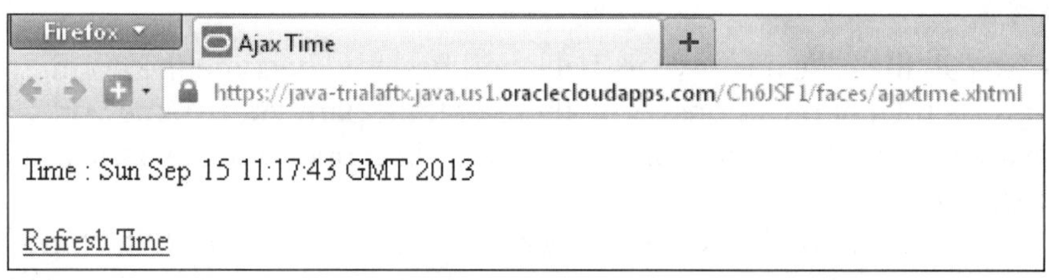

FIGURE 6-9. *Ajax time*

The <f:ajax> usage in Listing 6-12 conveys that on the link being clicked, we want the component with ID timetext to be rendered. Therefore, the whole page will not reload, but only that one component will get rendered again. As we are getting the **time** property in the component with ID timetext, the new **time** value will get updated on every click of the link, as shown in Figure 6-9.

Templates

Most web applications tend to follow a consistent look and feel across the site. For example, there's usually a constant header and footer and at times even a sidebar present on all pages. The Facelets tags in JSF provide templating capability that enables you to use a page as the template for other pages in the application.

To add a new template to our project, right-click the project and select New | Other | JavaServer Faces | Facelets Template. Select the layout with a header and a left sidebar, as shown in Figure 6-10. NetBeans will not only create the newTemplate.xhtml file, but will also create a resources directory with a couple of .css files within.

The code generated by NetBeans includes the CSS using standard HTML tags. However, because "resources" under the root of your web application is a special directory for JSF, where it expects all your web resources files such as CSS, images, and JavaScript to be stored, we can use the tag <h:outputStylesheet> to refer to the CSS and the tag <h:outputScript> to refer to any JavaScript. We can even create subdirectories within the resources directory for various themes for our application, and even create subdirectories for versions of a theme. Our modified code for the template is shown in Listing 6-14.

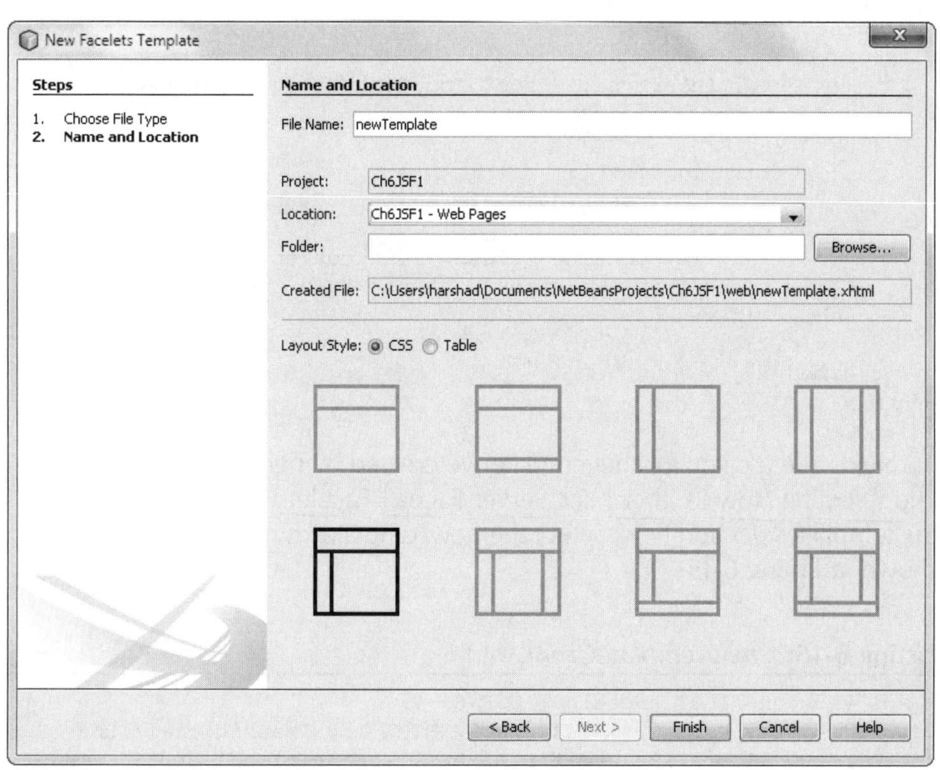

FIGURE 6-10. *Template layout styles*

Listing 6-14: *Template*

```
<?xml version='1.0' encoding='UTF-8' ?>
<!DOCTYPE html PUBLIC "-//W3C//DTD XHTML 1.0 Transitional//EN"
"http://www.w3.org/TR/xhtml1/DTD/xhtml1-transitional.dtd">
<html xmlns="http://www.w3.org/1999/xhtml"
      xmlns:ui="http://java.sun.com/jsf/facelets"
      xmlns:h="http://java.sun.com/jsf/html">
    <h:head>
        <meta http-equiv="Content-Type" content="text/html;
charset=UTF-8" />
        <h:outputStylesheet name="css/default.css"/>
        <h:outputStylesheet name="css/cssLayout.css"/>
        <title>Facelets Template</title>
```

```
    </h:head>
    <h:body>
        <div id="top" class="top">
            <ui:insert name="top">Top Content</ui:insert>
        </div>
        <div>
            <div id="left">
                <ui:insert name="left">Left Content</ui:insert>
            </div>
            <div id="content" class="left_content">
                <ui:insert name="content">Main Content</ui:insert>
            </div>
        </div>
    </h:body>
</html>
```

Next, add a client for the template we created by right-clicking the project and selecting New | Other | JavaServer Faces | Facelets Template Client. In the template selection field, select the newTemplate.xhtml file we created, as shown in Listing 6-15.

Listing 6-15: *newTemplateClient.xhtml*

```
<?xml version='1.0' encoding='UTF-8' ?>
<!DOCTYPE html PUBLIC "-//W3C//DTD XHTML 1.0 Transitional//EN"
"http://www.w3.org/TR/xhtml1/DTD/xhtml1-transitional.dtd">
<html xmlns="http://www.w3.org/1999/xhtml"
      xmlns:ui="http://java.sun.com/jsf/facelets">
    <body>
        <ui:composition template="./newTemplate.xhtml">
            <ui:define name="top">
                top
            </ui:define>
            <ui:define name="left">
                left
            </ui:define>
            <ui:define name="content">
                content
            </ui:define>
        </ui:composition>
    </body>
</html>
```

Run newTemplateClient.xhtml, and you will get the page shown in Figure 6-11. As expected, the page layout and styling are as per the template, whereas the text is from the client.

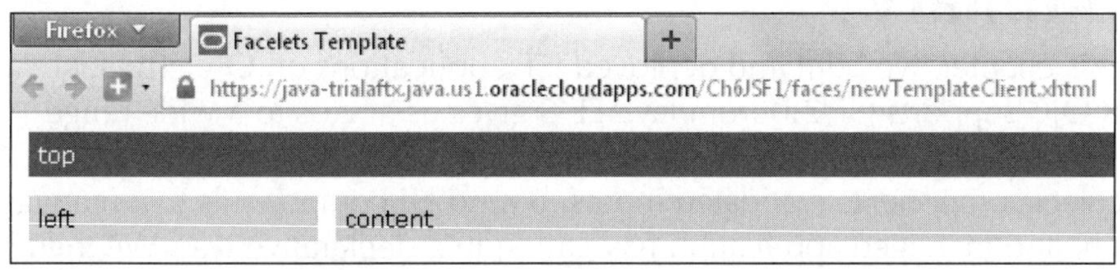

FIGURE 6-11. *Template client page*

You can try creating a consistent, template-based look and feel for all examples in this chapter by converting the earlier JSF pages into template client pages. Although the code for the functionality would remain the same, the layout and the look and feel would be that of the template. Therefore, our Ajax example in Listing 6-12 could be modified as shown in Listing 6-16 by creating a new template client file called ajaxTimeTemplateClient.xhtml.

Listing 6-16: *Ajax Time Using the Facelets Template*

```
<?xml version='1.0' encoding='UTF-8' ?>
<!DOCTYPE html PUBLIC "-//W3C//DTD XHTML 1.0 Transitional//EN"
"http://www.w3.org/TR/xhtml1/DTD/xhtml1-transitional.dtd">
<html xmlns="http://www.w3.org/1999/xhtml"
      xmlns:ui="http://java.sun.com/jsf/facelets"
      xmlns:h="http://java.sun.com/jsf/html"
      xmlns:f="http://java.sun.com/jsf/core">
    <body>
        <ui:composition template="./newTemplate.xhtml">
            <ui:define name="top">
                Ajax With JSF
            </ui:define>
            <ui:define name="left">
                <h:link value="Refresh Time" >
                    <f:ajax render="timetext"/>
                </h:link>
            </ui:define>
            <ui:define name="content">
                Time : <h:outputText value="#{welcome.time}"
id="timetext" />
            </ui:define>
        </ui:composition>
    </body>
</html>
```

Summary

In this chapter, we built and deployed JSF applications on OJC. The fact that OJC supports JSF 2.0 from Java EE 6 gives us access to a wide range of features as well as ease of use using annotations. We used several JSF Facelets components, validated inputs, bound UI components to a managed bean, and managed application navigation in a declarative way. We then used a template to create a consistent look and styling for our application. As you will have noticed, running our JSF application on OJC did not limit the scope or capability of our JSF application in any way. In the next chapter, we will venture into Enterprise JavaBeans (EJBs) and use them with JSF.

CHAPTER 7

Enterprise JavaBeans (Session Beans)

We have looked at using various Java EE technologies to handle the HTTP and the web part of the application. However, arguably, the most critical component of any software is the functioning of the actual business logic. In this chapter, we look at Enterprise JavaBeans, a technology whose primary aim is running business logic code efficiently, accurately, and securely.

Enterprise JavaBeans (EJB) was perhaps the technology that truly marked the arrival of Java EE (or J2EE as it was known as back then) to the software development world. There was tremendous buzz around EJB at the dawn of the twenty-first century. EJB was expected to deliver almost magical results and, as such, was the most prized skill on the job market. Although it did deliver on some of its promise, it was also extremely complex and tedious for developers to work with. Hardly any developer could confidently say they understood EJB inside out. Fortunately, EJB has been greatly simplified over the years.

Containers

EJBs run in a specialized part of the application server known as the EJB container. Whereas all the examples in the previous chapters used the web container part of the application server, in this chapter, we use the EJB container and then the web and EJB containers working together.

Many of the commonly used application servers such as WebLogic, GlassFish, WebSphere, Geronimo, and JBoss include both an EJB container and a web container. There are, however, application servers that do not include an EJB container, so you'll want to be mindful of this when choosing a server.

If an application server is listed in the Java EE Full Platform Compatible section on the Java EE Compatibility page, found at

www.oracle.com/technetwork/java/javaee/overview/compatibility-jsp-136984.html

it will have both an EJB container and a web container. If a server is not listed on the Java EE Compatibility page, refer to the server documentation for EJB support.

EJB in OJC

The Oracle Java Cloud runs WebLogic server, and WebLogic includes an EJB container and a web container. However, before we start building EJBs for OJC, we need to be aware of the exact specifications supported and what you can and cannot do with EJBs in OJC.

OJC supports the EJB 2.1 and EJB 3.0 specifications. The focus of EJB 3.0 was on simplifying EJBs for developers, with the key feature being the introduction of annotations as an option for XML deployment descriptor files. Therefore, EJB 3.0 was a significant improvement over 2.1 and will be the version we use in this chapter.

Until EJB 3.0, persistence using Entity Beans was an integral part of EJBs. However, with EJB 3.0, persistence was moved out to Java Persistence API (JPA). (We will look further at JPA in Chapter 9 on persistence.) Although OJC supports EJB 2.1, do note that EJB 2.1 Entity Beans, which dealt with persistence, are not supported. For persistence on OJC, we use JPA.

OJC only supports local EJB invocations and not remote invocations. As such, you can invoke an EJB only from within the same deployment archive or within a deployment archive that is deployed to the same Java Cloud Service instance. This is an important point to remember while using OJC for EJBs. Therefore, if you find the need at all to call a remote EJB, you would have to look at alternatives such as web services. This could also be a challenge if you are looking to migrate existing EJB-based applications that use remote EJBs.

There are two types of beans—session beans and message-driven beans. OJC does not support any Java Message Service (JMS) services, so to utilize message-driven beans, we need to use the Oracle Messaging Cloud along with OJC. OJC will otherwise mark any application with JMS dependencies as a whitelist violation.

TIP

Appendix C contains a detailed list of all technologies supported and not supported on OJC.

Why EJB?

EJBs in 3.x and later are pretty much Plain Old Java Objects (POJOs) with a few annotations that tell the EJB container to provide EJB-specific services and capabilities. However, one of the first questions to arise is why use EJB at all and not just use simple Java classes?

The reason to use EJB lies entirely in the capabilities of the EJB container. Your code as such is nothing very different, complex, or more capable. It is the container that is supposed to weave in its magic and provide additional capabilities that are of value to an enterprise application. Those additional capabilities are

- **Scalability** EJBs are a good option if you expect an application to have to scale to tens of thousands of users. EJBs include pooling and other features for optimum management of available resources.
- **Distributed environment** EJBs are built to run over a distributed environment. Their transition to the cloud is seamless, and they perform just as well in a distributed environment.
- **State management** Session beans include a stateful option you can utilize to manage state in your application. If you wish to hold data over multiple invocations or share data for a user, this is possible using stateful beans.
- **Transaction management** Transaction management is of great importance in enterprise applications. Instead of coding the transaction management, it is much more efficient to use EJBs' annotation-based transaction management to ensure your transaction works as expected with the least amount of frustration.
- **Reusable services** EJBs containing business logic are great for use across multiple applications and for sharing as web services. Code and functionality reuse is easily possible with EJBs.

Session Beans

Session beans are business logic classes. A real-world application might have tens of session beans, each dealing with a subset of the application's business logic and functionality. EJB 3.0 includes two types of session beans: stateless and stateful.

NOTE

A third type, the singleton session bean, has been introduced in EJB 3.1 (not yet supported on OJC). As the word singleton suggests, this kind of session bean gets instantiated once per application and only that one instance exists throughout the lifecycle of the application.

Stateless

A stateless session bean is one that retains any specific information only for the duration of an invocation. Once the method call is done, none of the client-specific state is retained.

This means you cannot rely on instance variables to store and retrieve information. Even repeated calls to a bean using the same reference might get you a new object each time. This is because stateless session beans rely on object pooling so as to achieve optimum performance, and on each invocation, you could very well get a different object from the pool. How this object pool is managed is up to the EJB container, but most application servers will let you tweak the parameters a bit. However, with OJC being a PaaS environment, you do not get such fine-grained access to pooling configuration for the server.

However, the pooled-stateless approach leads to optimum utilization of memory and significant performance gains. So the rule of thumb is that unless there's a strong case to recall data/state across invocations, you use stateless beans.

Stateful

A stateful session bean will maintain state information for the duration of the client-bean session. Stateful beans are used in cases where maintaining state is required for the bean and client interaction to be executed, or when you wish to hold some client information across multiple method invocations—the classic example is the shopping cart, where a shopper keeps adding and removing objects from the same cart.

Whereas you cannot rely on instance variables in the case of stateless beans, you can use instance variables with stateful beans, because the same instance will be used each time as long as the session is active.

We will look at the stages in the life of a session bean in the section "Lifecycle of a Session Bean."

Interfaces: Local or Remote

Client code can access a session bean using the business interface provided. The business interface for a session bean is like any other Java interface. You only need to add the requisite annotations to mark the interface as a business interface for your session bean.

NOTE

EJB 3.1 introduced a no-interface view option, by which all the public methods of the session bean are exposed to local clients. In the case of no-interface, you need not provide a local interface and state which methods you wish to expose. Although no-interface does simplify things, system architects often prefer having the interfaces in place. The no-interface option is part of EJB 3.1 and therefore is not currently available in OJC.

The reasons for using an interface with session beans are no different from why you would use an interface with any Java classes. A key consideration is that you can change the session bean without affecting the client code. The types of business interfaces are the local interface and the remote interface. A session bean can have both a local and a remote interface.

Remote access is required where you want the bean to be accessed by remote clients that are not running in the same application server. However, remote calls involve significant overhead due to the marshaling and unmarshaling of data over the wire, network latency, and the actual transportation over the network.

Local access is a good choice when you have tightly coupled functionality for which it would make sense to have the beans running on the same application server. Remote access is used when you are looking to build a system that could have bits of functionality divided over multiple servers, machines, or even locations.

For many years, EJB only had a remote access option, so each call to an EJB would have to be a remote call. It now seems rather strange that until EJB 2.0, EJB did not have a local access option. These days, local access seems to be the more prevalent use.

There isn't much difference in the actual code of the local and remote interfaces. Local interfaces are marked with the annotation @Local, whereas remote interfaces are marked by the @Remote annotation.

As mentioned earlier, OJC only supports local EJB invocations, so the client code invoking an EJB application's interface must be either within the same deployment archive as the EJB implementation code itself or within a deployment archive that is deployed to the same Java Cloud Service instance. Let's now create an application with a session bean and delve further into its working.

Developing an Enterprise Application with EJBs

We have been working with web applications that are packaged into WAR files. However, in cases where your application has more than just the web application, you have an EAR file (enterprise archive). This is the file in which you are to package your enterprise applications, which can contain one or more EJB modules and web applications.

The EJB module is packaged into a JAR file (Java archive). The web application is packaged into a WAR file (web archive). The entire enterprise application, including the JAR and WAR files, is packaged into an EAR file (enterprise archive). Note that all three types of files have the same format as a regular JAR file in Java. The compression is the same as a ZIP file, so all the files can be opened and viewed with any common zip/unzip tool.

To create our enterprise application, start NetBeans, select New Project, and then select Java EE | Enterprise Application, as shown in Figure 7-1.

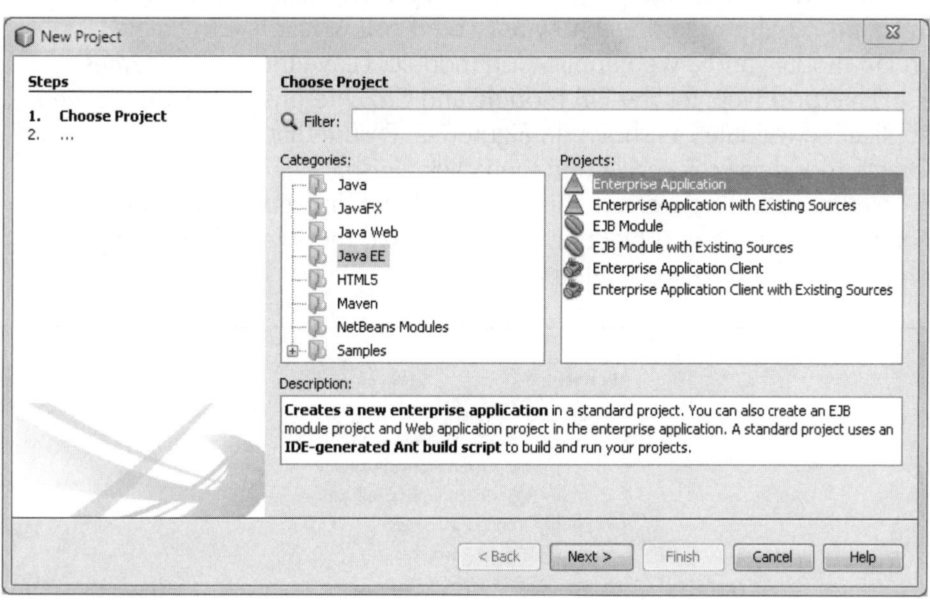

FIGURE 7-1. *A new enterprise application*

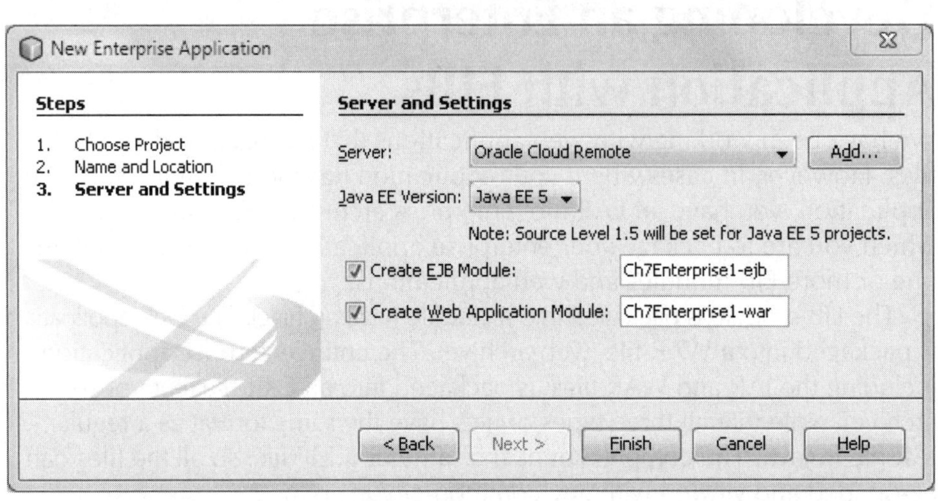

FIGURE 7-2. *Web and EJB modules*

Click Next. Name the project **Ch7Enterprise1**. Click Next. As shown in Figure 7-2, the wizard will now ask you if you would like to create an EJB module and a web application module. Leave the default names (Ch7Enterprise1-ejb for the EJB module and Ch7Enterprise1-war for the web application module), as shown in Figure 7-2. Ensure that you have selected Oracle Cloud as your server and then click Finish.

NetBeans will now create the projects shown in Figure 7-3. There's the enterprise application project, including the two modules, along with the EJB project and the web application project.

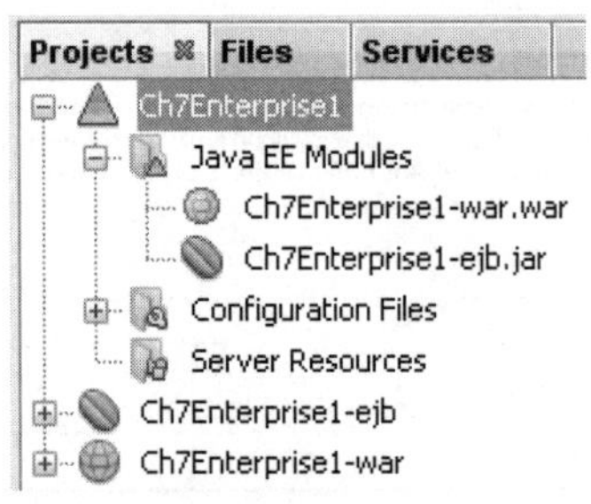

FIGURE 7-3. *Ch7Enterprise1 projects*

Right-click Ch7Enterprise1 and select Clean and Build. The Output log will show that a new Ch7Enterprise1.ear file is created at <YourNetBeansProjectsDirectory>\Ch7Enterprise1\dist\Ch7Enterprise1.ear.

Open the file using any zip/unzip tool, and you will see that the file includes the WAR file for the web application, the JAR file for the EJB application, and a couple of configuration XML files.

Our project is currently empty, so let's add a session bean to our EJB module.

New Session Bean

Right-click Ch7Enterprise1-ejb and select New | Enterprise JavaBeans | Session Bean. Name the bean **AuthenticateSessionBean** and the package **beans**, as shown in Figure 7-4. Under Create Interface, the Local check box will be checked by default so that NetBeans will create the appropriate

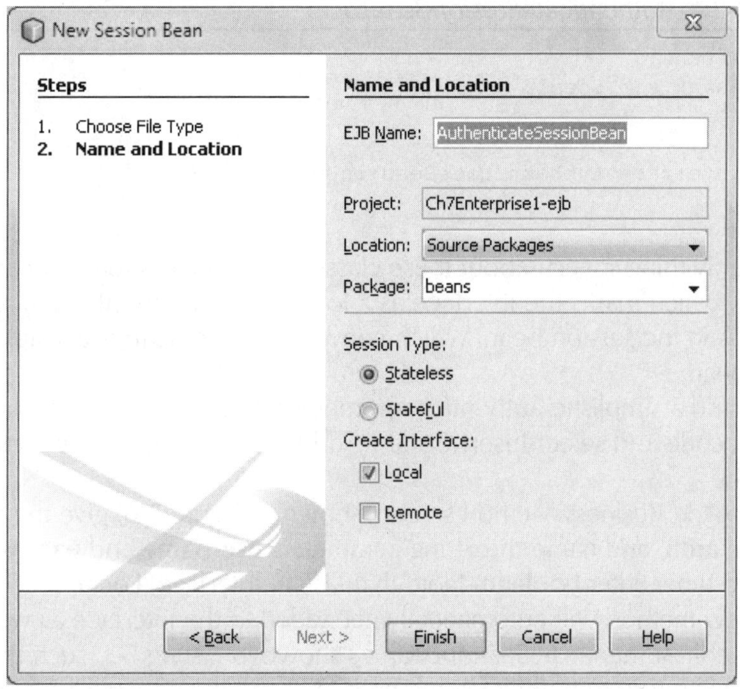

FIGURE 7-4. *The new session bean AuthenticateSessionBean*

interface along with the bean class. As mentioned earlier, only local access is permitted in OJC, so creating the remote interface would not serve much purpose. Note that the Stateless session type is selected by default, which we will use for this example.

NetBeans will now generate the AuthenticateSessionBean class, shown in Listing 7-1, which implements the local interface AuthenticateSessionBeanLocal, shown in Listing 7-2.

Listing 7-1: *AuthenticateSessionBean*

```
package beans;
import javax.ejb.Stateless;
@Stateless
public class AuthenticateSessionBean
 implements AuthenticateSessionBeanLocal {
}
```

Listing 7-2: *AuthenticateSessionBeanLocal*

```
package beans;
import javax.ejb.Local;

@Local
public interface AuthenticateSessionBeanLocal {
}
```

The only thing special about these classes is the annotation @Local in the interface, which marks the interface as a local interface, and the annotation @Stateless in the session bean, which conveys that the bean is a stateless session bean.

Let's add a simplistic authentication method to our bean. Right-click in the bean code and select Insert Code | Add Business Method, as shown in Figure 7-5.

In the Add Business Method screen, shown in Figure 7-6, give the method the name **auth**, and name the String parameters **username** and **password**. For the return type, enter **boolean**. Note that Use in Interface (Local) is selected, so this new method will automatically get added to the interface as well.

Now edit AuthenticateSessionBean as shown in Listing 7-3, such that the method will return true if the username is java and the password is cloud. (Hardcoded, programmatic authentication is not ideal and is only used as a simple demonstration of business logic in a session bean.)

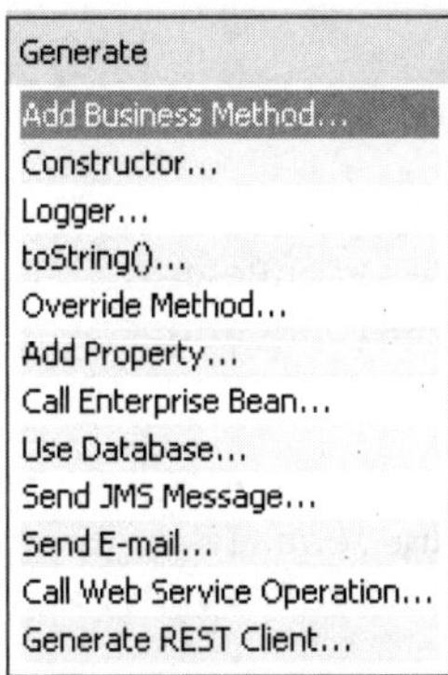

FIGURE 7-5. *Insert Code | Add Business Method*

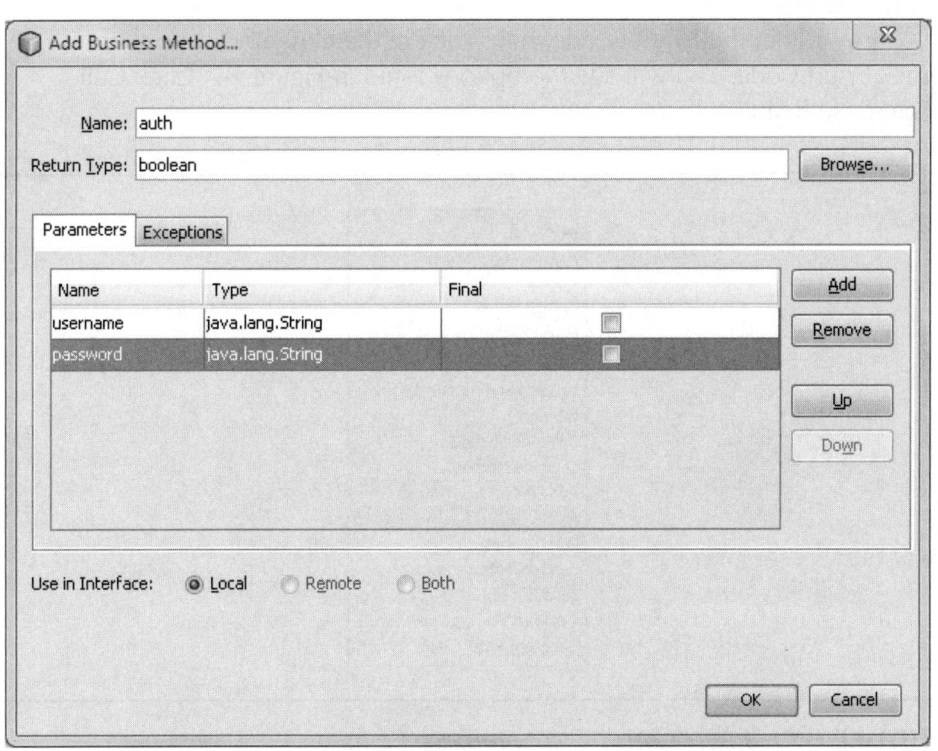

FIGURE 7-6. *The Add Business Method screen*

Listing 7-3: *AuthenticateSessionBean*

```
package beans;
import javax.ejb.Stateless;

@Stateless
public class AuthenticateSessionBean
 implements AuthenticateSessionBeanLocal {

    @Override
    public boolean auth(String username, String password) {
            return (username.equals("java")
            && password.equals("cloud"));
    }
}
```

Now let's create a new Servlet and then access and use this session bean from the Servlet. Right-click Ch7Enterprise1-war and select New | Servlet. Name the Servlet **LoginServlet** and the package **servlets** with the URL pattern **/LoginServlet**.

Now within the Servlet code, right-click in the class body and then click Insert Code. You will see the options listed in Figure 7-7. Click Call Enterprise Bean.

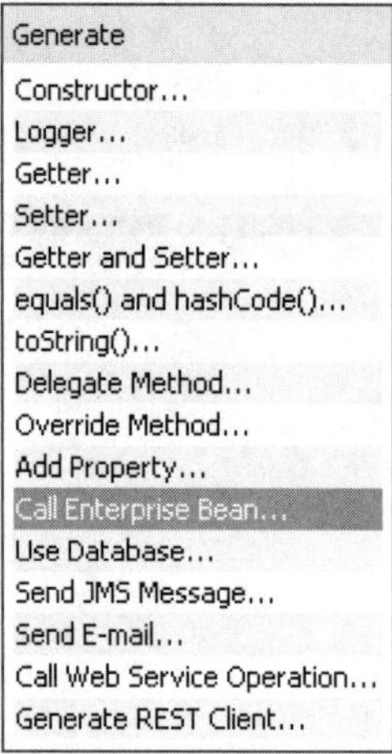

FIGURE 7-7. *Insert Code | Call Enterprise Bean*

In the screen displayed, select the session bean we have created in this chapter. You will find that the lines shown in Listing 7-4 are added to the Servlet.

Listing 7-4: *Dependency Injection of a Session Bean Instance*

```
@EJB
private AuthenticateSessionBeanLocal authenticateSessionBean;
```

The @EJB annotation here is a manifestation of dependency injection, a concept that has rapidly grown in popularity and adoption in a fairly short period of time.

Inject the Session Bean into the Servlet

Dependency injection in the context of Java EE is when a component is provided its dependencies by the container. Therefore, the annotation tells the container what kind of object to inject, and the container does all the hard work to create the instance and inject it into the component.

Those new to dependency injection are usually flummoxed when they see methods being called on an object without there being any object initialization code in place. The reason why this works and does not throw a NullPointerException, like many would expect, is that the relevant object has been injected by the container and therefore isn't null.

The advent of dependency injection was wonderful news for Java EE because it led to smarter application servers that no longer had to be told obvious information, but could figure out and get mundane tasks done based on simple annotations in the code.

In our Servlet example, the @EJB annotation is a request for an injection of the EJB instance into the Servlet. There's no code in the Servlet to look up or actually instantiate the EJB; the annotation is merely a request to the container to do the required task. The @EJB annotation can be provided additional information via parameters such as beanInterface, beanName, description, mappedName, and name.

Once the EJB is injected into the Servlet, we can use it in the processRequest method, as shown in Listing 7-5.

Listing 7-5: *Access Injected Session Bean in the Servlet*

```
@EJB
private AuthenticateSessionBeanLocal authenticateSessionBean;

protected void processRequest(HttpServletRequest request
                , HttpServletResponse response)
                throws ServletException, IOException {
```

```
    response.setContentType("text/html;charset=UTF-8");
    PrintWriter out = response.getWriter();
    try {
            out.println("<h1>Auth -> "
                             + authenticateSessionBean.auth("java", "cloud")
                             + "</h1>");
    } finally {
              out.close();
    }
}
```

Here, we call the auth method in the injected bean instance and print the output received. Note that we can even inject an EJB into another local EJB using the same dependency injection technique we used for the Servlet.

Package and Run from NetBeans

Considering that we are now working with an enterprise application that includes a web application module and an EJB module, directly running the Servlet from the web application will not work. We need to deploy the enterprise application. We can do that by right-clicking the enterprise application and selecting Deploy. Because NetBeans is aware of the Java EE modules in the enterprise application, NetBeans will build the web and the EJB module projects, followed by packing them up together in an EAR file.

Deploy Using the Java Cloud Services Control

To deploy using the Java Cloud Services Control, log in using your credentials at http://cloud.oracle.com. In the Applications widget, which is located at the top right of the page by default, you will find the Deploy New button, as shown in Figure 7-8. The other buttons are grayed out if no application is listed or if none of the listed applications is selected.

FIGURE 7-8. *The Deploy New button*

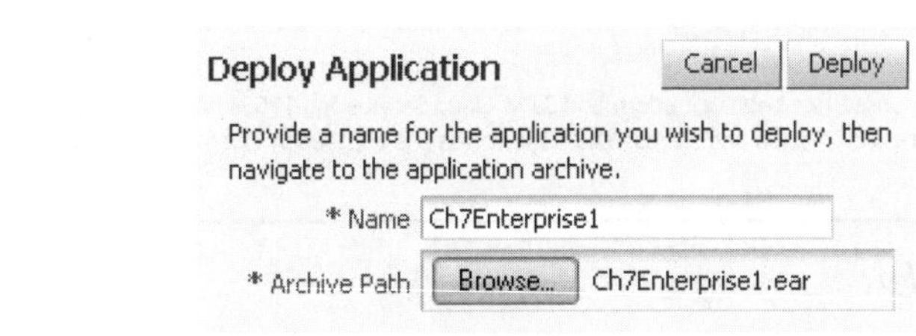

FIGURE 7-9. *The Deploy Application screen for uploading the archive*

You will now get the screen shown in Figure 7-9. Here, you can name the application and provide the relevant application archive (that is, the JAR, WAR, or EAR file for the application).

To get the EAR for our enterprise application, right-click the Ch7Enterprise1 project in NetBeans and select the Clean and Build option, which will delete any previously compiled files and other build outputs. It will then recompile the application—in this case, both the web application module and the EJB module that are part of our enterprise application. The entire application is then packed into an EAR file.

While we're on the topic of building an application, note that upon right-clicking the project, you get three build options: Build, Clean and Build, and Clean. Running Clean and Build is a good safeguard against outdated compiled files. However, for large projects, Clean and Build can take much longer than Build.

Before you deploy using the Java Cloud Services Control website, it's a good idea to first run the Verify tool to check for any whitelist violations. It's much easier to catch and deal with whitelist violations using the Verify tool than having a failed deployment on the cloud, going through the log, and discovering the whitelist violation. To verify, right-click the project and click Verify. A new White List Tool log window will open up and list any warnings and errors in the application. Warnings are not show-stoppers; however, if you get an error, your application will not get deployed.

Coming back to the Ch7Enterprise1 application, select the EAR file and click the Deploy button shown in Figure 7-9. You will get an Uploading Archive prompt and then be redirected to the main screen for the Java Cloud Services Control, where you will get an alert like the one shown in Figure 7-10.

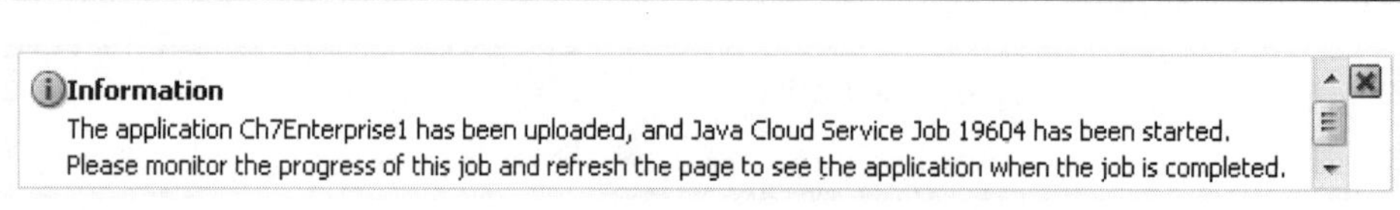

FIGURE 7-10. *Alert*

For more information about the deployment process, you need to head over to the Java Cloud Service Jobs widget, which is, by default, at the bottom of the page. As shown in Figure 7-11, select the last job ID, which is our deployment job. Depending on the size of your application, it might take a while for the deployment to complete and the logs to be available.

Figuring out how to view the log is somewhat unintuitive. Click View Java Cloud Service Job Logs. In the drop-down that appears, as shown in Figure 7-12, you can choose to view the log for the Virus Scan, Application Whitelist Validation, WLS Compile, Cloud Compile, or Deploy Application. Click any one of these options, and your browser will pop up a window to view/save the log file.

If you select the Deploy Application log and the application deployment has succeeded, you will get a log like the one in Listing 7-6. The WLS Compile option will get you the WebLogic Application Compilation logs that will list the WebLogic libraries being referred to and their versions, along with some WebLogic-specific compilation information. The Cloud Compile option will get you the Cloud Application Compilation logs, which will list how OJC is detecting, injecting, and assembling your application for deployment. If all has gone well, both these logs should end with the status SUCCESS.

Java Cloud Service Jobs

View Java Cloud Service Job Logs ▾ Refresh Manual

Java Cloud Service Job ID	Java Cloud Service Job Type	Name	Submitted Time	End Time	Status
19604	Deploy Application	Ch7Enterprise1	Jul 4, 2014 10:30:56 PM		Running

FIGURE 7-11. *View the job log*

FIGURE 7-12. *View/save the log file*

Listing 7-6: *Deploy Application Log*

```
2014-07-05 00:31:27 CDT: Starting action "Deploy Application"
2014-07-05 00:31:27 CDT: Deploy Application started
2014-07-05 00:31:28 CDT: [Deployer:149034]An exception occurred for
task [Deployer:149026]deploy application Ch7Enterprise1 on c1.: .
2014-07-05 00:31:28 CDT: WL action state: completed
2014-07-05 00:31:28 CDT: Application deployment succeeded.
2014-07-05 00:31:28 CDT: "Deploy Application" complete: status SUCCESS
```

Once the application is deployed (which can take a few minutes), click the link in the Applications widget on the Java Cloud Services Control, and you will get the page shown in Figure 7-13.

As you can see, apart from some information about the application, you can also delete, redeploy, start, and stop the application. Click the application name and you will get a screen like the one shown in Figure 7-14, which provides further information about the application.

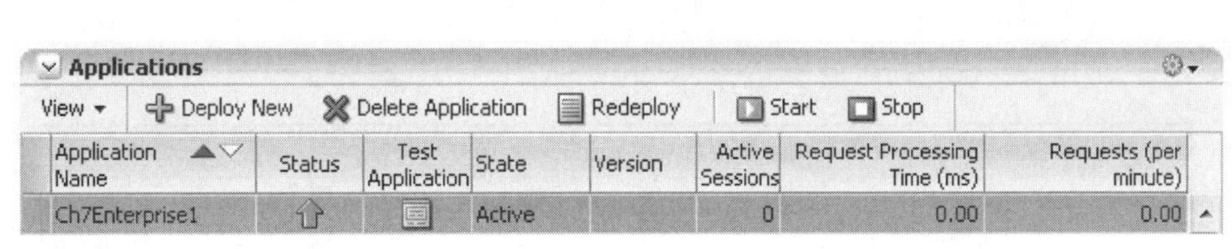

FIGURE 7-13. *Ch7Enterprise1 application listing*

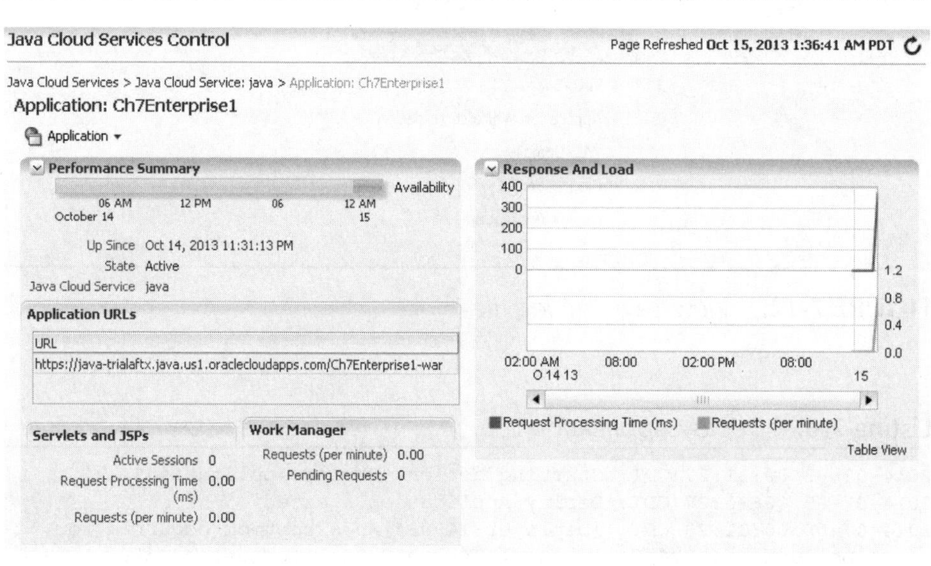

FIGURE 7-14. *Application summary*

Click the URL listed in the Application URLs widget (it's https://java-trialaftx.java.us1.oraclecloudapps.com/Ch7Enterprise1-war for my trial). This will display the index.jsp page with "Hello World." To access the Servlet, change the URL to the URL pattern for the Servlet https://java-trialaftx.java.us1.oraclecloudapps.com/Ch7Enterprise1-war/LoginServlet. You will get the output shown in Figure 7-15.

This shows that the session bean was injected and accessed by the Servlet and we got the desired output.

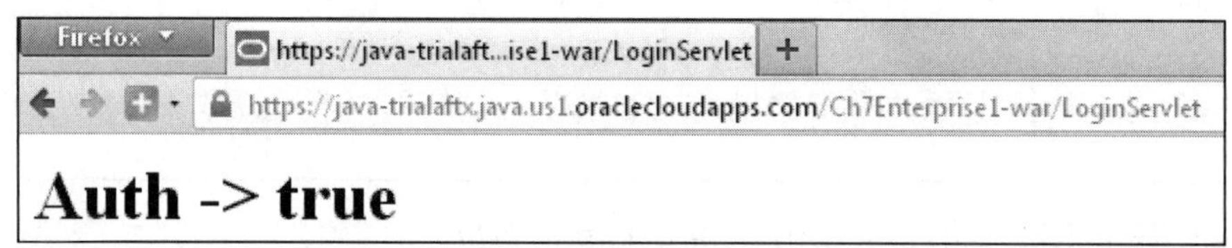

FIGURE 7-15. *Run the Servlet*

The code to create and use a stateful session bean is the same as that for a stateless bean, except for the @Stateful annotation. However, the difference is in the working of the bean. For example, if you were to use a stateful bean for a shopping cart, you could have the bean injected into a Servlet, as shown in Listing 7-7, and if you keep adding items to a collection instance variable, the state will be maintained and you will keep getting the same object back each time. If you were to use a stateless bean, you could very well get a different instance of the bean for all three method calls. To continue using our shopping cart analogy, it would be as though each time you wanted to add something to your cart, you found that the earlier contents of your cart had been lost or you found unexpected items in your cart that you never added.

Listing 7-7: *Stateful Session Bean*

```
shopBean.add("phone");
shopBean.add("laptop");
shopBean.add("tv");
```

In our example, we used a web application and a single EJB, but in most real-world applications using EJB, you would have many EJB modules in the enterprise application, with the EJBs generally being used from various segments of the web application.

Lifecycle of a Session Bean

All EJBs are managed by the EJB container; however, it is important to know the lifecycle of any EJB, the stages it goes through, and the things you can and cannot do at each stage.

The lifecycle of a stateless session bean is fairly simple:

1. The bean is created by the container. Any dependencies are injected by the container. Any PostConstruct callbacks are made. The bean is now ready.

2. Before the bean instance is destroyed, the container makes any PreDestroy callbacks. The bean instance is removed and is later garbage-collected.

The PostConstruct callback is useful if you wish to perform any actions before the bean starts responding to client requests. The PreDestroy callback is useful if you wish to perform any cleanup actions before the bean is destroyed.

All you need to use a callback is to mark a method with the annotation @PostConstruct or @PreDestroy. As shown in Listing 7-8, you can choose any method name, but the method signature must return a void and take no arguments. The reason for this is that the method is being called by the EJBContainer on the occurrence of a lifecycle event, so there isn't a possibility of the user passing a parameter or getting a return value.

Listing 7-8: *Callback Methods*

```
@PostConstruct
public void initialize() {
      // Code to initialize resources
}

@PreDestroy
public void release() {
      //Code to release resources
}
```

Stateless session beans also utilize a pooling capability, where all instances of the stateless session beans are equivalent and the container can pick objects from the pool and return them back to the pool as required.

The lifecycle of a stateful session bean involves a couple more steps:

1. The bean is created by the container. Any dependencies are injected by the container. Any PostConstruct callbacks are made. The bean is now ready.
2. Based on the usage of a bean and the available resources, the EJB container may at times decide to passivate a bean by moving it from memory to secondary storage. Before passivating, the EJB container will make any PrePassivate callbacks.
3. If a client calls a method on a passivated bean, the EJB container will activate the bean. On activation, the container will make any @PostActivate callbacks. The bean is now ready.
4. Before the bean instance is destroyed, the container makes any PreDestroy callbacks. The bean instance is removed and is later garbage-collected.

Transaction Management

Transaction management is the assurance that either the entire transaction with all the intermediate steps will execute or nothing will get executed. Imagine that you are transferring money from one bank account to another account. This involves two steps:

1. Withdraw money from one account.
2. Deposit money to another account.

You want either the entire transaction to get executed or nothing at all. In other words, you never want a scenario where money is withdrawn from one account, but it never gets deposited into the other account.

Although you can manually write the code for transaction management, container-managed transactions using annotations are just so much easier and cleaner to write and maintain. You annotate methods that are party to a transaction, and the EJB container will do the rest.

Let's add a stateless session bean to our enterprise application. This bean will transfer money in a transaction-safe manner. We could add this bean to the existing EJB module, but let's instead create a new EJB Module project so as to highlight how an enterprise application can have multiple EJB modules working together.

Select New Project | Java EE | EJB Module. Name the project **Ch7EJBMoneyTransfer** and click Next. In the next screen, shown in Figure 7-16, add the project to the enterprise application Ch7Enterprise1

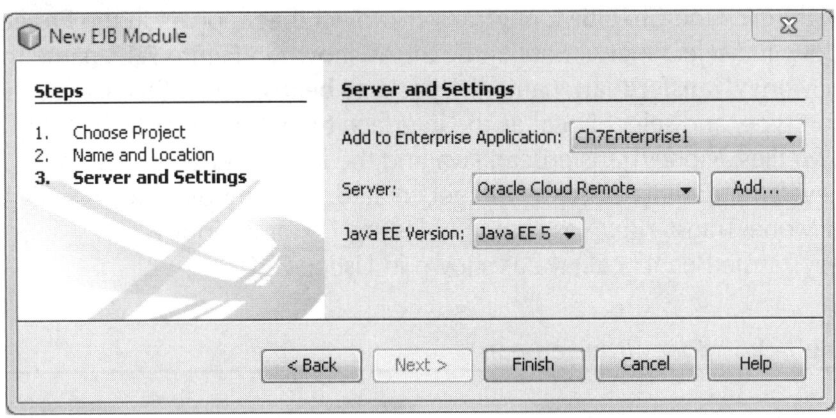

FIGURE 7-16. *The new EJB module*

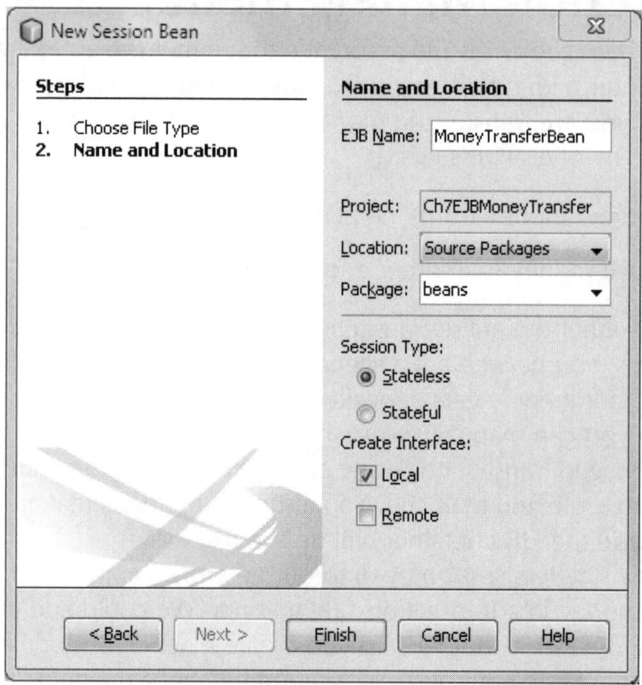

FIGURE 7-17. *The new MoneyTransferBean session bean*

and select the Oracle Cloud Remote Server. Click Finish. Our enterprise application now has two EJB modules and one web application module.

Right-click the Ch7EJBMoneyTransfer project that appears in the Projects window and select New | Session Bean. As shown in Figure 7-17, name the bean **MoneyTransferBean**, name the package **beans**, select Stateless as the session type, and select Local as the interface type. Click Finish.

Two files, MoneyTransferBean.java and the local interface MoneyTransferBeanLocal.java, will get created. Now modify the bean MoneyTransferBean as shown in Listing 7-9, and modify MoneyTransferBeanLocal.java as shown in Listing 7-10.

Listing 7-9: *MoneyTransferBean*

```
package beans;
import javax.ejb.Stateless;
import javax.ejb.TransactionAttribute;
```

```
import javax.ejb.TransactionAttributeType;

@Stateless
public class MoneyTransferBean implements MoneyTransferBeanLocal {

    @TransactionAttribute(TransactionAttributeType.REQUIRES_NEW)
    public void moveMoney() {
        //Amount withdrawn from A
        pullMoneyFromA();

        //If something fails here, the transaction is rolled back
        //and A's amount will be restored.
        depositInB();
    }

    @TransactionAttribute(TransactionAttributeType.MANDATORY)
    public void pullMoneyFromA() {
        //Perform actions to pull  money from A
        //Update database record for A - Reduce account balance
    }

    @TransactionAttribute(TransactionAttributeType.MANDATORY)
    public void depositInB() {
        //Perform actions to deposit money into B
        //Update database record for B - Increase account balance
    }
}
```

Listing 7-10: *MoneyTransferBeanLocal*

```
package beans;
import javax.ejb.Local;

@Local
public interface MoneyTransferBeanLocal {
    void moveMoney();
}
```

Here, we have introduced a public method, moveMoney, to the bean and declared it in the local interface. This method uses two other methods, pullMoneyFromA and depositInB, to transfer money from A to B. The annotations are the key to this transaction. Note the use of the REQUIRES_NEW and MANDATORY attributes. REQUIRES_NEW tells the container that it needs to create a new transaction, and MANDATORY tells the container that the method will throw an exception if it is not part of a transaction. Therefore, in this case, moveMoney will create a new transaction that pullMoneyFromA and depositInB will join in. The whole thing will get executed as one single transaction. Therefore, if pullMoneyFromA succeeds but depositInB fails, even pullMoneyFromA will be rolled back.

The other transaction attributes and their behaviors are detailed in the following table, which explains how a method with the stated attribute will work if it is called by a method with a transaction (second column) or called by a method without a transaction (third column).

Attribute	Transaction Exists	Transaction Does Not Exist
NOT_SUPPORTED	Suspends transaction	No transaction
SUPPORTS	Uses transaction	No transaction
REQUIRED	Uses transaction	Starts new transaction
REQUIRES_NEW	Suspends transaction and starts new transaction	Starts new transaction
MANDATORY	Uses transaction	Exception
NEVER	Exception	No transaction

Now let's create a new Servlet from which we will call the moveMoney method in the bean. Right-click the Ch7Enterprise1-war project and select New | Servlet. Name the Servlet **MoneyTransferServlet**, the package **servlets**, and the URL pattern **/MoneyTransferServlet**. Now modify MoneyTransferServlet as shown in Listing 7-11. In this code, we inject an instance of the MoneyTransferBean into the Servlet and then add a call to the moveMoney method in the processRequest method.

Listing 7-11: *MoneyTransferServlet*

```
@EJB
private MoneyTransferBeanLocal moneyTransferBean;

protected void processRequest(HttpServletRequest request
                 , HttpServletResponse response)
                 throws ServletException, IOException {
        response.setContentType("text/html;charset=UTF-8");
        PrintWriter out = response.getWriter();
        try {
```

```
                moneyTransferBean.moveMoney();
                out.println("<h1>Money Transferred From A to B</h1>");
        } finally {
                out.close();
        }
}
```

NetBeans will auto-add the dependency on the Ch7EJBMoneyTransfer to the project properties if you use the Call Enterprise Bean wizard to inject the EJB. However, if you directly add the code to the Servlet, you will have to add Ch7EJBMoneyTransfer to project libraries. You can get to the project properties either by right-clicking the project name in the Project window and selecting Properties, or from the File | Project Properties menu. If you do not see the library listed, add it as shown in Figure 7-18.

Clean and build the Ch7Enterprise1 project and redeploy the application using the Java Cloud Service Control. The Redeploy button is shown in Figure 7-13 and can also be found in the drop-down on the Application

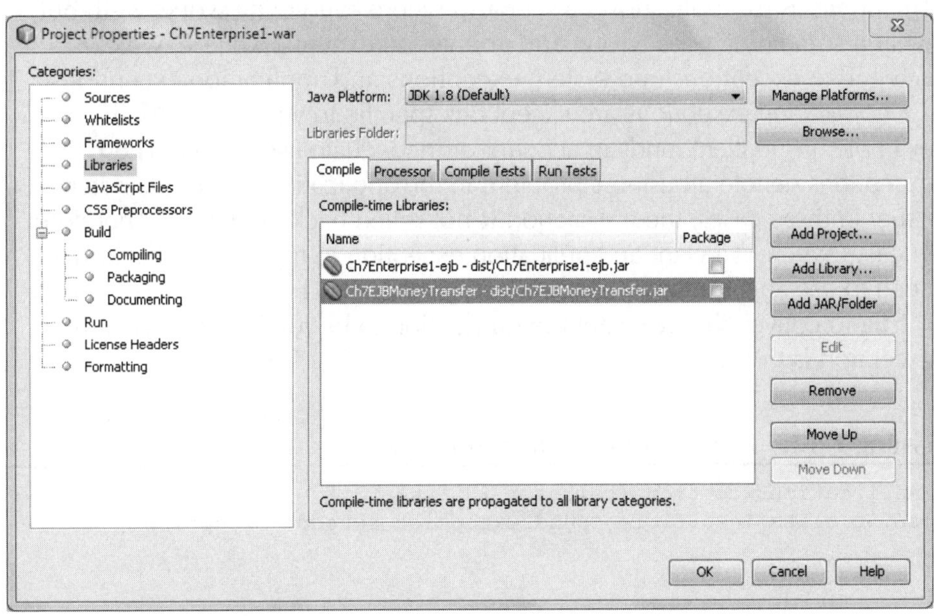

FIGURE 7-18. *Project libraries*

FIGURE 7-19. *MoneyTransferServlet output*

Summary page in Figure 7-14. Upon redeploying the EAR file, we can access the Servlet at https://java-trialaftx.java.us1.oraclecloudapps.com/Ch7Enterprise1-war/MoneyTransferServlet and will get the output shown in Figure 7-19. This example shows the ease of container-managed transactions and the significant value added to any EJB-based application.

Rollback and Exception Handling

The previous example shows a scenario where everything works well, but what if something goes wrong and you get an exception. Here, we can categorize exceptions into system exceptions and application exceptions.

Application exceptions are exceptions specific to your application (for example, insufficient funds in account or inadequate user rights). These exceptions denote a business problem in the application and not a system issue. In these cases, the transaction is not rolled back by default. Therefore, in cases where we want an application exception to trigger a rollback, we need to use an annotation, as shown in Listing 7-12. Here, we state **rollback = true** to convey that we want the transaction to be rolled back when the exception is thrown.

Listing 7-12: *ApplicationException Rollback*

```
@ApplicationException (rollback = true)
public class InsufficientFundsException extends Exception {
...
}
```

System exceptions include java.lang.RuntimeException, java.rmi.RemoteException, and their subclasses. The transaction will get rolled back in the case of any system exception. For example, NullPointerException is one of the most common exceptions encountered. Because NullPointerException is a RuntimeException, the transaction will get rolled back. You can tell the container to not roll back the transaction, even in the case of a run-time exception, by using the ApplicationException annotation and setting the **rollback** element value to **false**, as shown in Listing 7-13.

Listing 7-13: *Do Not Roll Back RuntimeException*

```
@ApplicationException(rollback = false)
public class CreateException extends RuntimeException {
    //...
}
```

Summary

In this chapter, we looked at building enterprise applications that include multiple EJBs and web applications, all packed together into one application. We saw the rich functionality offered by stateless and stateful session beans and also how container-managed transactions are a great asset to have while building any application that relies on transactions. EJBs are critical for enterprise application development, and with the greatly simplified EJB development over the past few years, EJBs are certainly something to look at while building your enterprise applications for the cloud. The rich EJB support is also a major plus for OJC because not all cloud vendors offer the same level of support for EJB.

Summary

CHAPTER 8

Web Services

Web services are the chosen mode for communication over disparate technologies. The W3C group on Web Services Architecture defines a *web service* as a software system designed to support interoperable machine-to-machine interaction over a network. Because a web service is software that is meant to have all-encompassing reach, it relies on the HTTP protocol, a standard supported across technologies and locations. Web services also rely on XML, which again is a technology that is supported across technologies. Although the underlying idea of communication across platforms is the same, two types of web services are in use:

- Web services that rely on XML messages as per the Simple Object Access Protocol (SOAP) standard
- Web services that use Representational State Transfer (RESTful) and leverage the HTTP methods GET, POST, PUT, and others for communication

We will look at developing and deploying both types of web services on OJC.

NOTE
OJC supports a mix of Java EE 5 and Java EE 6 technologies. Even with web services, OJC supports Java API for XML-based Web Services (JAX-WS)–based SOAP-XML web services from Java EE 5, as well as Java API for RESTful Web Services (JAX-RS) from Java EE 6. OJC supports JAX-WS version 2.1 and JAX-RS version 1.1. OJC does not support Java API for XML-based RPC (JAX-RPC)–based web services. JAX-WS was the successor to JAX-RPC, so OJC recommends converting any JAX-RPC web services to JAX-WS. OJC supports JAX-WS and JAX-RS annotations as well as Jersey 1.9 annotations, Jersey being the reference implementation of JAX-RS. Let's begin by building web services examples with SOAP and JAX-WS.

In Chapter 7, we discussed that because OJC restricts remote access to your bean, you can use web services as an alternative. Because web services rely on basic HTTP, you can expose functionality in your EJB beyond the boundaries of OJC. You could have remote clients calling your bean with SOAP-based or RESTful web services.

Developing a SOAP Web Service

The first wave of web services was built around the SOAP standard, which uses XML extensively for defining the web service as well as for the actual communication. Except for the actual business logic code, which we will write in Java, the rest of the web service is XML. Therefore, the web service operations are defined in an XML-based Web Services Definition Language (WSDL) file. The communication between the web service and the web service client will be in XML, as per the SOAP standard.

Let's build two web applications—one SOAP web service application and one web service client application—and then analyze the code to better understand how they work. We begin by creating a new web application by selecting File | New Project | Java Web | Web Application. Name the application **Ch8SoapWebService**, and ensure that the server selected is Oracle Cloud Remote. Now, right-click the project and select New, or select File | New File, and then select Web Services | Web Service. Click Next. You should now get a screen like the one shown in Figure 8-1. Name the web service **DateTimeService** and the package **ws**. Click Finish.

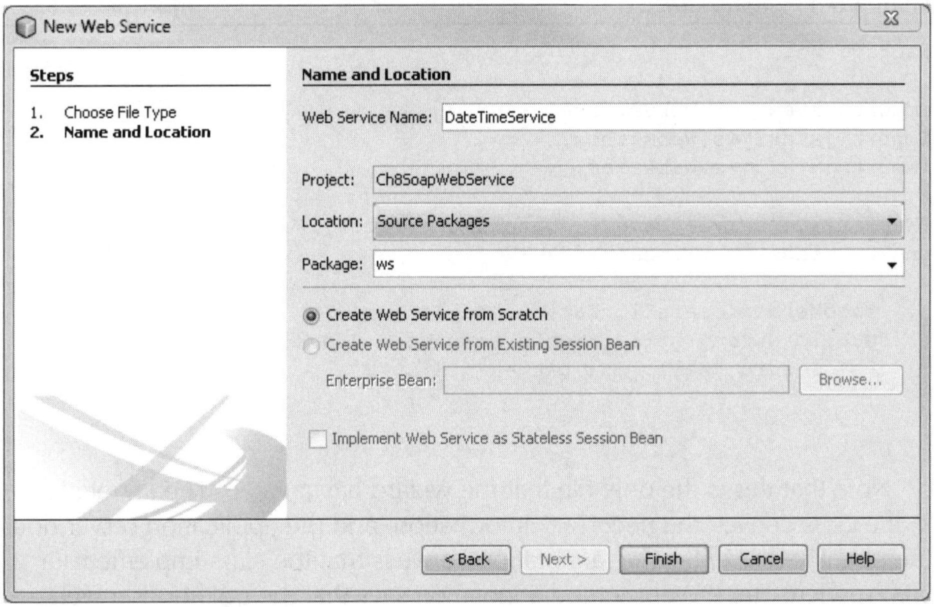

FIGURE 8-1. *Creating a new web service*

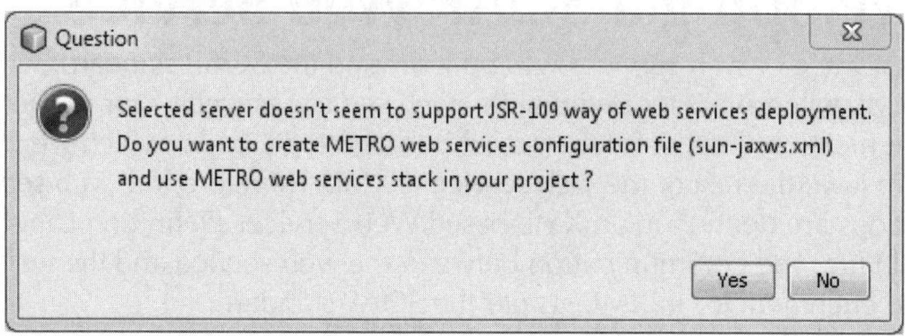

FIGURE 8-2. *An alert about creating sun-jaxws.xml*

NetBeans may now pop up an alert, as shown in Figure 8-2. As mentioned earlier, OJC supports standard web services deployment with JAX-WS, so we do not need the sun-jaxws.xml file. Click No.

The DateTimeService.java file should have now been created, as shown in Listing 8-1.

Listing 8-1: *DateTimeService*

```
package ws;

import javax.jws.WebService;
import javax.jws.WebMethod;
import javax.jws.WebParam;

@WebService(serviceName = "DateTimeService")
public class DateTimeService {

    @WebMethod(operationName = "hello")
    public String hello(@WebParam(name = "name") String txt) {
        return "Hello " + txt + " !";
    }
}
```

Note that this is the only file that the wizard has created. The annotations in the class convey the necessary information, and the application server does the rest. The @WebService annotation conveys that the class implements a web service. The @WebMethod annotation says that the method is a web service method that is to be exposed to web service clients.

NetBeans, by default, creates a hello method. We now want to add another method that will return the date and time, the functionality that our web service is meant to provide. You could write the code directly with the necessary annotation, along the same lines as the hello method. However, NetBeans offers a simpler way. Click the Design tab and you will get the screen shown in Figure 8-3.

Now click the Add Operation button to get the screen shown in Figure 8-4. Name the method **fetchDateTime** and then click OK.

Switch back to Source view and you will find that a new method, fetchDateTime, has been added to the class DateTimeService. Modify the method as shown in Listing 8-2, and you now have the web service, ready for use.

FIGURE 8-3. *Web service design view*

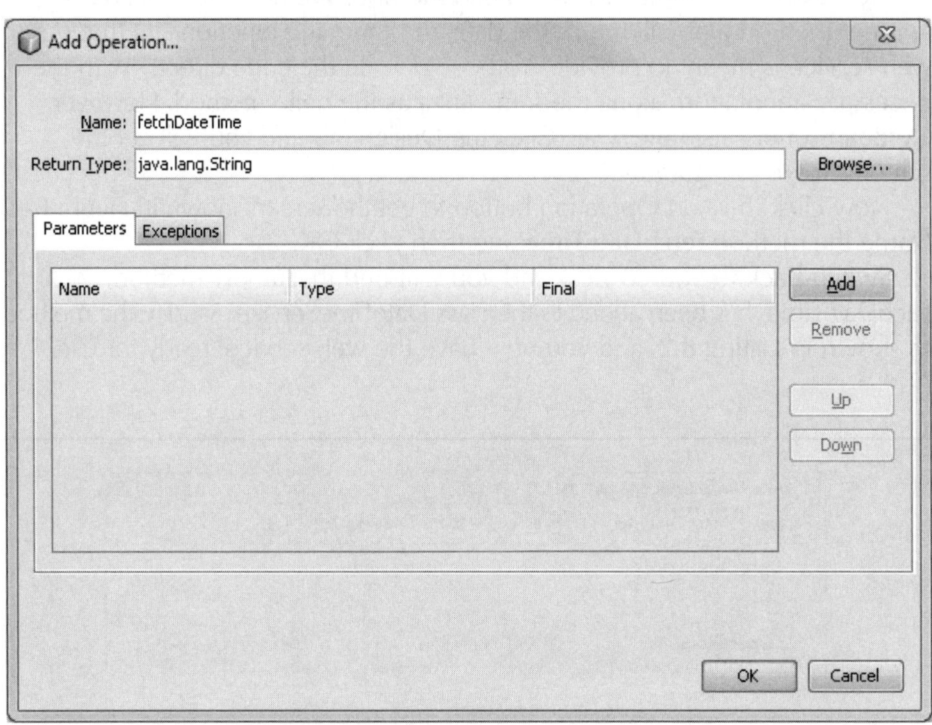

FIGURE 8-4. *The Add Operation screen*

Listing 8-2: *The fetchDateTime Method*

```
@WebMethod(operationName = "fetchDateTime")
public String fetchDateTime() {
    return new java.util.Date().toString();
}
```

In this method, we instantiate a new object of java.util.Date and then return a String representation of the object. Our web service is now ready to start serving web service clients. However, before we begin building the client, we can choose to run the web service, not just as a Java class, but even as an EJB, as discussed in the previous chapter.

You can convert your Java class web service into an EJB web service by simply adding the @Stateless annotation to the code. Your code is shown in Listing 8-3. To highlight the usage of the annotation parameters and how they are distinct from the class name or method name, tweak the parameter values as shown in Listing 8-3, changing the serviceName parameter to DateTimeServiceWS and the operationName parameters to helloOp and fetchDateTimeOp.

Listing 8-3: *DateTimeService*

```
package ws;

import javax.ejb.Stateless;
import javax.jws.WebService;
import javax.jws.WebMethod;
import javax.jws.WebParam;

@Stateless
@WebService(serviceName = "DateTimeServiceWS")
public class DateTimeService {

    @WebMethod(operationName = "helloOp")
    public String hello(@WebParam(name = "name") String txt) {
        return "Hello " + txt + " !";
    }

    @WebMethod(operationName = "fetchDateTimeOp")
    public String fetchDateTime() {
        return new java.util.Date().toString();
    }
}
```

We need to remove the login requirement in this case. Unlike the examples in previous chapters, the web services will usually not be used (consumed) via a browser, but rather by another piece of code. So as to keep our web service public and accessible, and to avoid adding any login functionality to the web service client code, we will edit the web.xml file to add an empty login-config tag, as shown in Listing 8-4.

Listing 8-4: *web.xml*

```
<?xml version="1.0" encoding="UTF-8"?>
<web-app version="2.5" xmlns="http://java.sun.com/xml/ns/javaee"
xmlns:xsi="http://www.w3.org/2001/XMLSchema-instance"
xsi:schemaLocation="http://java.sun.com/xml/ns/javaee
```

```
http://java.sun.com/xml/ns/javaee/web-app_2_5.xsd">
    <login-config></login-config>
    <session-config>
        <session-timeout>
            30
        </session-timeout>
    </session-config>
    <welcome-file-list>
        <welcome-file>index.jsp</welcome-file>
    </welcome-file-list>
</web-app>
```

Now that our web service is in place, let's deploy it to OJC. Right-click the project and select Deploy. As with previous applications in this book, NetBeans will build and deploy the application to OJC.

Once the application is deployed, you can access the web service page at https://<CloudServiceName>-<IdentityDomain>.java.<DataCenter>.oraclecloudapps.com/Ch8SoapWebService/DateTimeServiceWS. You will see a screen like the one shown in Figure 8-5. Note that the URL as well as the service name is DateTimeServiceWS, as stated in the annotation, and not DateTimeService, which is the Java class name.

WSDL

In Figure 8-5, https://java-trialaftx.java.us1.oraclecloudapps.com/Ch8SoapWebService/DateTimeServiceWS?wsdl is a link to a dynamically generated WSDL file. WSDL stands for Web Services Description Language

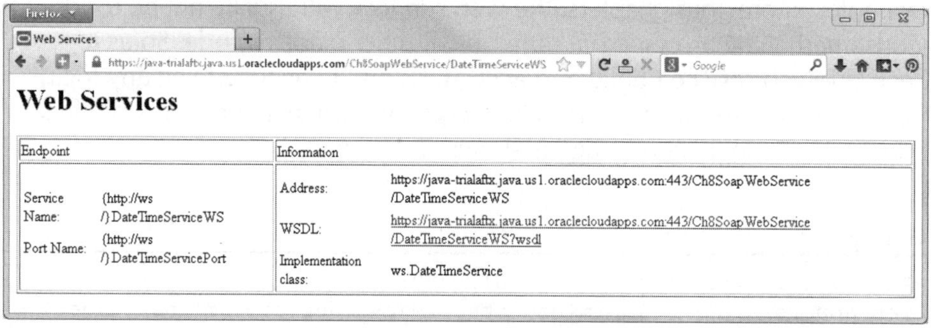

FIGURE 8-5. *The web service information page*

and is a standard format used to describe a web service. It states the name of the service, the operation, parameters, the data structures, and the output. The WSDL definition is useful to web service clients to know how to access a web service and what operations it performs. WSDL is often pronounced as *wizdul*.

Click the link, and you will get a WSDL file. The WSDL is not included here because it would take up multiple pages, and most of the XML tags are self-explanatory anyway. You will find the service name, soap address, and the operations declared in the XML. Do note the xsd:schema tag with the schema location URL, which will be in the following format: https://<CloudServiceName>-<IdentityDomain>.java.<DataCenter>.oraclecloudapps.com/Ch8SoapWebService/DateTimeServiceWS?xsd=1.

Note that both the schema and the WSDL begin with the line "Published by JAX-WS RI at http://jax-ws.dev.java.net. RI's version is Oracle JAX-WS 2.1.5," which tells us that these files are generated by JAX-WS 2.1.5 running on the WebLogic server on OJC.

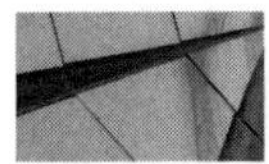

NOTE

You could have generated the WSDL, and even modified it, by right-clicking the web service in NetBeans and selecting Generate and Copy WSDL. However, unless there's a strong case for modifying WSDL, it's easiest to just put in the annotations and have the WSDL generated by the server.

Web Service Client

Now that our web service is up and running, let's create a second web application that will act as the web service client. We could have created the web service client in the same application, but it will be closer to a real implementation to build the client in a separate application.

We begin by creating a new web application named **Ch8SoapWebServiceClient**. As in previous cases, ensure that you select the Oracle Cloud server. Right-click the Ch8SoapWebServiceClient project and select New | Web Services | Web Service Client.

As shown in Figure 8-6, select the WSDL URL radio button and provide the URL to the WSDL for the web service. Name the package **wsclient** and click Finish. You will now get the popups shown in Figures 8-7 and 8-8. Click Yes for both.

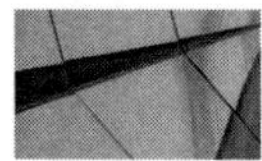

CAUTION
You are likely to get an "Unable to connect" popup if you take too long to accept the popups shown in Figures 8-7 and 8-8. The log will show "Error: An I/O error occurred. Connection reset." In such a case, just repeat the web service client creation steps.

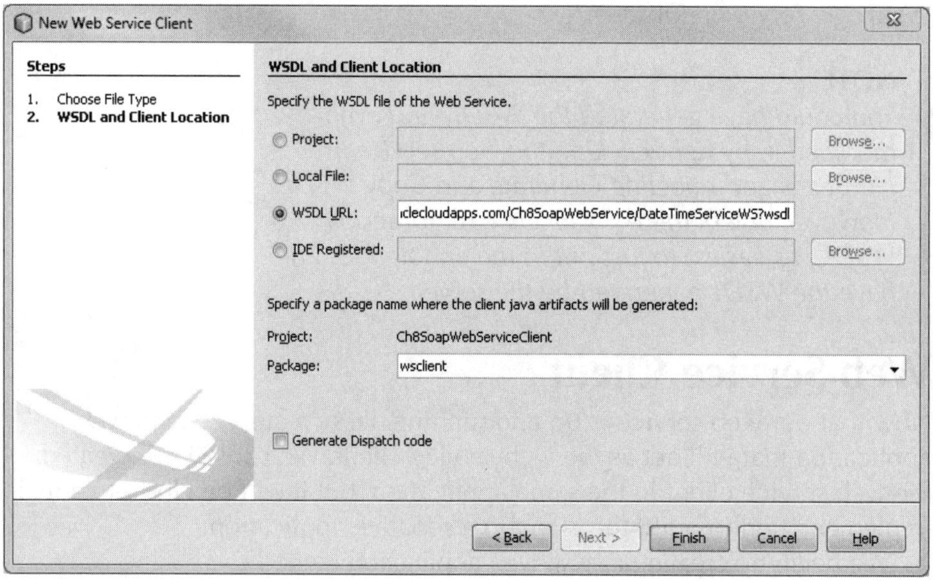

FIGURE 8-6. *Creating a new web service client*

FIGURE 8-7. *Accept the website certificate.*

NetBeans will now create the necessary directories and then run the wsimport tool, which parses the WSDL and generates the appropriate JAX-WS code. As shown in Figure 8-9, a new directory is listed under the Ch8SoapWebServiceClient project in NetBeans.

Now let's create a Servlet in the project and use the web service client code generated. Although we are using a Servlet here, this could

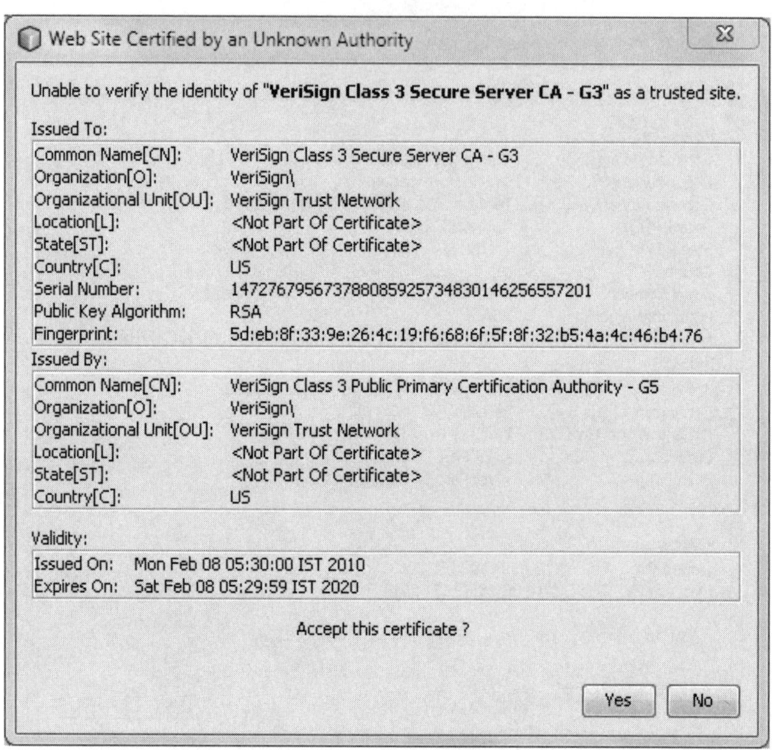

FIGURE 8-8. *The website is certified by an unknown authority.*

very well be a JSP, a managed bean, an EJB, or any other class. Right-click Ch8SoapWebServiceClient and create a new Servlet named **DateTimeClientServlet** in the package **servlets**. Now, right-click in the Servlet and select Insert Code | Call Web Service Operation. Because we already have the JAX-WS-generated client code in place, you will get a screen like the one shown in Figure 8-10.

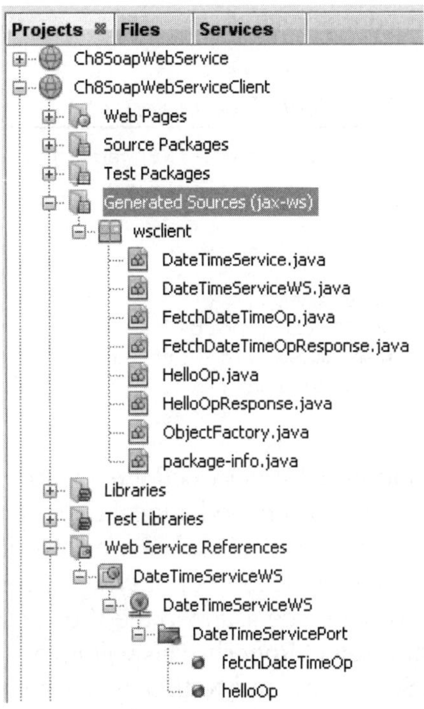

FIGURE 8-9. *A new project listed in the Projects view*

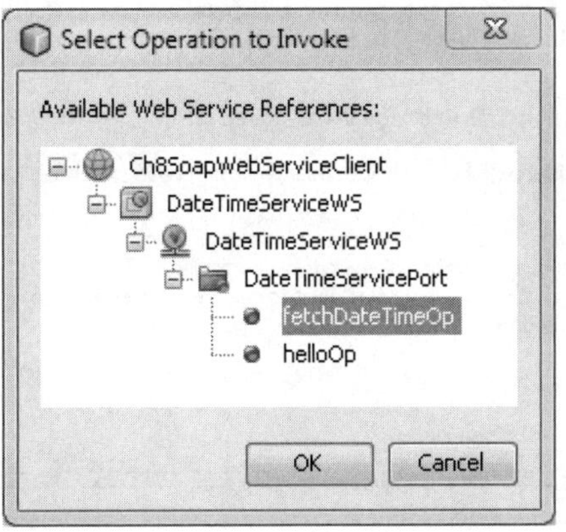

FIGURE 8-10. *Selecting the web service operation*

Select fetchDateTime and click OK. NetBeans will now add the code shown in Listing 8-5 to your Servlet class.

Listing 8-5: *Web Service Client Code in Servlet*

```
@WebServiceRef(wsdlLocation = "WEB-INF/wsdl/java-trialaftx.java.
us1.oraclecloudapps.com/Ch8SoapWebService
/DateTimeService.wsdl")
private DateTimeServiceWS service;

private String fetchDateTimeOp() {
      wsclient.DateTimeService port
      = service.getDateTimeServicePort();
      return port.fetchDateTime ();
}
```

Note that the annotation @WebServiceRef refers to a local WSDL file, which means that NetBeans has created a local copy of the WSDL file. Although a local copy is good for fast and easy access, it could also mean that the local and remote copies could get out of sync. To remedy this, you can always right-click the Web Service listing in the Web Service References, as shown in Figure 8-9, and select Refresh. This will invoke a popup screen as shown in Figure 8-11. Select Yes, and NetBeans will get the latest WSDL and regenerate the Java code accordingly.

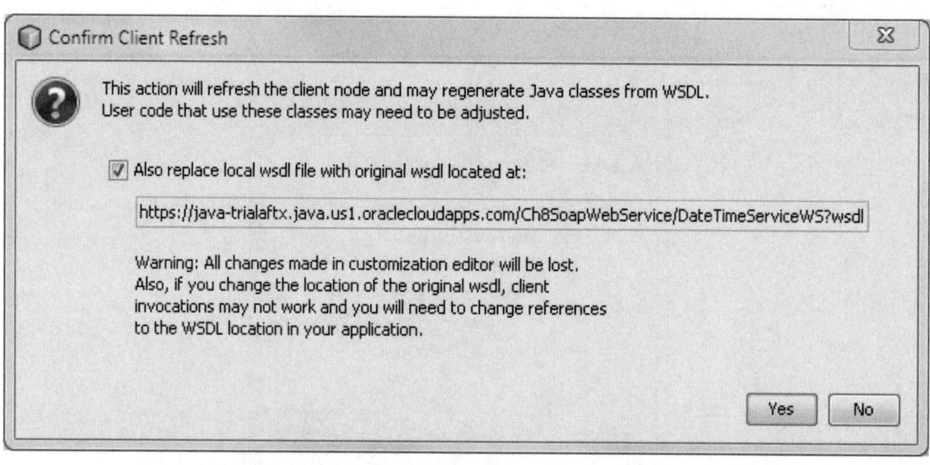

FIGURE 8-11. *Refreshing the WSDL*

Now, all we need to do to use the web service—that is, to send it a SOAP XML message and get back a SOAP XML message—is to add a line to our Servlet to call the fetchDateTime method inserted in the Servlet. Therefore, update the process request method as shown in Listing 8-6.

Listing 8-6: *Servlet Web Service Client Code*

```
protected void processRequest(HttpServletRequest request
, HttpServletResponse response)
            throws ServletException, IOException {
      response.setContentType("text/html;charset=UTF-8");
      PrintWriter out = response.getWriter();
      try {
            out.println("<h1>Date - Time Is -> "
            + fetchDateTime () + "</h1>");
      } finally {
            out.close();
      }
}
```

Now run the Servlet. NetBeans will package the project into a WAR file and deploy to OJC. Note that along with our Servlet, the WSDL, as well as the classes for the JAX-WS-generated web service's client code, are packaged into the WAR. The Servlet output is shown in Figure 8-12. What's happening underneath is that a SOAP XML message is sent to our DateTimeService web service in the application Ch8SoapWebService. This web service responds with a SOAP XML message containing the current server date and time.

In this example, we created an EJB-based web service and used the WSDL to generate the web service client. Note that because of the platform and technology independence of web services, our web service can be accessed

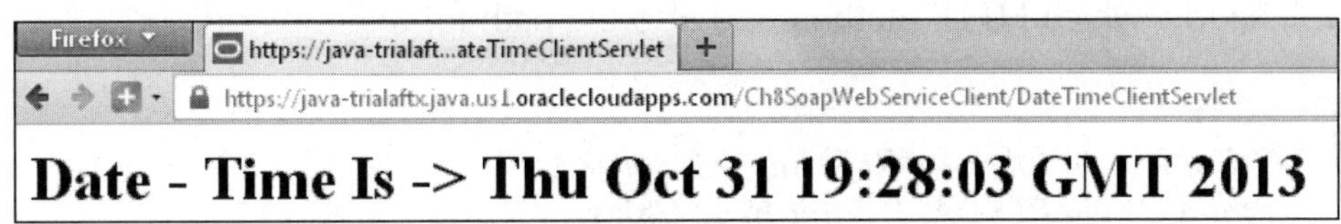

FIGURE 8-12. *The web service client Servlet in a browser*

from another platform using another technology. Similarly, our web service client can utilize a web service developed in another technology by referring to the WSDL and communicating using SOAP XML messages.

RESTful Web Services Using JAX-RS API

RESTful web services are often referred to as "lightweight" web services because, unlike SOAP, which requires a lot of XML going back and forth, REST is a much simpler and more straightforward way of developing web services. As compared to SOAP web services, there's hardly any overhead with REST. Also, consuming RESTful web services is as simple as accessing a URL. The primary limitation of REST involves support for the web services security standards that have evolved over the past decade.

The OJC support for RESTful web services uses the JAX-RS API. Jersey is the reference implementation of JAX-RS and is the implementation used on the OJC.

The key to the REST way of building applications is to access data and functionality of resources with standard HTTP methods using unique identifiers, which in most cases, are web URLs. Therefore, if you want to get the data for employee number 22, you could do something as simple as firing an HTTP GET request to the URL in the form <WebApplicationPath>/resources/employee/22/. In response, you could get information about employee number 22 in a format such as HTML, XML, Text, JSON, or PDF, among others. Using RESTful web services is often the preferred mode lately because calling a URL seems so much simpler and more intuitive than exchanging XML-based SOAP messages.

The usual CRUD (Create-Read-Update-Delete) is covered by the HTTP methods PUT, GET, POST, and DELETE. Annotations convey which method will handle which HTTP method and also the path for that method.

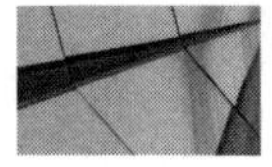

NOTE

A simple example of a RESTful web service is the Google REST API. Enter ***http://ajax.googleapis.com/ajax/services/search/web?v=1.0&q=Oracle%20Java%20Cloud*** *in your browser, and you get the response in the JSON format. In the URL, change* ***web*** *to* ***news***, ***video***, *or* ***images*** *to use the different Google search services.*

Building RESTful Web Services on the OJC

Let's begin building our RESTful web service application by creating a new web application project named **Ch8RestWebService** in NetBeans with Oracle Cloud selected as the server. Right-click the project and select New | Web Services | RESTful Web Services From Patterns. Click Next. NetBeans now provides multiple patterns for creating the resource. Choose Simple Root Resource and click Next.

Set the package name to **rest**, name the path **employees**, and name the class **EmployeeWS**. Then, select the MIME type **text/html** and name the representation class **java.lang.String**, as shown in Figure 8-13.

NetBeans will create ApplicationConfig.java, which extends javax.ws.rs.core.Application to create our JAX-RS application. ApplicationConfig includes the @javax.ws.rs.ApplicationPath annotation, which declares the path as "webresources." Also, the addRestResourceClasses method adds all REST resources to a collection.

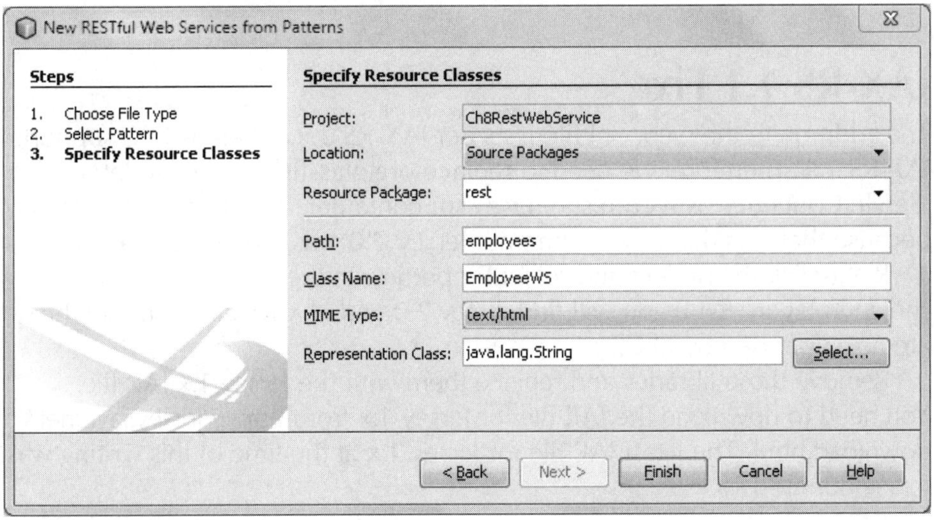

FIGURE 8-13. *Creating a new RESTful web service*

NetBeans also creates EmployeeWS.java, which has the code for our resource. Also, note the modifications to the web.xml file. You will find that a new Servlet and mapping are created, as shown in Listing 8-7.

Listing 8-7: *web.xml*

```
<login-config></login-config>
<servlet>
      <servlet-name>ServletAdaptor</servlet-name>
      <servlet-class>
            org.glassfish.jersey.servlet.ServletContainer
      </servlet-class>
      <init-param>
            <param-name>javax.ws.rs.Application</param-name>
            <param-value>rest.ApplicationConfig</param-value>
      </init-param>
      <load-on-startup>1</load-on-startup>
</servlet>
<servlet-mapping>
      <servlet-name>ServletAdaptor</servlet-name>
      <url-pattern>/webresources/*</url-pattern>
</servlet-mapping>
```

JAX-RS 1.1 Fix

The addition to the web.xml file is as per JAX-RS 2.x, whereas OJC supports JAX-RS 1.1. Therefore, we need to replace org.glassfish.jersey.servlet.ServletContainer with com.sun.jersey.spi.container.servlet.ServletContainer because that was the class name until Jersey 2.0 was moved to GlassFish.

Right-click the project and select Properties. In the Libraries section, shown in Figure 8-14, you will find Jersey 2.0 and JAX-RS 2.0, both of which are not supported by OJC.

Remove these libraries and replace them with the Jersey 1.x JAR file. You need to download the JAR file for Jersey 1.x from https://jersey.java.net/download.html. The latest JAR file for Jersey 1.x at the time of this writing was jersey-bundle-1.18.

NOTE

You can quickly verify that our application follows the OJC specifications and complies with the white list by right-clicking the project and selecting Verify.

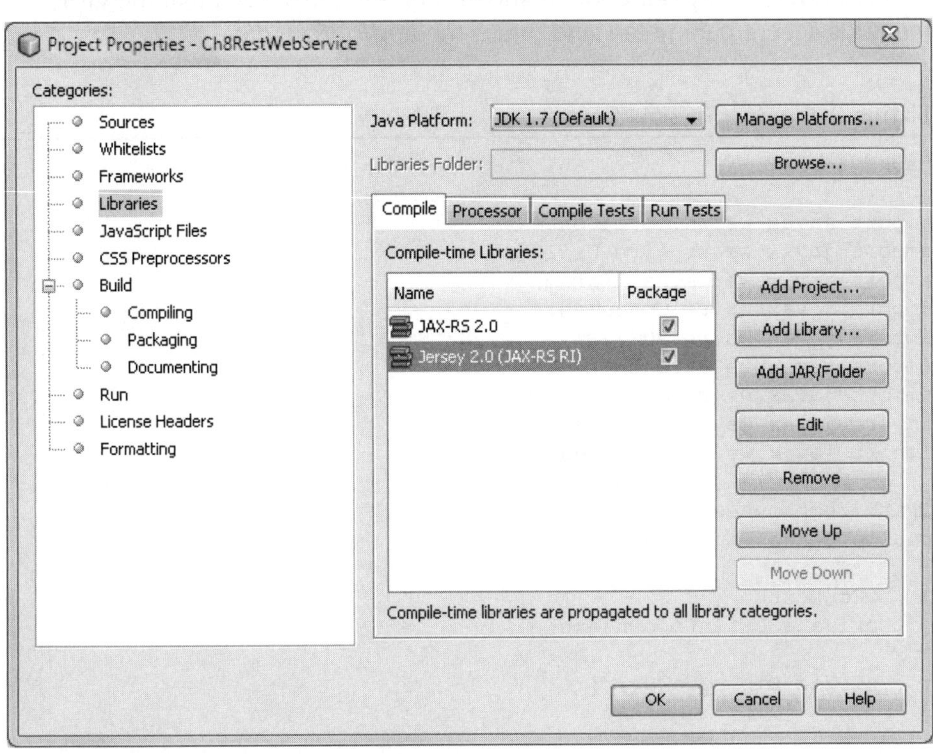

FIGURE 8-14. *A view of the project libraries*

Modify the REST Resource

Now let's look at EmployeeWS.java and modify it as appropriate. The first thing you'll note is the @Path annotation value **employees**, so based on the path in ApplicationConfig and EmployeeWS, we will be accessing this resource with the path /webresources/employees/. Next is the @GET annotation, which marks a method as the one to respond to HTTP GET requests. Similarly, the methods annotated with @PUT, @POST, @HEAD, and @DELETE handle the HTTP requests of the same name. Thus, CRUD (Create-Read-Update-Delete) is covered by PUT, GET, POST, and DELETE, respectively. Also, note the annotations @Produces and @Consumes, which define the MIME type produced and consumed by those methods.

Let's now modify our code as shown in Listing 8-8, such that the GET methods accept parameters and return the appropriate data.

Listing 8-8: *EmployeeWS*

```
package rest;

import javax.ws.rs.core.Context;
import javax.ws.rs.core.UriInfo;
import javax.ws.rs.PathParam;
import javax.ws.rs.Consumes;
import javax.ws.rs.PUT;
import javax.ws.rs.Path;
import javax.ws.rs.GET;
import javax.ws.rs.Produces;
import javax.ws.rs.core.MediaType;

@Path("employees")
public class EmployeeWS {

    @Context
    private UriInfo context;

    public EmployeeWS() {
    }

    @GET
    @Produces(MediaType.APPLICATION_XML)
    public String getHtml() {
        return "<employees><employee>Employee Data</employee>
        </employees>";
    }

    @PUT
    @Consumes("MediaType.TEXT_HTml")
    public void putHtml(String content) {
    }

    @GET
    @Path("/1")
    @Produces(MediaType.TEXT_HTML)
    public String getEmployeeOne() {
        return "<h1>EMP ONE</h1>";
    }

    @GET
```

```
    @Path("/{name}")
    @Produces("MediaType.TEXT_PLAIN")
    public String getEmployeeByName
          (@PathParam("name") String name) {
          return "<h1>Got Data For Employee: " + name + " </h1>";
    }

}
```

We have modified the @Produces annotation to use MediaType constants instead of the string MIME types, and we have modified the getHtml method to produce XML. We have also introduced two new GET methods—one that takes the path /1 and returns data for employee one, and one that accepts a parameter that we process in the code and generates the output accordingly.

Note that for the method getEmployeeByName, we have generated HTML tags, but the @Produces annotation says MediaType.TEXT_PLAIN. Therefore, the browser will not process the HTML, but instead will show the tags as plain text. These various methods show the flexibility of RESTful web services to accept varying input and generate variable output. Exposing some functionality as a RESTful web service is as simple as adding the method and marking it with the necessary annotations.

NetBeans lists the RESTful Web Services shown in Figure 8-15. It also provides the option to right-click the listing and select Test Resource URI. However, as of this writing, NetBeans generates the URI presuming a local server and was not able to produce the correct URI for OJC.

Right-click the project and select Deploy. Once the project is deployed, you can access our RESTful web services directly from the browser. Enter the URL https://<CloudServiceName>-<IdentityDomain>.java.<DataCenter>.oraclecloudapps.com/Ch8RestWebService/webresources/employees/Example, and you get the output shown in Figure 8-16.

Accessing the web service from the browser is simple enough, so let's also look at accessing it programmatically from your Java code.

RESTful Web Service Client

Calling a RESTful web service is as simple as making an HTTP request. You can use an HTTP library such as HttpClient from Apache HttpComponents, or you can use the client library functionality in JAX-RS/Jersey. NetBeans has a wizard to auto-generate the RESTful Java client; however, the code

FIGURE 8-15. *RESTful Web Services listing in NetBeans*

generated is as per JAX-RS 2.0, so we will not be using it here. The code for JAX-RS 1.1 is simple enough.

We could create a new project in NetBeans for our client, but we would then have to again follow the steps mentioned earlier in the "JAX-RS 1.1 Fix" section. Instead, let's create the client code in the Ch8RestWebService project

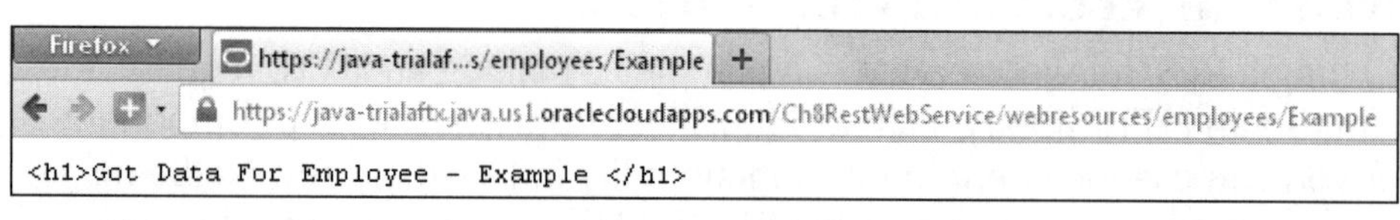

FIGURE 8-16. *Output generated by getEmployeeByName*

itself. For that, create a new Servlet named **RestClientServlet** in the package **servlets**. Modify the code as shown in Listing 8-9.

Listing 8-9: *RESTful Client*

```
protected void processRequest(HttpServletRequest request
           , HttpServletResponse response)
           throws ServletException, IOException {
    response.setContentType("text/html;charset=UTF-8");
    PrintWriter out = response.getWriter();
    try {
             Client c = Client.create();
             WebResource r = c.resource
                ("https://java-trialaftx.java.us1.oraclecloudapps.com/"
                + "Ch8RestWebService/webresources/");
             out.println("RESTful WS Output: "
                              + r.path("employees").path("1")
                                       .accept(MediaType.TEXT_HTML)
                                       .get(String.class).toString());
    } finally {
              out.close();
    }
}
```

You will also need to add the import statements for com.sun.jersey.api.client.Client, com.sun.jersey.api.client.WebResource, and javax.ws.rs.core.MediaType. Run the Servlet and you will get the output shown in Figure 8-17.

The client code accesses the web service and fetches data for employee one.

FIGURE 8-17. *RestClientServlet output*

Summary

In this chapter, we looked at building web services with SOAP and REST and deploying them on OJC. We also looked at how to get around some of the limitations of OJC when it comes to web services.

CHAPTER 9

Persistence Using the Oracle Database Cloud Service

We have so far looked at various Java EE technologies, such as JSP, JSF, and EJB; however, the key missing element is the ability to persist data. Most applications need the capability to store and retrieve data from a persistent store, so Java and Java EE provide a set of standards and tools for persistence. In this chapter, we look at Java Persistence and the persistence capabilities of the Oracle Cloud.

Persistence on the Oracle Cloud

When most people think of Oracle, they think of the Oracle Database. So naturally, a major focus area of the Oracle Cloud is around the Oracle Database Cloud. The Oracle Java Cloud uses the Oracle Database Cloud to provide the persistence capabilities required for Java EE applications. The Oracle Java Cloud currently does not support any database other than the Oracle Database Cloud, which is based on Oracle Database 11*g* Release 2, Enterprise Edition.

That you can only use the Oracle Database is certainly something to consider while adopting OJC; however, many enterprises already use Oracle Database extensively and are comfortable with committing to the Oracle Database even on the cloud.

Oracle Database Cloud Service

Oracle Database Cloud Service is not an Oracle Database installation on a remote server that you can tweak endlessly. It is very much a PaaS offering, where you get a database instance to use but with restrictions and abstractions. The benefit is that you do not have to bother about installing, configuring, patching, or managing the database.

The Oracle Database Cloud Service runs on Oracle Exadata hardware and therefore benefits from the Exadata features and optimizations. It uses schema isolation for multitenancy, and all data is encrypted while being stored on disk.

You cannot just connect to a Database Cloud Service with SQL*Net or add it as a connection in any other remote tool or IDE. Even to upload data for Oracle Database Cloud, you need to send the data loads to a Secure FTP server, where they are scanned for viruses before the data in the files is loaded into the Database Cloud Service.

The Oracle Database Cloud Service provides Oracle Application Express (Apex), which is a database-centric development tool that is installed on all editions of the Oracle Database and also on the Oracle Database Cloud. Apex serves as the dashboard for the Oracle Database Cloud.

Explore Database Cloud

A trial of the Oracle Database Cloud is included in the trial for the Oracle Java Cloud. Therefore, no additional forms need to be filled out and no approval is required. Do note that this is true only for the trial period for commercial use; the Java Cloud Service and the Database Cloud Service need to be bought separately. To access the Oracle Database Cloud, on the services page that you encounter upon login to the Oracle Cloud, click the Database Service link shown in Figure 9-1. You will get to a screen, as shown in Figure 9-2, showing the current service status as well as information about start date, end date, SFTP, and more. In the left panel, you will find sections titled Overview, Administration, Exports, Metrics, and Associations.

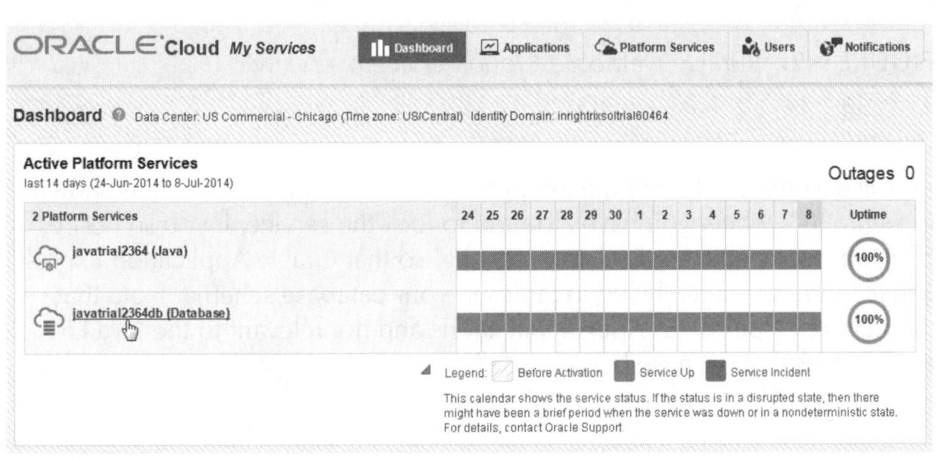

FIGURE 9-1. *Launching the Oracle Cloud Services*

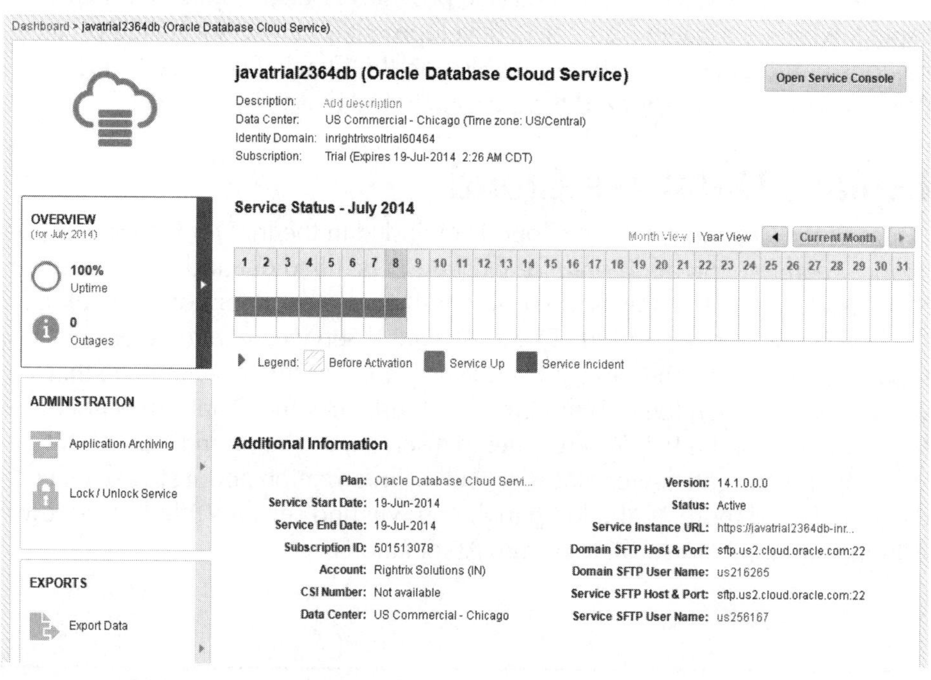

FIGURE 9-2. *Oracle Database Cloud Service overview*

Click Administration in the left panel and you will get a screen as shown in Figure 9-3, where you have a button to lock the service, if you so desire. You can also enable application archiving, so that Oracle Application Express applications can be archived to tables in your database schema. Note that this feature is specific to Apex applications and not relevant to the Java EE applications that we have built.

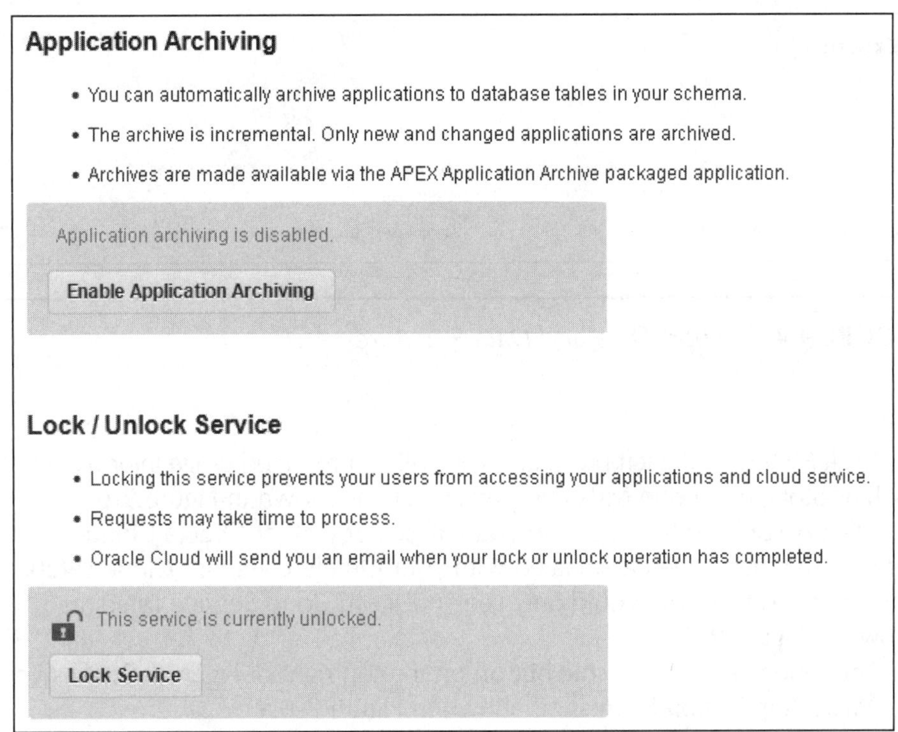

Application Archiving
You can automatically archive applications to database tables in your schema.
The archive is incremental. Only new and changed applications are archived.
Archives are made available via the APEX Application Archive packaged application.
Application archiving is disabled.
Enable Application Archiving
Lock / Unlock Service
Locking this service prevents your users from accessing your applications and cloud service.
Requests may take time to process.
Oracle Cloud will send you an email when your lock or unlock operation has completed.
This service is currently unlocked.
Lock Service

FIGURE 9-3. *Application Archiving - Lock/Unlock Service*

Click Exports in the left panel and you will get a screen as shown in Figure 9-4. Click the Export button and you will get a popup as shown in Figure 9-5. You can choose if you want to export just the data structure or include the data as well. Click Create Data Export. The exported content will be available via SFTP for two days.

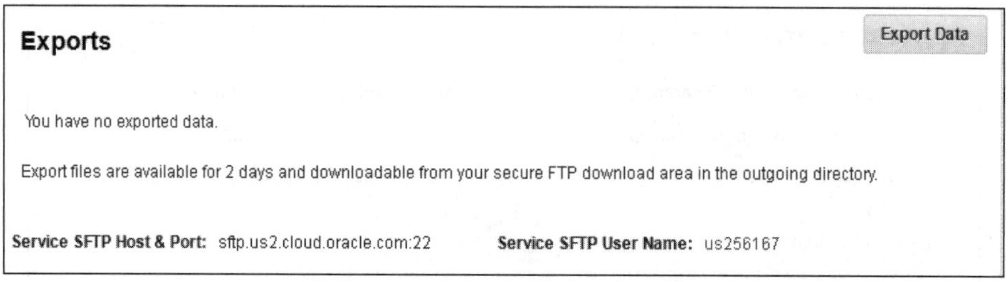

Exports

Export Data

You have no exported data.

Export files are available for 2 days and downloadable from your secure FTP download area in the outgoing directory.

Service SFTP Host & Port: sftp.us2.cloud.oracle.com:22 **Service SFTP User Name:** us256167

FIGURE 9-4. *Export Data and Data Structure*

Click Metrics in the left panel and you will be presented usage information such as Storage Used in MBs and percentage, as shown in Figure 9-6.

Click Associated Services and you will see any other Oracle Cloud services that have been associated with your Oracle Database Cloud setup. For the trial setup, you would only see your Java Cloud Service listed, as shown in Figure 9-7.

The Open Service Console button on the top right of Figure 9-2 takes you to Oracle Application Express, as shown in Figure 9-8.

You will see the main icons, as well as a tabbed menu at the top of the screen to access the various features and to administer your Database Cloud.

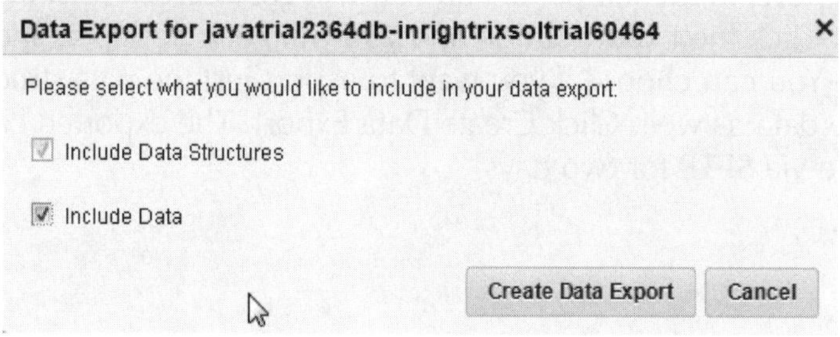

Data Export for javatrial2364db-inrightrixsoltrial60464

Please select what you would like to include in your data export:

Include Data Structures

Include Data

Create Data Export Cancel

FIGURE 9-5. *Create Data Export*

Latest Usage (as of 25 hr 1 min ago)

Storage	
Storage Used (MB)	2.75
Storage Percent	0.27%

Historical Usage

No utilization data for last 7 days.

FIGURE 9-6. *Metrics - Usage*

Associated Services

FIGURE 9-7. *Associated Services*

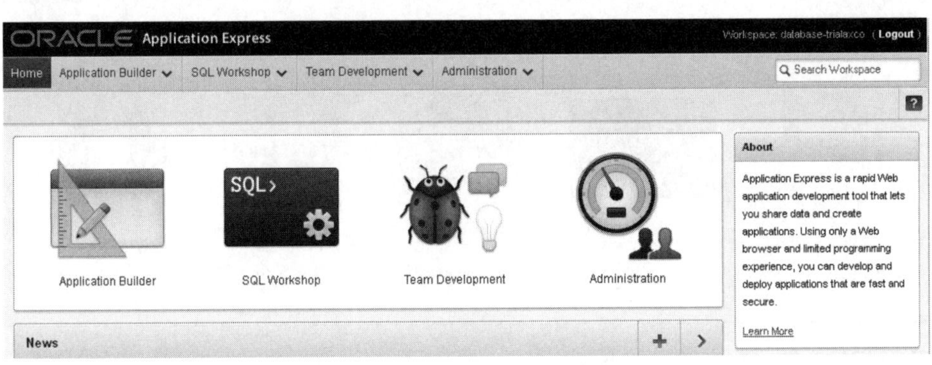

FIGURE 9-8. *Oracle Application Express*

Oracle Apex

Oracle Application Express (Apex) is your primary tool for working with the Database Cloud. As shown in Figure 9-8, Apex has four major sections:

- **Application Builder** The Application Builder provides a browser-based development environment with wizards and tools to build data-centric applications with relative ease. It also comes with packaged applications and the ability to import applications.
- **SQL Workshop** The SQL Workshop provides a bunch of tools to manage your data. The SQL Workshop, as shown in Figure 9-9, is what we would use most while using the Oracle Database Cloud along with OJC. Of special note are the utilities, shown in Figure 9-10, and the ability to expose data in the form of RESTful services.
- **Team Development** Team Development provides the ability to track features, to-do tasks, milestones, and bugs. It also helps manage the application development lifecycle.
- **Administration** Administration provides the ability to manage users and groups, monitor activity and utilization, and manage the service.

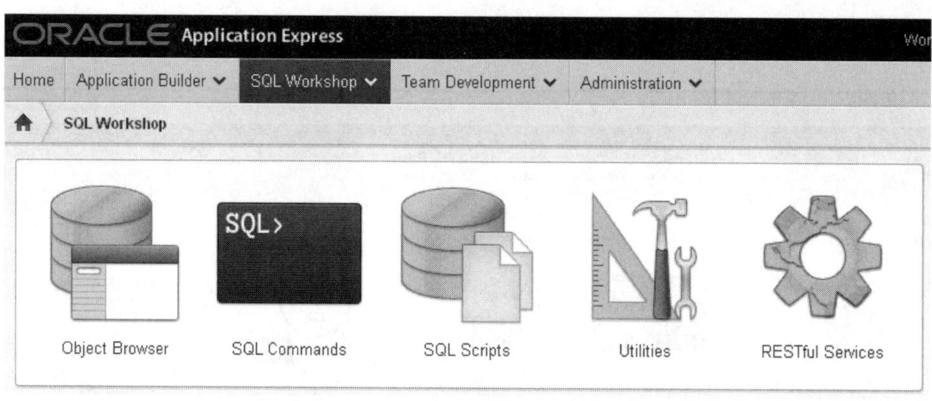

FIGURE 9-9. *SQL Workshop*

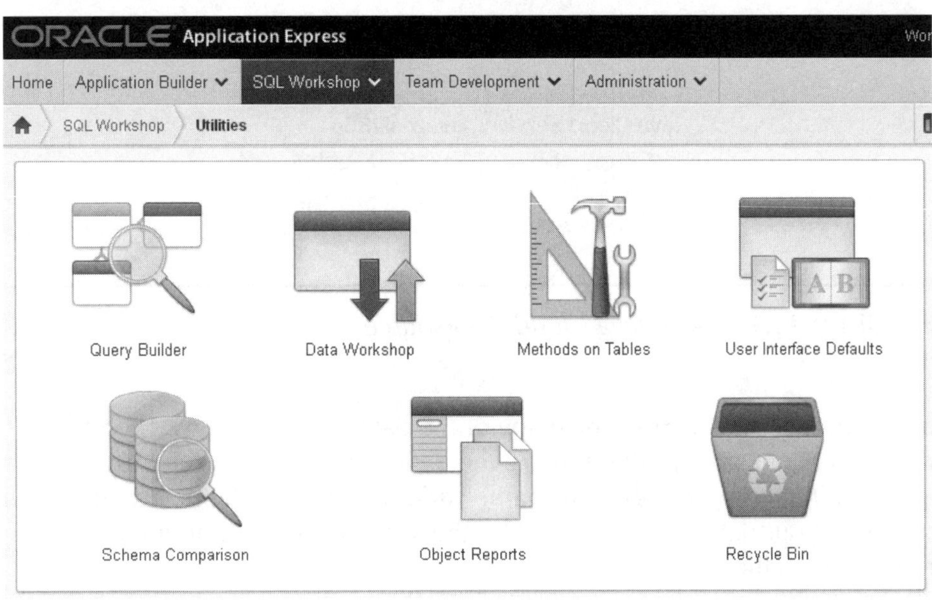

FIGURE 9-10. *SQL Workshop's utilities*

NOTE
Your data source in the Oracle Database Cloud cannot be accessed directly from a remote DB tool on your desktop. Therefore, we also cannot just add the cloud DB as a service in NetBeans. However, you can use SFTP with SQL Developer, Oracle's integrated development environment (IDE) for SQL, to upload data to the Database Cloud.

Java Cloud: Database Cloud Integration

The Oracle Database Cloud instance is available as a JDBC data source to all applications deployed on OJC. As shown in Figure 9-11, the "javatrial2364db" JNDI location listed under Data Sources in the Java Cloud Services Control is the only data source available to OJC. You cannot add

FIGURE 9-11. *Oracle Java Cloud data sources*

a new data source or customize any of the data source settings. Therefore, all applications on OJC that require the data source need to refer to the same JNDI name. Note that this name varies across installations, so the JNDI name for your data source will not be the same as that seen in the figure or referred to in the text.

NOTE
A common question is whether it is possible to add a third-party database or a remote data source to OJC. As of now, you cannot do so. You would have to use the data source for the Oracle Database Cloud.

The Oracle Database Cloud Service supports JPA 2.0 and JDBC 4.0 APIs. Note that OJC supports the JPA 2.0 specification that is part of Java EE 6.

NOTE
OJC supports EJB 2.1, excluding entity beans. So although you can use EJB 2.1 on OJC, you cannot use the entity beans Container-Managed Persistence (CMP) from EJB 2.x.

JPA

Java Persistence API (JPA) is the API for persistence and object/relational mapping (ORM). The origins of JPA lie in the popularity of the Hibernate object/relational framework. In Chapter 6, we talked about how Apache

Struts was so popular that it had become the de facto standard for Java web frameworks; similarly for object/relational mapping, there was Hibernate.

Hibernate offered Java developers the option to stick to developing with Java, while the framework took care of mapping the Java objects to the corresponding database tables. Java developers loved it and flocked to Hibernate by the thousands. Even though object/relational mapping wasn't a new idea, as such, Hibernate clicked big time as Java developers found it a much easier and better alternative to writing Java Database Connectivity (JDBC) code and firing SQL queries along with all the exception handling required. Also, working with Java objects seems like the more intuitive thing to do for Java developers.

Java, due to its emphasis on collaboration and standardization, is great at adopting a good idea and building a standard around it. So JPA became the specification for managing data between Java objects and relational databases.

NOTE

JPA is not a "Java EE–only" specification, but it works for Java EE and Java SE. Java developers need to write their Java class and annotations as per the JPA specification. They need not bother with the actual mapping to the database because the JPA implementation will take care of it on their behalf.

Persistence Providers

As with all Java specifications, JPA states how you need to write your classes and how the persistence is to be managed. However, JPA does not include any actual implementation. Therefore, it is up to various persistence providers to build the JPA implementations. As always, the beauty of a specification with multiple implementations is that if you code as per the specification, you can later switch your JPA implementation if required. Hibernate, OpenJPA, and EclipseLink are some of the popular implementations of JPA.

Entity

Entities are Plain Old Java Objects (POJOs) that represent tables in the database. So to add a new row, you create a new instance of the entity class and persist it. Similarly, to update a row, you can get the appropriate row as an entity instance, update it, and persist it. Let's now build an application with an entity named "Device," which maps to a database table of the same name. We will use the table to record some information about multiple devices. We will also look at how we can use this entity from a Servlet, as well as perform CRUD applications using JSF.

Developing an Entity Application

First, create a new web application project named **Ch9JPA1** in NetBeans. Ensure that you choose Oracle Cloud as the server. Next, right-click the project and select New File | Persistence | Entity Class. As shown in Figure 9-12, name the class **Device** and the package **entities**. Note that the primary key is Long, by default. Keep the Create Persistence Unit box checked. Click Next.

Next, as shown in Figure 9-13, the wizard will ask for more information on the persistence provider and the database. EclipseLink (JPA 2.0) is selected

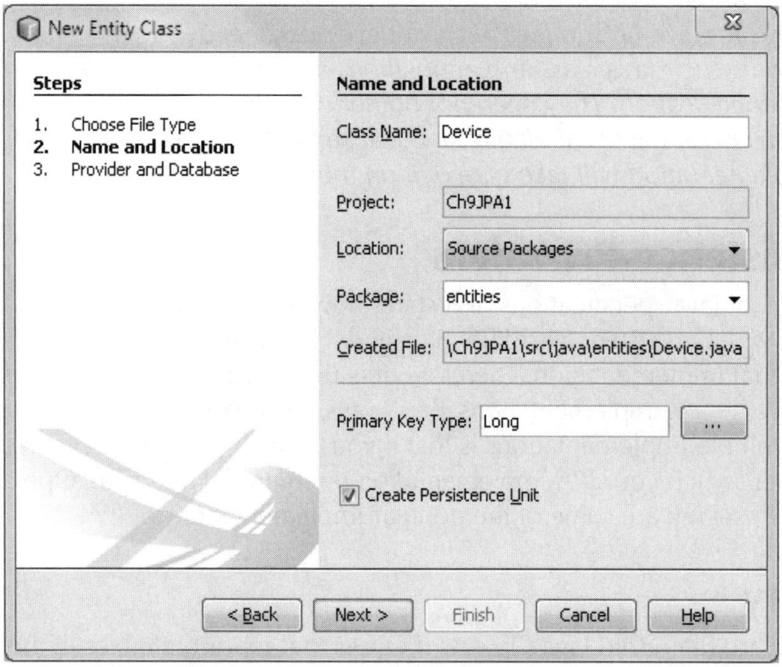

FIGURE 9-12. *Creating a new entity class*

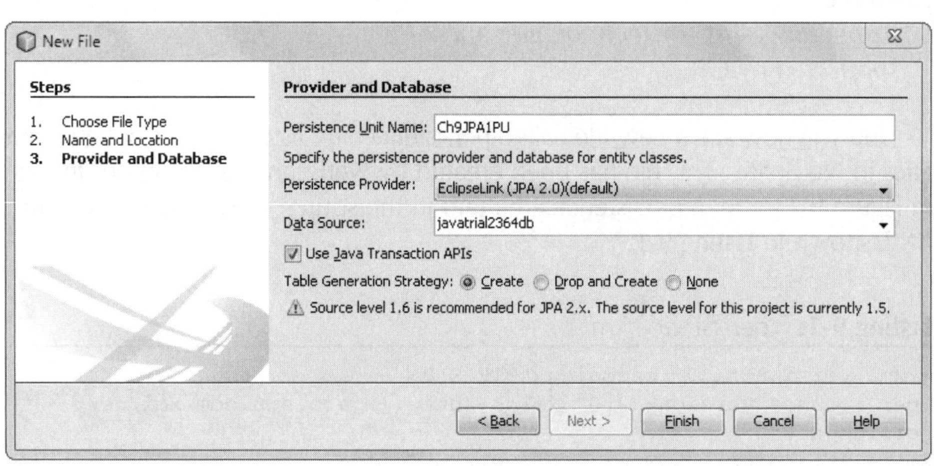

FIGURE 9-13. *Entity provider and database*

as the persistence provider by default. We will use it because that's the one supported by OJC out of the box. You can select another JPA 2.0 provider such as Hibernate from the drop-down. However, in that case, you would have to provide the library files as well, because OJC won't have them set up otherwise.

The data source name is "database," as shown in Figure 9-13. The Table Generation Strategy option gives us the choice to create a new table, to drop the earlier table and then create a new one, or not to attempt to create the table. Select the Create option because we want the table to be created based on the properties in our entity class. Click Finish.

You should now have an entity class in place.

NOTE

OJC supports Java SE 6 APIs as long as the usage passes the whitelist check. Therefore, considering the caution shown in Figure 9-9, you could change the source level in File | Project Properties | Sources to JDK 6. However, the example in this chapter will work fine even without the change.

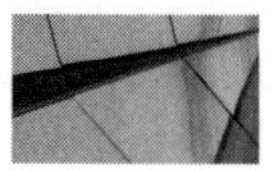

NOTE
Appendix C lists the technologies and APIs supported by OJC.

You will now see a new file called persistence.xml listed under Configuration Files in NetBeans. This file has been created by NetBeans based on our inputs in Figure 9-13. Open persistence.xml, and in the source view, you will see the XML shown in Listing 9-1.

Listing 9-1: *persistence.xml*

```
<?xml version="1.0" encoding="UTF-8"?>
<persistence version="2.0" xmlns="http://java.sun.com/xml/ns/
persistence"
xmlns:xsi="http://www.w3.org/2001/XMLSchema-instance"
xsi:schemaLocation="http://java.sun.com/xml/ns/persistence
http://java.sun.com/xml/ns/persistence/persistence_2_0.xsd">
  <persistence-unit name="Ch9JPA1PU" transaction-type="JTA">
    <provider>org.eclipse.persistence.jpa.PersistenceProvider
    </provider>
    <jta-data-source>javatrial2364db</jta-data-source>
    <exclude-unlisted-classes>false</exclude-unlisted-classes>
    <properties>
      <property name="eclipselink.ddl-generation"
       value="create-tables"/>
    </properties>
  </persistence-unit>
</persistence>
```

You can try clicking the Design tab and changing the persistence provider and some properties so as to better understand the usage of this configuration file. To repeat, JTA data source name "javatrial2364db" refers to the JNDI name shown previously in Figure 9-11. This name could be different for your installation.

The Device.java file created for the entity class has the id property and some annotations and default implementations of the toString, hashcode, and equals method. You will note that the id property has the annotation `@GeneratedValue(strategy = GenerationType.AUTO)`, which specifies the generation strategies for the primary key value. AUTO, here, indicates that the persistence provider should pick an appropriate strategy for the particular database. The other options are IDENTITY, SEQUENCE, and TABLE. You will find that for the Oracle Database on the cloud, the persistence provider (EclipseLink) creates a table called SEQUENCE, which is used for generating the primary key.

Let's now modify the entity class to add a few properties, which will become columns in our table. You can write the code yourself or autogenerate it by right-clicking and selecting Insert Code. Add the properties "String name" and "int cost", along with the corresponding getter and setter methods, so that your entity class appears as shown in Listing 9-2. Adding suitable constructors is also a good idea.

Listing 9-2: *Device.java*

```
package entities;

import java.io.Serializable;
import javax.persistence.Column;
import javax.persistence.Entity;
import javax.persistence.GeneratedValue;
import javax.persistence.GenerationType;
import javax.persistence.Id;

@Entity
public class Device implements Serializable {

    private static final long serialVersionUID = 1L;
    @Id
    @GeneratedValue(strategy = GenerationType.AUTO)
    private Long id;

    @Column(name = "DEVICENAME")
    private String name;
    private int cost;

    public Device(String name, int cost) {
        this.name = name;
        this.cost = cost;
    }

    public Device() {
    }

    public Long getId() {
        return id;
    }
```

```
    public void setId(Long id) {
        this.id = id;
    }

    public String getName() {
        return name;
    }

    public void setName(String name) {
        this.name = name;
    }

    public int getCost() {
        return cost;
    }

    public void setCost(int cost) {
        this.cost = cost;
    }

    @Override
    public int hashCode() {
        int hash = 0;
        hash += (id != null ? id.hashCode() : 0);
        return hash;
    }

    @Override
    public boolean equals(Object object) {
        // TODO: Warning - this method won't work in the case
        the id fields are not set
        if (!(object instanceof Device)) {
            return false;
        }
        Device other = (Device) object;
        if ((this.id == null && other.id != null)
        || (this.id != null && !this.id.equals(other.id))) {
            return false;
        }
        return true;
    }

    @Override
    public String toString() {
        return "entities.Device[ id=" + id + " ]";
    }
}
```

We want the persistence provider to create a table called DEVICE that maps to the objects of our Device entity class. By default, the persistence provider will name the columns the same as the property names in the entity class. However, we can use the @Column annotation to provide different column names.

Add Entity from a Servlet

Let's look at how we can programmatically add a new device to the table from a Servlet. For that, first add a new Servlet named **DeviceServlet** in the package **servlets** to our Ch9JPA1 project. To work with entities, we use the EntityManager API. Using the EntityManager, we can create and remove entity instances as well as find and query them, as required.

To use the EntityManager, right-click in the Servlet code and select Insert Code | Use Entity Manager. This will lead to code for injecting an EntityManager and adding a UserTransaction to the class. A "persist" method will also be added to the class. Although the EntityManager is what we will use to work with our entities, the UserTransaction is required because there is no built-in transaction support in Servlets. Therefore, we have to programmatically start and stop the transaction as shown in the persist method. Transaction support here is a must because without the transaction "begin" and "commit" code, the persist method of EntityManager will throw javax.persistence.TransactionRequiredException.

Adding a new device to the table using our Device entity is as simple as creating a new instance of Device and then calling the persist method in the Servlet, as shown in Listing 9-3. We also need to add an `import entities.Device;` statement for the Servlet class to compile.

Listing 9-3: *DeviceServlet*

```
@PersistenceContext(unitName = "Ch9JPA1PU")
private EntityManager em;
@Resource
private javax.transaction.UserTransaction utx;

protected void processRequest(HttpServletRequest request
, HttpServletResponse response)
            throws ServletException, IOException {
      response.setContentType("text/html;charset=UTF-8");
      PrintWriter out = response.getWriter();
      try {
            persist(new Device ("Android", 100));
```

```
                persist(new Device ("iPhone", 200));
                out.println("Added devices to the table");
        } finally {
                out.close();
        }
}

public void persist (Object object) {
        try {
                utx.begin();
                em.persist(object);
                utx.commit();
        } catch (Exception e) {
                Logger.getLogger(getClass().getName())
                .log(Level.SEVERE, "exception caught", e);
                throw new RuntimeException(e);
        }
}
```

The name **Ch9JPA1PU** refers to the persistence unit, as declared in the persistence.xml file. The EntityManager instance gets injected into the Servlet. We call the persist method in the Servlet. This method starts the transaction using the UserTransaction utx object injected; it then calls the EntityManager persist and finally commits the transaction.

NOTE
The transaction management code in this example is required because Servlets lack any built-in transaction management capability. You could instead use EJBs to interact with the entities, and the transactions could be managed by the EJB based on the annotation values you specify. Refer to Chapter 7 for EJBs and EJB transaction management.

Now run DeviceServlet. To check the tables that are created and the data entered, head over to the SQL Workshop | Object Browser on the Oracle Database Cloud. As shown in Figure 9-14, two new tables (DEVICE and SEQUENCE) are created. The other tables are used by the sample application on Oracle Database Cloud and are not related to our application. For the

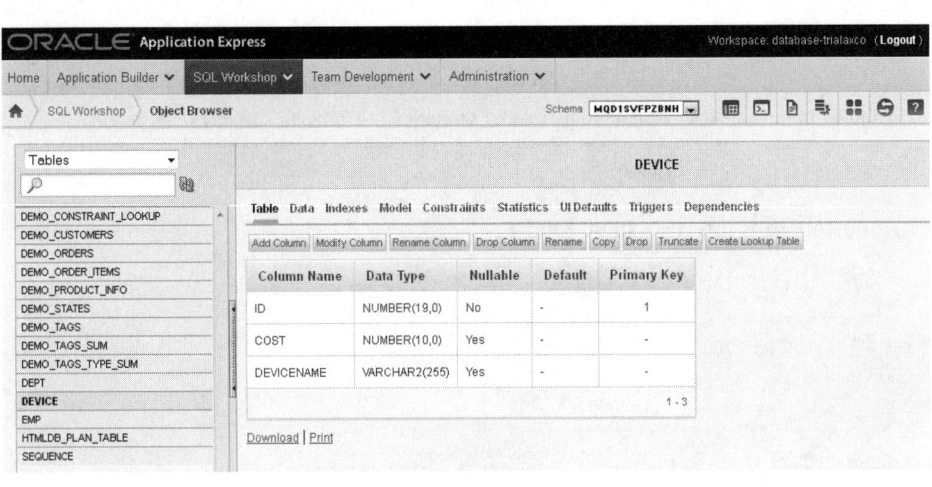

FIGURE 9-14. *Tables in the SQL Workshop's Object Browser*

DEVICE table, note that the column name is as specified in the annotation. So it's DEVICENAME and not the property name NAME. The SEQUENCE table will be used to autogenerate the primary key.

NOTE
NetBeans would have added the EclipseLink library to your project libraries. EclipseLink is the default JPA library on OJC, so it is not required to be bundled with our project. Therefore, you can remove that library for the project. Removing unnecessary libraries also leads to much faster deploys.

Click the Data tab for the DEVICE table and, as shown in Figure 9-15, you will see the two devices we added from the Servlet. Now that we have some data in the table, let's look at querying and retrieving that data.

DEVICE

Table Data Indexes Model Constraints Statistics UI Defaults Triggers Dependencies

Query Count Rows Insert Row

EDIT	ID	COST	DEVICENAME
	1	100	Android
	2	200	iPhone

row(s) 1 - 2 of 2

Download

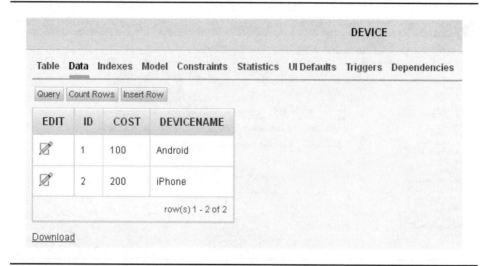

FIGURE 9-15. *The Data tab for the DEVICE table*

NOTE

Now that our Device table has been created as desired, you can edit the persistence.xml file by removing the property eclipselink.ddl-generation because you no longer want EclipseLink to attempt the creation of the tables. Changing the Table Generation Strategy to "None" in the persistence .xml editor should get you the same result, but I faced some issues with NetBeans where the XML wasn't getting updated. Therefore, you might have to manually delete the property from the XML.

Find and Update Entity

All entities can be found/retrieved using the class name and the primary key. Updating an entity is as simple as updating the value in the entity object and persisting the updated object. We will later look at using queries for bulk updates, but where you need to update a single entity, updating the value in the object is the easiest way to go about it.

Let's add the method shown in Listing 9-4 to our Servlet, which will first find an object, update it, and then persist the updated object.

Listing 9-4: *Find and Update Device*

```
public void findAndUpdateDevice(Long primaryKey) {
      try {
            utx.begin();
            Device foundDevice
            = em.find(Device.class, primaryKey);
            if (foundDevice != null) {
                  foundDevice.setCost(2000);
                  em.persist(foundDevice);
            }
            utx.commit();
      } catch (Exception e) {
            Logger.getLogger(getClass().getName())
            .log(Level.SEVERE, "exception caught", e);
            throw new RuntimeException(e);
      }
}
```

Note that this method is similar to the persist method in Listing 9-3. As with adding a new entity, even while updating the entity, we need a transaction for the EntityManager to not throw an exception when we call its persist method.

In the line `Device foundDevice = em.find(Device.class, 2L)`, we state that the class is Device.class and that the primary key is 2. Note that we state it as "2L" so as to convey that it is a Long. Without the L, it will be treated as an integer and thus lead to an exception. Once we find the device, we update the cost and persist the updated object. However just being able to *find* using the EntityManager won't suffice for most applications; therefore, you need a powerful querying mechanism such as the Java Persistence Query Language (JPQL).

Java Persistence Query Language

The JPQL is a SQL-like query language that lets you write portable queries without worrying about the underlying data store. You can perform SELECT, UPDATE, or DELETE queries, similar to SQL. You can declare JPQL queries using annotations in the Entity class, or you can use the createQuery method of EntityManager to state the query in the code itself. Declaring your queries as annotations is usually the easier, cleaner way to go about it.

SELECT NamedQuery

Let's look at an example where we declare one SELECT query as an annotation and a second one in the code.

In the Device.java Entity class, add an import statement for javax.persistence .NamedQuery and the NamedQuery annotation so that the top of the class is as shown in Listing 9-5.

Listing 9-5: *NamedQuery*

```
import javax.persistence.NamedQuery;

@Entity
@NamedQuery(name = "Device.findPricey"
, query = "SELECT d FROM Device d WHERE d.cost > :cost")
public class Device implements Serializable {
...
```

Here, we declare a query with the name Device.findPricey, which is meant to find all devices whose price is greater than the "cost" parameter we will be passing. The syntax is pretty similar to SQL except for ":cost" (which we use to pass the cost parameter). Next, we add the new method shown in Listing 9-6 and call it from the processRequest method in the DeviceServlet class, with 100 as the cost parameter. Add import statements for javax .persistence.Query and java.util.List.

Listing 9-6: *Select Using a NamedQuery*

```
private void findPriceyDevices(PrintWriter out, int cost) {
      //Select NamedQuery
      Query q = em.createNamedQuery("DeviceC.findPricey");
      out.println("<h2>* Listing all devices with
      cost greater than 100</h2>");

      List<Device> priceDevices
                = em.createNamedQuery("Device.findPricey")
                .setParameter("cost", cost)
                .getResultList();
      for (Device d : priceDevices) {
            out.println("<h4>Device Name:"
```

```
            + d.getName() + "</h4>");
        }
    }
```

In Listing 9-5, we created the NamedQuery *DeviceC.findPricey* using an annotation in the Entity class. In Listing 9-6, we use the same name to refer to the NamedQuery. Next, we set the cost parameter and get the devices as a list.

SELECT Query

Let's now look at how you can fire a query without having declared it as an annotation in the entity. Add the new method shown in Listing 9-7 to the DeviceServlet class and call the method from the processRequest method, passing the value A% as the pattern to match.

Listing 9-7: *Select Query*

```
private void deviceNameLike(PrintWriter out, String pattern) {
   //Select Query
   out.println
   ("<h2>* Listing all devices with names starting with A</h2>");

   List<Device> nameDevices = em.createQuery
                ("SELECT d FROM Device d WHERE d.name LIKE :devname")
                .setParameter("devname", pattern)
                .getResultList();

   for (Device d : nameDevices) {
            out.println("<h4>Device Name:" + d.getName() + "</h4>");
   }
}
```

Here we create the query in the code and get all devices whose name begins with *A*.

NOTE
Although the column name is DEVICENAME, as declared by us using an annotation in Device.java, we refer to the property name in the SELECT query.

UPDATE and DELETE Query

Earlier in this chapter, in the "Find and Update Entity" section, we looked at how to update the table by updating the entity object. Although that's an easy way to update a single record, it is not an efficient way when you want to update multiple records. You would much rather run an UPDATE query than iterate over many entities and update each one.

Let's add a few named queries to the Device entity class—one to raise the cost of all devices with a certain name and the second to delete all devices with a certain name. With multiple named queries, you can use the @NamedQueries annotation, as shown in Listing 9-8. You need to add an import statement for javax.persistence.NamedQueries.

Listing 9-8: *Update Delete Queries*

```
@Entity
@NamedQueries ({
    @NamedQuery(name = "Device.findPricey"
    , query = "SELECT d FROM Device d WHERE d.cost > :cost"),
    @NamedQuery(name = "Device.hikePrice"
    , query = "UPDATE Device d SET d.cost
    = d.cost+100 WHERE d.name = ?1"),
    @NamedQuery(name = "Device.deleteBasedOnName"
    , query = "DELETE FROM Device d WHERE d.name = :devname")
})
public class Device implements Serializable {
...
```

Note that for the UPDATE query, we pass a parameter based on position, whereas for DELETE, we have named the parameter.

Now we need to add code to our servlet to run the UPDATE and DELETE queries. We add a deleteDeviceByName method to delete a device and an updateDevicePrice method to update a device, as shown in Listing 9-9. Because UPDATE and DELETE queries need to run as part of a transaction, it's best to also create an updateDeleteInTxn method, as shown in Listing 9-9, and pass the query to be executed. We will call the deleteDeviceByName and updateDevicePrice methods from the processRequest method.

Listing 9-9: *Execute Update Delete*

```
private void deleteDeviceByName(PrintWriter out, String name) {
      //DELETE namedQuery
      Query deleteQuery =
      em.createNamedQuery("Device.deleteBasedOnName")
```

```
        .setParameter("devname", name);
        out.println("<h4>Deleted: " + updateDeleteInTxn(deleteQuery)
        + " </h4>");
}

private void updateDevicePrice(PrintWriter out, String name) {
        //Update namedQuery
        Query updateQuery = em.createNamedQuery("Device.hikePrice")
                    .setParameter(1, name);
        out.println("<h4>Updated: " + updateDeleteInTxn(updateQuery)
                    + " </h4>");

}

public int updateDeleteInTxn(Query q) {
        try {
              utx.begin();
              int count = q.executeUpdate();
              utx.commit();
              return count;
        } catch (Exception e) {
              Logger.getLogger(getClass().getName()).log(Level.SEVERE
              , "exception caught", e);
              throw new RuntimeException(e);
        }
}
```

We utilize the various methods by calling them from the processRequest method, as shown in Listing 9-10.

Listing 9-10: *processRequest*

```
protected void processRequest(HttpServletRequest request
, HttpServletResponse response)
            throws ServletException, IOException {
      response.setContentType("text/html;charset=UTF-8");
      PrintWriter out = response.getWriter();
      try {
            persist(new Device("Android", 100));
            persist(new Device ("iPhone", 200));
            out.println("Added devices to the table");
            // Find Devices priced over 100
            findPriceyDevices(out, 100);

            //Find Devices where name begins with A
            deviceNameLike(out, "A%");
```

```
            //Update iPhone price
            updateDevicePrice(out, "iPhone");

            //Delete Android devices
            deleteDeviceByName(out, "Android");

            //Find & Update cost of device with the primary key 2
            findAndUpdateDevice(2L);

        } finally {
            out.close();
        }
}
```

Now run the DeviceServlet, and you should get the output shown in Figure 9-16.

Visit the SQL Workshop | Object Browser on the Database Cloud to check whether your data has been created and updated as expected. In this example, we have looked at creating an entity as well as selecting, updating, and deleting it, as required, using the various JPA features as well as JPQL queries.

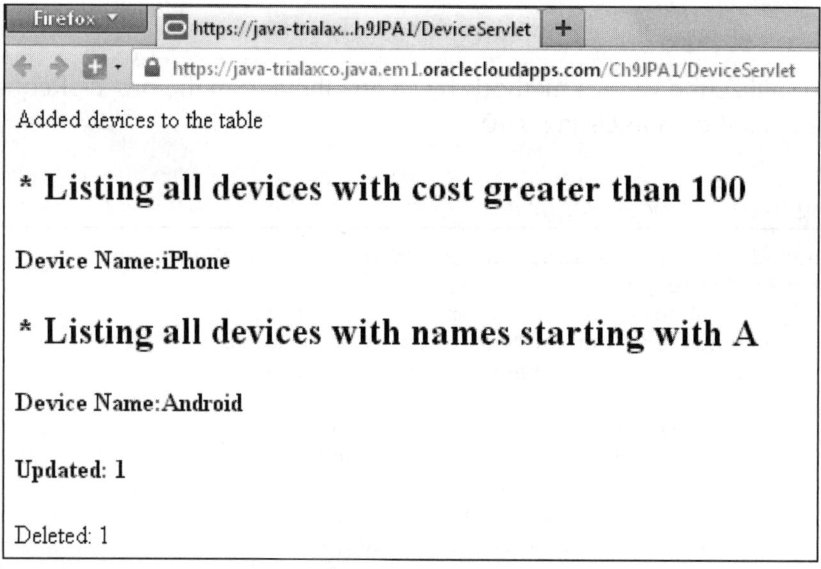

FIGURE 9-16. *DeviceServlet output*

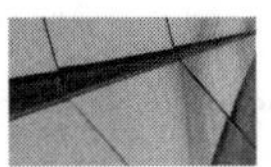

NOTE
We created the tables using the entity; however, you could just as well take the reverse approach and create your entity using the table. NetBeans, as well as many other IDEs, have neat wizards to autogenerate entities from tables. We won't get into the micro details of the JPQL syntax here. Although most of it is quite similar to SQL, I recommend that you refer to the detailed JPQL syntax listing at http://docs.oracle.com/javaee/6/tutorial/doc/bnbuf.html for more information.

CRUD JSF for Entity

A large majority of applications provide Create-Read-Update Delete (CRUD) functionality for data. Now that we have an entity in place that maps to a table, let's use a neat NetBeans feature to create a JSF CRUD application for our entity. Although the created application can be used as is, it can also serve as a good base for you to modify depending on the requirements of your application.

To generate the JSF CRUD application, right-click the Ch9JPA1 project and select New | Other | Persistence | JSF Pages from Entity Classes. You will get the screen shown in Figure 9-17.

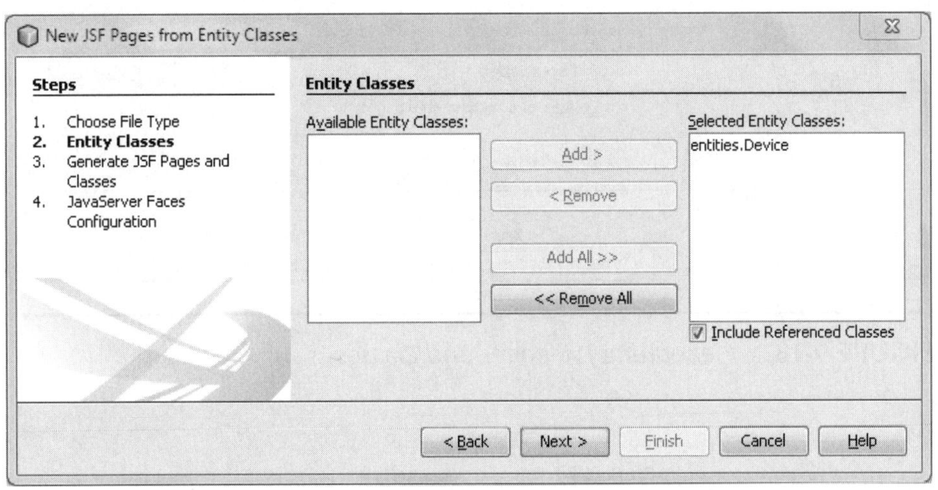

FIGURE 9-17. *The New JSF Pages from Entity Classes screen*

Add the Device entity and click Next. On the next screen, shown in Figure 9-18, set the JPA controller package to **jpacontroller** and the JSF classes package to **jsfclasses**. Click Next.

As shown in Figure 9-19, NetBeans will now ask you for the server library to use. JSF 2.0 will be selected by default because that's the version supported by OJC. You need not change this, so click Finish.

NetBeans will generate multiple classes and JSF .xhtml files. It will also create the managed bean jsfclasses.DeviceController and modify the weblogic.xml file to add a library reference to JSF 2.0. You will find a few other classes generated as well as a new device directory in Web Pages. We will not get into the nitty-gritty of the autogenerated app here, but these are essentially classes to get the basic CRUD application going.

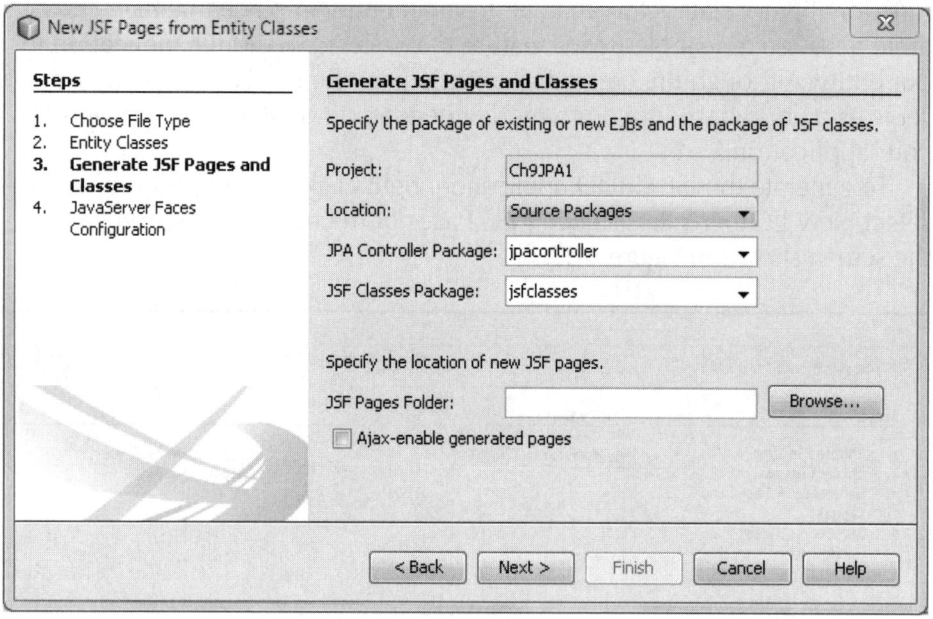

FIGURE 9-18. *Generating JSF pages and classes*

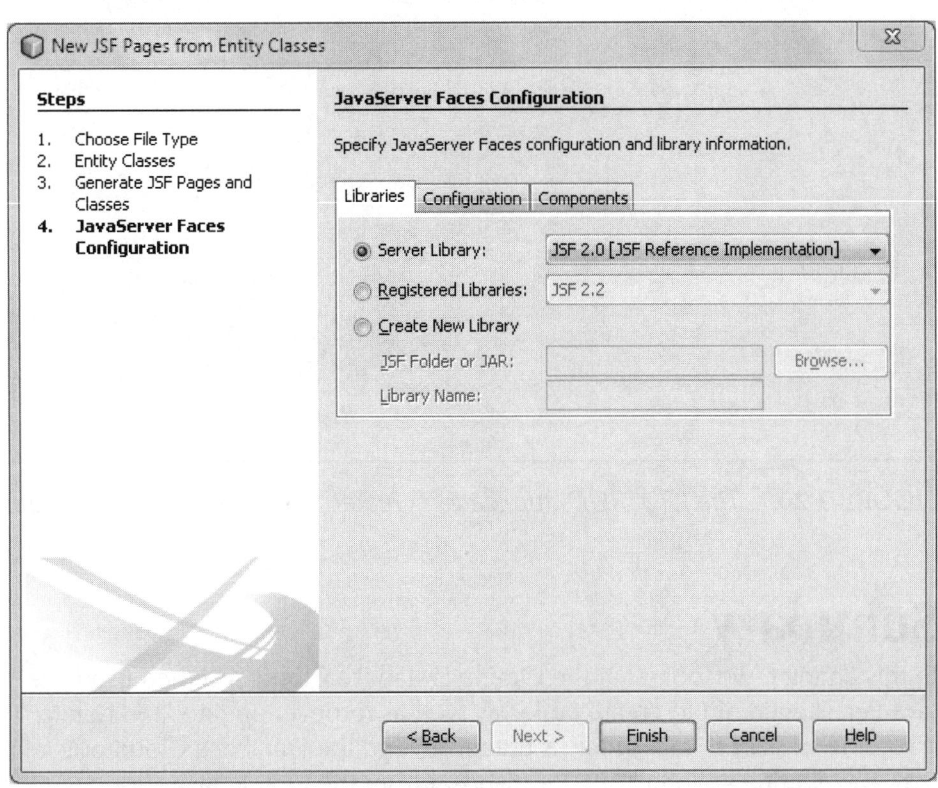

FIGURE 9-19. *The JSF library selection*

Now run the index.xhtml file that has been generated, and you will get a screen with the link Show All Device Items. Click the link and you get the screen shown in Figure 9-20, with all the basic CRUD functionality in place.

We looked at JSF earlier in the book, so try to analyze the code generated because it will enhance your understanding of JSF.

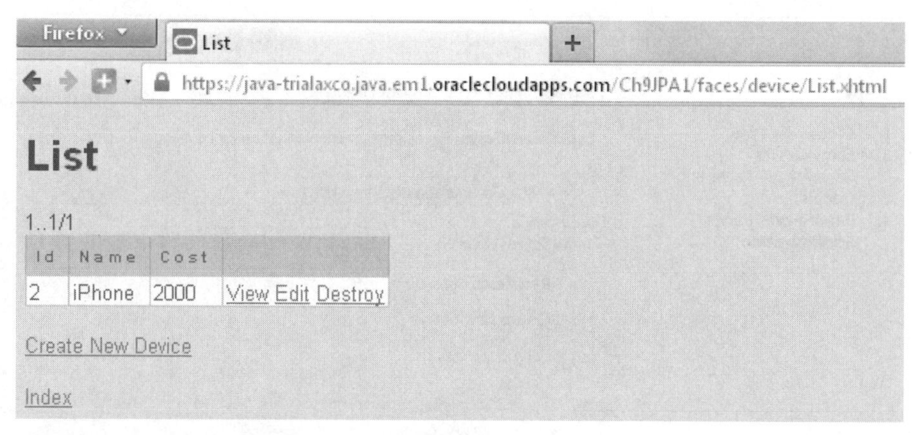

FIGURE 9-20. *The JSF CRUD application created from the entity ClassPages*

Summary

In this chapter, we looked at the Oracle Database Cloud and then used the Java Persistence API to create tables as well as retrieve, update, and delete data. Oracle is best known for its database, and the Database Cloud puts all that power and capability at your disposal from the Oracle Java Cloud.

APPENDIX A

Java EE Technologies and JSRs

This appendix provides a listing of all Java EE 5, 6, and 7 technologies and their corresponding Java Specification Requests (JSRs). Also listed are the Web Profile technologies for Java EE 6 and 7. Web Profile is discussed in Chapter 1. You will find the detailed documents for each JSR at https://jcp.org/en/jsr/detail?id=<JSR-Number>.

The Oracle Java Cloud Service runs on Oracle WebLogic Server and runs a mix of Java EE 5 and Java EE 6 technologies. So although not all the technologies listed are supported by the Oracle Java Cloud Service, the information in this appendix is important for an understanding of Java EE and its evolution over versions 5, 6, and 7.

You will find a list of technologies supported on the Oracle Java Cloud Service in Appendix C and a discussion about Oracle Java Cloud support for various technologies in Chapter 2.

Java Platform, Enterprise Edition 5 (Java EE 5) JSR 244

J2EE 1.4 was the version prior to Java EE 5. Although J2EE 1.4 was popular, it also got a lot of flak for being complex and difficult to use. So based on the feedback from developers, Java EE 5 was a major effort at simplification across all enterprise Java technologies. The "2" in the version name was dropped, and the version jumped from J2EE 1.4 to Java EE 5.

Java EE 5 introduced annotations, looked to cut down on XML configuration, and made XML optional wherever possible. Java EE 5 also introduced dependency injection, which reduced the need to look up and create resources and led to more concise, easy-to-understand code.

The Java Persistence API (JPA) was another important addition to Java EE 5. JPA standardized object relational mapping for managing relational data using Plain Old Java Objects (POJOs).

The following is a listing of the various APIs in Java EE 5, broadly classified into technologies that deal with Web Services, Web Applications, Enterprise Applications, and Management and Security.

Web Services Technologies

Implementing Enterprise Web Services	JSR 109
Java API for XML-Based Web Services (JAX-WS) 2.0	JSR 224

Java API for XML-Based RPC (JAX-RPC) 1.1	JSR 101
Java Architecture for XML Binding (JAXB) 2.0	JSR 222
SOAP with Attachments API for Java (SAAJ)	JSR 67
Streaming API for XML	JSR 173
Web Service Metadata for the Java Platform	JSR 181

Web Application Technologies

JavaServer Faces 1.2	JSR 252
JavaServer Pages 2.1	JSR 245
JavaServer Pages Standard Tag Library	JSR 52
Java Servlet 2.5	JSR 154

Enterprise Application Technologies

Common Annotations for the Java Platform	JSR 250
Enterprise JavaBeans 3.0	JSR 220
J2EE Connector Architecture 1.5	JSR 112
JavaBeans Activation Framework (JAF) 1.1	JSR 925
JavaMail	JSR 919
Java Message Service API	JSR 914
Java Persistence API	JSR 220
Java Transaction API (JTA)	JSR 907

Management and Security Technologies

J2EE Application Deployment	JSR 88
J2EE Management	JSR 77
Java Authorization Contract for Containers	JSR 115

Java Platform, Enterprise Edition 6 (Java EE 6) JSR 316

Java EE 6 was focused on continuing the simplification of the platform with extensive use of annotations to add functionality to Plain Old Java Objects (POJOs).

Java EE 6 also introduced application-specific forms of the Java EE platform known as Profiles, the first being the lightweight Web Profile, which included a subset of Java EE 6 technologies, targeted at building web applications. Therefore, developers could now choose to use the Web Profile or the Full Platform.

Java EE 6 also introduced Contexts and Dependency Injection (CDI), which took dependency injection further by giving developers the choice to inject an instance based on the context for that injection.

Considering the growing popularity of RESTful web services, Java EE 6 also introduced the Java API for RESTful Web Services (JAX-RS).

The following is a listing of the various APIs in Java EE 6, broadly classified into technologies that deal with Web Services, Web Applications, Enterprise Applications, Management and Security, and Java SE technologies of relevance to Java EE.

Web Services Technologies

Java API for RESTful Web Services (JAX-RS) 1.1	JSR 311
Implementing Enterprise Web Services 1.3	JSR 109
Java API for XML-Based Web Services (JAX-WS) 2.2	JSR 224
Java Architecture for XML Binding (JAXB) 2.2	JSR 222
Web Services Metadata for the Java Platform	JSR 181
Java API for XML-Based RPC (JAX-RPC) 1.1	JSR 101
Java APIs for XML Messaging 1.3	JSR 67
Java API for XML Registries (JAXR) 1.0	JSR 93

Web Application Technologies

Java Servlet 3.0	JSR 315	(Included in Web Profile)
JavaServer Faces 2.0	JSR 314	(Included in Web Profile)
JavaServer Pages 2.2/Expression Language 2.2	JSR 245	(Included in Web Profile)
Standard Tag Library for JavaServer Pages (JSTL) 1.2	JSR 52	(Included in Web Profile)
Debugging Support for Other Languages 1.0	JSR 45	(Included in Web Profile)

Enterprise Application Technologies

Contexts and Dependency Injection for Java (Web Beans 1.0)	JSR 299	(Included in Web Profile)
Dependency Injection for Java 1.0	JSR 330	(Included in Web Profile)
Bean Validation 1.0	JSR 303	(Included in Web Profile)
Enterprise JavaBeans 3.1 (includes Interceptors 1.1)	JSR 318	(EJB 3.1 Lite and Interceptors 1.1 is included in Web Profile)
Java EE Connector Architecture 1.6	JSR 322	
Java Persistence 2.0	JSR 317	(Included in Web Profile)
Common Annotations for the Java Platform 1.1	JSR 250	
Java Message Service API 1.1	JSR 914	
Java Transaction API (JTA) 1.1	JSR 907	(Included in Web Profile)
JavaMail 1.4	JSR 919	

Management and Security Technologies

Java Authentication Service Provider Interface for Containers	JSR 196
Java Authorization Contract for Containers 1.3	JSR 115
Java EE Application Deployment 1.2	JSR 88
J2EE Management 1.1	JSR 77

Java EE–Related Specs in Java SE

Java API for XML Processing (JAXP) 1.3	JSR 206
Java Database Connectivity 4.0	JSR 221
Java Management Extensions (JMX) 2.0	JSR 255
JavaBeans Activation Framework (JAF) 1.1	JSR 925
Streaming API for XML (StAX) 1.0	JSR 173

Java Platform, Enterprise Edition 6 (Java EE 6) Web Profile

This specification lists the technologies that need to be supported by Web Profile products. However, Web Profile products may choose to support some of the technologies present in the full Java EE platform and not listed in "Required Components" for Web Profile.

Required Components:

- Servlet 3.0
- JavaServer Pages (JSP) 2.2
- Expression Language (EL) 2.2
- Debugging Support for Other Languages (JSR-45) 1.0
- Standard Tag Library for JavaServer Pages (JSTL) 1.2
- JavaServer Faces (JSF) 2.0
- Common Annotations for the Java Platform (JSR-250) 1.1
- Enterprise JavaBeans (EJB) 3.1 Lite
- Java Transaction API (JTA) 1.1
- Java Persistence API (JPA) 2.0
- Bean Validation 1.0
- Managed Beans 1.0
- Interceptors 1.1
- Contexts and Dependency Injection for the Java EE Platform 1.0
- Dependency Injection for Java 1.0

Java Platform, Enterprise Edition 7 (Java EE 7) JSR 342

Java EE 7 introduced the Java API for WebSocket, which offers a lightweight, full-duplex communication channel for use in applications that require real-time updates and frequent exchange of data. WebSocket, along with HTML5, looks to deliver a rich and interactive user experience.

CDI, which was introduced in Java EE 6, has become an even more integral part of Java EE 7. Considering the widespread use of JSON for data exchange, Java EE 7 introduced the Java API for JSON Processing, which can be used to parse and generate JSON. Java EE 7 also introduced APIs for Batch Applications and Concurrency Utilities. It includes updated versions of the JMS and the JAX-RS APIs.

Considering the widespread use of RESTful web services, the Web Profile has been updated in Java EE 7 to include the JAX-RS API.

The following is a listing of the various APIs in Java EE 7, broadly classified into technologies that deal with Web Applications, Enterprise Applications, Web Services, Management and Security, and Java SE technologies of relevance to Java EE.

Web Application Technologies

Java API for WebSocket	JSR 356	(Included in Web Profile)
Java API for JSON Processing	JSR 353	(Included in Web Profile)
Java Servlet 3.1	JSR 340	(Included in Web Profile)
JavaServer Faces 2.2	JSR 344	(Included in Web Profile)
Expression Language 3.0	JSR 341	(Included in Web Profile)
JavaServer Pages 2.3	JSR 245	(Included in Web Profile)
Standard Tag Library for JavaServer Pages (JSTL) 1.2	JSR 52	(Included in Web Profile)

Enterprise Application Technologies

Batch Applications for the Java Platform	JSR 352	
Concurrency Utilities for Java EE 1.0	JSR 236	
Contexts and Dependency Injection for Java 1.1	JSR 346	(Included in Web Profile)
Dependency Injection for Java 1.0	JSR 330	(Included in Web Profile)
Bean Validation 1.1	JSR 349	(Included in Web Profile)

Enterprise JavaBeans 3.2	JSR 345	(Included in Web Profile)
Interceptors 1.2	JSR 318	(Included in Web Profile)
Java EE Connector Architecture 1.7	JSR 322	
Java Persistence 2.1	JSR 338	(Included in Web Profile)
Common Annotations for the Java Platform 1.2	JSR 250	(Included in Web Profile)
Java Message Service API 2.0	JSR 343	
Java Transaction API (JTA) 1.2	JSR 907	(Included in Web Profile)
JavaMail 1.5	JSR 919	

Web Services Technologies

Java API for RESTful Web Services (JAX-RS) 2.0	JSR 339	(Included in Web Profile)
Implementing Enterprise Web Services 1.3	JSR 109	
Java API for XML-Based Web Services (JAX-WS) 2.2	JSR 224	
Web Services Metadata for the Java Platform	JSR 181	
Java API for XML-Based RPC (JAX-RPC) 1.1 (Optional)	JSR 101	
Java APIs for XML Messaging 1.3	JSR 67	
Java API for XML Registries (JAXR) 1.0	JSR 93	

Management and Security Technologies

Java Authentication Service Provider Interface for Containers 1.1	JSR 196	
Java Authorization Contract for Containers 1.5	JSR 115	
Java EE Application Deployment 1.2 (Optional)	JSR 88	
J2EE Management 1.1	JSR 77	
Debugging Support for Other Languages 1.0	JSR 45	(Included in Web Profile)

Java EE–Related Specs in Java SE

Java Architecture for XML Binding (JAXB) 2.2	JSR 222
Java API for XML Processing (JAXP) 1.3	JSR 206
Java Database Connectivity 4.0	JSR 221
Java Management Extensions (JMX) 2.0	JSR 003
JavaBeans Activation Framework (JAF) 1.1	JSR 925
Streaming API for XML (StAX) 1.0	JSR 173

Java Platform, Enterprise Edition 7 (Java EE 7) Web Profile

The Web Profile specification lists the technologies that need to be supported by Web Profile products. However, Web Profile products may choose to support some of the technologies present in the full Java EE platform and not listed in "Required Components" for Web Profile.

Required Components:

- Servlet 3.1
- JavaServer Pages (JSP) 2.2
- Expression Language (EL) 3.0
- Debugging Support for Other Languages (JSR-45) 1.0
- Standard Tag Library for JavaServer Pages (JSTL) 1.2
- JavaServer Faces (JSF) 2.2
- Java API for RESTful Web Services (JAX-RS) 2.0
- Common Annotations for the Java Platform (JSR-250) 1.1
- Enterprise JavaBeans (EJB) 3.2 Lite
- Java Transaction API (JTA) 1.2
- Java Persistence API (JPA) 2.1
- Bean Validation 1.1
- Managed Beans 1.0

- Interceptors 1.1
- Contexts and Dependency Injection for the Java EE Platform 1.1
- Dependency Injection for Java 1.0

Sources

www.oracle.com/technetwork/java/javaee/tech/javaee6technologies-1955512.html
www.oracle.com/technetwork/java/javaee/tech/index.html

APPENDIX B

Application Servers Compatible with Java EE 5, 6, and 7

Java EE compatibility is discussed in detail in Chapter 1. Basically, a Java EE implementation (application server) is considered Java EE compatible only if it passes the tests in the Java EE Compatibility Test Suite (CTS). Do note that the CTS is meant to be used by Java EE licensees looking to build Java EE–compatible application servers and not by Java EE application developers.

The Oracle Java Cloud Service runs Oracle WebLogic Application Server, so you won't need to evaluate and pick from all available servers. However, for understanding Java EE, it's important to be aware of the many other application servers and the different versions of Java EE supported by each server. This list is also useful to compare the various cloud vendors, because, as discussed in Chapter 1, most vendors support one or more of the servers listed. The Java EE 7 implementations list is likely to grow as more vendors support the latest Java EE version.

Java EE 5–Compatible Implementations

- Apache Geronimo-2.1.4
- Apusic Application Server (v5.0)
- Fujitsu Interstage Application Server Enterprise Edition 9.2
- GlassFish Application Server v2
- IBM WASCE 2.0
- IBM WebSphere Application Server v7
- JBoss Application Server 5.0
- JBoss Enterprise Application Platform 5
- NEC WebOTX 8.1
- Oracle Application Server 11
- Oracle WebLogic Server 10g R3
- OW2 JOnAS 5.1

- SAP NetWeaver 7.1
- Sun GlassFish Enterprise Server 9.1
- TmaxSoft JEUS 6
- TongWeb Application Server 5.0

Java EE 6 Full Platform–Compatible Implementations

- Apache Geronimo 3.0-beta-1
- Fujitsu Interstage Application Server powered by Windows Azure
- Fujitsu Interstage Application Server v10.1
- Hitachi uCosminexus Application Server v9.0
- IBM WebSphere Application Server 8.x
- IBM WebSphere Application Server Community Edition 3.0
- JBoss Application Server 7.x
- JBoss Enterprise Application Platform 6
- NEC WebOTX Application Server v9.x
- Oracle GlassFish Server 3.x
- Oracle WebLogic Server 12.1.1
- TMAX JEUS 7

Java EE 6 Web Profile–Compatible Implementations

- Apache Geronimo 3.0-beta-1
- Apache TomEE 1.0
- Caucho Resin 4.0.17

- IBM WebSphere Application Server Version 8.5.5 (Liberty Profile)
- JBoss Application Server 7.x
- JBoss Enterprise Application Platform 6
- JOnAS
- Oracle GlassFish Server 3.x
- SAP NetWeaver Cloud

Java EE 7 Full Platform–Compatible Implementations

- GlassFish Server Open Source Edition 4.0
- TMAX JEUS 8
- Wildfly 8.0.0

Java EE 7 Web Profile–Compatible Implementations

- GlassFish Server Open Source Edition 4.0 Web Profile
- Wildfly 8.0.0 Web Profile

Source

www.oracle.com/technetwork/java/ javaee/overview/compatibility-jsp-136984.html

APPENDIX C

Supported and Unsupported Technologies, Services, and APIs

Technologies and Services Supported

The Java Cloud Service supports the deployment of the following types of applications:

- Web Application Archive (WAR) and Enterprise Archive (EAR) deployments.
- Web applications: Applications using Servlet 2.5, JavaServer Pages (JSP) 2.1, and JavaServer Faces (JSF) release 1.2 and release 2.0.
- Web Services applications: Applications using Java API for XML Web Services (JAX-WS) 2.1–based web services. Applications providing REST-based APIs through Java API for RESTful Web Services (JAX-RS) 1.1 and Jersey 1.9 annotations are supported.
- Enterprise Java Beans (EJB) containers: Applications using EJB 2.1 and EJB 3.0 specifications. Only local EJB invocations are supported. EJB 2.x Entity Beans are not supported.
- JDBC services: Applications using Java Persistence API (JPA) 2.0 specifications and JPA persistence.xml elements with EclipseLink 2.1.3–specific extensions.
- Direct use of Java Database Connectivity (JDBC) 4.0 APIs.
- Use of Oracle Database 11*g*–compatible SQL statements.
- Java Platform Standard Edition (SE) 1.6 APIs: Applications can use the set of Java SE 1.6 public APIs as long as they pass the Java Cloud Service whitelist tool and their use is in line with Java EE best practices.
- ADF 11.1.1.6 applications.

Java EE 5 and 6 Specifications Supported

The following is a list of Java EE 5 and 6 specifications that are supported on the Oracle Java Cloud:

- JavaServer Pages Standard Tag Library (JSTL) 1.2
- Java Database Connectivity (JDBC) 4.0
- Java Persistence API 2.0
- Web Services Metadata for the Java Platform 2.0

- Java Naming and Directory Interface Specification (JNDI) 1.2
- Java Transaction API (JTA) 1.1
- Streaming API for XML (StAX) 1.0
- SOAP with Attachments API for Java (SAAJ) 1.3
- JavaBeans Activation Framework Specification (JAF) 1.1
- Java API for XML Processing (JAXP) 1.3
- Java Management Extensions (JMX) 1.2
  JMX is only supported for exposure of MBeans within a deployment archive and access to these MBeans from the deployment archive itself or other archives deployed to the same Java Cloud Service instance.
- Java API for XML-based Web Services (JAX-WS) 2.1
- Java API for RESTful Web Services (JAX-RS) 1.1
- Java Architecture for XML Binding (JAXB) 2.0

Public WebLogic Server 10.3.6 APIs and Capabilities Supported

The Oracle Java Cloud supports WebLogic server–specific APIs and capabilities that are included in the following packages:

- weblogic.logging.*
- weblogic.jsp.*
- weblogic.cache.*
- weblogic.application.*
- weblogic.i18n.*
- weblogic.i18ntools.*
- weblogic.jndi.*
- weblogic.jws.*
- weblogic.servlet.*
- weblogic.transaction.*

Unsupported Features and APIs

Oracle Java Cloud does not support the features and APIs listed here. In most cases, the reason for this is a) constraints due to a common-shared environment, b) Oracle's Cloud products strategy, or c) security concerns.

- Any API deprecated in WebLogic Server release 10.3.6 or lower.
- Any API deprecated in ADF release 11.1.1.6 or lower.
- Direct JAR deployment.
- WebLogic Server shared libraries, deployments, and references, except for references to libraries predefined in Java Cloud Service, as described in "Understanding On-Premise and Java Cloud Service Portability."
- Java EE Connector Architecture (JCA) Container—RAR deployments.
- Java Message Service (JMS) services. Any application that has JMS dependencies, including the use of WebLogic Server application-scoped JMS modules.
- JAX-RPC-based web services.
- Applications exposing or invoking asynchronous web services.
- Use of WS-* specifications other than WS-Security (through OWSM policies).
- Remote invocations with a transport protocol other than HTTPS (including plain-text HTTP).
- Coherence applications managed or used through WebLogic Server ActiveCache.
- Direct use of any JRF API components other than ADF. For example, the direct use of Oracle Platform Security Services (OPSS) and ODL APIs.
- Direct use of Oracle JDBC Driver APIs.
- Use of SQL statements specific to a database instance other than Oracle Database 11*g* (11.2).
- JavaMail API specification.
- Direct modification of the Java command-line parameters, including for the specification of system properties.

- Application-scoped JDBC modules.
- Run-time OWSM policy attachments.
- Setting of operating system environment variables, Java system properties, and JVM/Server command-line parameters.
- File system access by deployed applications.
- EJB 2.x Entity Beans.
- ADF features: Desktop Integration, mBeans, seeded customizations or cross-session personalization (MDS), Mobile, Active Data Services, Data Controls for BI, Essbase, BAM, JMX, and Business Components services, interfaces (web services), and events.
- Application deployment archives that have a size of more than 95MB.

Unsupported WebLogic Server 10.3.6 APIs and Capabilities

WebLogic Server 10.3.6 APIs and capabilites that are not supported on Oracle Java Cloud. In some cases, the APIs are quite old, from the days prior to WebLogic being an Oracle product. Also, it's a best practice to avoid using vendor-/server-specific APIs.

- weblogic.wtc.*
- com.bea.logging
- com.bea.httppubsub
- com.bea.security.*
- commonj.*
- weblogic.apache.*
- weblogic.webservice.*
- weblogic.cluster.*
- weblogic.connector.*
- weblogic.deploy.*
- weblogic.management.*

- weblogic.rmi.*
- weblogic.security.*
- weblogic.time.*
- weblogic.uddi.*
- weblogic.workarea.*
- weblogic.xml.*
- .NET and C APIs for JMS

Whitelist Violations

You will encounter whitelist violations when an application uses functionality from any of the following:

Java SE	Java nonblocking IO Java Networking Executing a new process Direct SQL connection Java media Java Mail Java Compiler Java RMI Java Native Interface (JNI) Java Desktop accessibility JDK Log Management. (You can use JDK loggers to log messages.) CORBA API (org.omg.*) Overriding Java Security Manager
Java EE	Remote EJB Java Messaging Service Remote JMX Management

Sources

http://docs.oracle.com/cloud/CSJSU/feat_implement.htm#CSJSU7149
http://docs.oracle.com/cloud/CSJSU/dev_app.htm#BCEEFEBF

Index

Symbols

A

B

C

D

L

M

N

O

P

Q

R

S

T

U

V

W

X

Z